VELOPMENT
OF COMPONENT-BASED
INFORMATION SYSTEMS

Advances in Management Information Systems

Advisory Board

DEVELOPMENT OF COMPONENT-BASED INFORMATION SYSTEMS

SERGIO DE CESARE
MARK LYCETT
ROBERT D. MACREDIE

EDITORS

ADVANCES IN MANAGEMENT
INFORMATION SYSTEMS
VLADIMIR ZWASS SERIES EDITOR

LONDON AND NEW YORK

First published 2006 by M.E. Sharpe

Published 2015 by Routledge
2 Park Square, Milton Park, Abingdon, Oxon OX14 4RN
711 Third Avenue, New York, NY 10017, USA

Routledge is an imprint of the Taylor & Francis Group, an informa business

Library of Congress Cataloging-in-Publication Data

References to the AMIS papers should be as follows:

Janssen, M., and Wagenaar, R. Business engineering of component-based systems.
S. de Cesare, M. Lycett, and R.D. Macredie, eds., *Development of Component-Based
Information Systems: Advances in Management Information Systems,* Volume 2
(Armonk, NY: M.E. Sharpe, 2005), 166–186.

ISBN 0-7656-1248-8
ISSN 1554-6152

ISBN 978-0-7656-1248-9 (hbk)

**ADVANCES IN
MANAGEMENT INFORMATION SYSTEMS**

AMIS Vol. 1: Richard Y. Wang, Elizabeth M. Pierce, Stuart E. Madnick, and Craig W. Fisher.
Information Quality
ISBN 0-7656-1133-3

AMIS Vol. 2: Sergio de Cesare, Mark Lycett, and Robert D. Macredie.
Development of Component-Based Information Systems
ISBN 0-7656-1248-8

CONTENTS

Part II. Managing Component-Based Development

Part III. Component-Based Development with Commercial Off-the-Shelf Products

SERIES EDITOR'S INTRODUCTION

Vladimir Zwass

This second volume of *Advances in Management Information Systems (AMIS)* is devoted to the fundamental contemporary methodology of information systems (IS) development. It is the objective of *AMIS* to bring together the knowledge about IS and, by exemplifying the research methods in the domain, serve as a tool in the continuing generation of new knowledge. The present volume furthers this goal.

As a scholarly field, the IS discipline offers a panoply of well-developed analytical research domains. Equally, the field of IS encompasses the research methods aiming at synthesis: the design of information systems that meet specified objectives in novel and superior ways. These methods of a design science include disciplined construction of artifacts with the explicit goal of generating new knowledge (Nunamaker et al. 1990/91; Hevner et al. 2004). Experimentation with the new design exemplars leads to further theory-building. Indeed, the inclusion of these methods inheres in the nature of the IS discipline as one of the sciences of the artificial (Simon 1996). It is notable, however, that the scholarly disciplines not generally counted among the design-oriented are also evolving their own synthesis research. Economics, for example, has been accommodating research streams deploying its well-honed analytical tools in researching the optimal designs of marketplaces and reputation systems (Roth 2002). We like to think that some of the motivation for this new research direction has been furnished by the ubiquitous use of information systems, such as the Internet-Web compound.

Component-based development (CBD) is a broad paradigm for the development of software. It was discovered very early in the software-development game that systems ought to be built in modular fashion, rather than as monoliths incapable of work subdivision and incremental development, as well as devilishly difficult to modify as the requirements for them inevitably evolve. Software is built to be modified and thus needs to be modifiable. With time, the ideas regarding modules, each encapsulating a relatively independent aspect of the overall design, have evolved into the concept of software components. Components are independent software units with contractually specified interfaces and with only explicit dependencies on the context of their use (Szyperski 2002). CBD offers such benefits as the potential for software reuse, faster time-to-market, and lowered costs of system maintenance and integration, which drive the organizational IS expenditures in the highly fluid business environment. In their most regimented form, commercial off-the-shelf components (COTS) can be furnished by software markets or under open-source licenses.

Software reuse, a systematic practice of developing software from a stock of components, as well as building the component stocks themselves, is of great interest to the practice and study of IS. The idea of software reuse imitates, mutatis mutandis, the development of the commonly known hardware artifacts, be they cars or bridges (Kim and Stohr 1998). The difficulties involved are reflected in slow progress despite the apparent advantages of progressing. Software, whose main strengths are flexibility and malleability, invites variety rather than regimentation. Technologically, reuse grounded in CBD is predicated on the highly disciplined deployment of components within software frameworks, which are combinations of system software and protocols that provide services for "framing" the components into the system under development. Well-known frameworks include those following the CORBA standard and the newer Java platform J2EE as well as .NET. The technological underpinnings of CBD alone are vastly insufficient to ensure successful reuse, however. The principal causes of the organizational failure of software reuse programs are the absence of reuse-specific development processes along with human factors (Morisio et al. 2002). This is why the accumulated behavioral and organizational knowledge of the IS discipline can be of vital service here—and why we can further our knowledge of IS by studying CBD.

As the present volume indicates, we are witnessing several important emerging directions in CBD. New initiatives keep coming. The creation of component-based software able to adapt its structure and behavior to the execution environment is of the moment with the growth of ubiquitous computing and the need for the software to adapt itself to the delivery device and the deployment environment (McKinley et al. 2004). Another form of adaptation being researched is the tailoring of component-based software at run time by end-user developers (Mørch et al. 2004). New and powerful frameworks, such as IBM's WebSphere, support the distributed, federated model of component deployment (Herness et al. 2004). Other research attempts to ensure that component-based IS satisfy a given set of properties (Vecellio and Thomas 2003). Web services, if supported by further standardization, can lead to extensive component-based reuse. However, the vision of "business-component factory" (Herzum and Sims 2000) remains as yet just that—a vision, worth striving for.

Consistent with the objectives of *AMIS,* the editors of this volume discuss in their introduction the domain of CBD as well as the research methods in the domain, illustrating them with papers from general literature as well as from the present monograph. The work should help in further development of IS as a scholarly discipline with a rich multimethod research program—and serve the progress in CBD.

REFERENCES

Herness, E.N., R.J. High, and J.R. McGee. 2004. WebSphere Application Server: A foundation for on-demand computing. *IBM Systems Journal* 43, no. 2: 213–237.

Herzum, P., and O. Sims. 2000. *Business Component Factory: A Comprehensive Overview of Component-Based Development for the Enterprise.* Chichester, UK: Wiley.

Hevner, A.R., S.T. March, and J. Park. 2004. Design science in information systems research. *MIS Quarterly* 28, no. 1 (March): 75–104.

Kim, Y., and E.A. Stohr. 1998. Software reuse: Survey and research directions. *Journal of Management Information Systems* 14, no. 4 (Spring): 113–147.

McKinley, P.K., S.M. Sadjadi, E.P. Kasten, and B.H.C. Cheng. 2004. Composing adaptive software. *Computer* 37, no. 7 (July): 56–64.

Mørch, A.I., G. Stevens, M. Won, M. Klann, Y. Dittrich, and V. Wulf. 2004. Component-based technologies for end-user development. *Communications of the ACM* 47, no. 9 (September): 59–62.

Morisio, M., M. Ezran, and C. Tully. 2002. Success and failure factors in software reuse. *IEEE Transactions on Software Engineering* 28, no. 4 (April): 340–357.

Nunamaker, J.F., Jr., M. Chen, and T.D.M. Purdin. 1990/91. Systems development in information systems research. *Journal of Management Information Systems* 7, no. 3 (Winter): 89–106.

Roth, A. 2002. The economist as engineer: Game theory, experimentation, and computation as tools for design economics. *Econometrica* 70 (4): 1341–1378.

Simon, H.A. 1996. *The Sciences of the Artificial.* 3rd ed. Cambridge, MA: MIT Press

Szyperski, C. 2002. *Component Software: Beyond Object-Oriented Programming.* 2nd ed. London: Addison-Wesley.

Vecellio, G.J., and W.M. Thomas. 2003. Infrastructure support for predictable policy enforcement. *Proceedings of the 6th ICSE Workshop on Component-Based Software Engineering*, ed. I. Crnkovic, H. Schmidt, J. Stafford, and K. Wallnau, www.csse.monash.edu.au/~hws/cgi-bin/CBSE6/Proceedings/papersfinal/p10.pdf.

ACKNOWLEDGMENTS

This book is the result of the collaborative effort of many individuals. First, we would like to thank all the authors who have contributed with their research work to the chapters of this book. Without them this book would not have been possible. We are grateful to the reviewers who with their valuable and constructive feedback have contributed in improving the quality and content of the volume. Finally we wish to thank Carolyn Bailey of Brunel University for her help in managing the whole administrative process, Elizabeth Granda and Harry Briggs of M.E. Sharpe for their support in the successful completion of the project, and Professor Vladimir Zwass, series editor, who provided us with this opportunity, supporting and reviewing our work along the way.

DEVELOPMENT
OF COMPONENT-BASED
INFORMATION SYSTEMS

CHAPTER 1

DEVELOPMENT OF COMPONENT-BASED INFORMATION SYSTEMS

AN INTRODUCTION

SERGIO DE CESARE, MARK LYCETT, AND ROBERT D. MACREDIE

Abstract: Information systems (IS) development is a complex endeavor. Notwithstanding significant advances achieved in a number of areas, including methodologies, techniques, architectures, and project management, the rate of unsuccessful or failed projects continues to be high. Development paradigms have evolved in an attempt to reduce the effort and cost of IS change necessitated by continuous demands of systems maintenance and integration. This has led IS developers to rethink systems design in terms of independent but collaborating components, each charged with specific responsibilities. Component-based development promises considerable benefits such as reuse, increased interoperability, and less costly software evolution. Such benefits are not easily achievable and require simultaneous work along multiple dimensions: organizational, methodological, and technological.

This chapter serves two purposes. First, it provides an overview of the concepts, issues, and dimensions underlying component-based information systems development. Second, it serves as an introduction to the remaining chapters, providing the reader with the necessary foundation to critically appreciate the research work presented throughout the volume. A discussion of research methods on the development of component-based information systems is also presented, with particular emphasis on design research.

Keywords: Software Component, Component-Based Development, Component Development, Component Assembly, Organizational Implications, Design Research

INTRODUCTION

Information systems (IS) development is at the core of the IS field (Fitzgerald et al. 2002). Approaches to IS development have evolved significantly in an attempt to overcome the difficult problems of delivering IS projects on time, within budget, and with the desired level of quality. Notwithstanding the advances achieved in a number of areas (e.g., methodologies, techniques, architectures, and the organization and management of projects), systems development as a whole is still characterized by a high rate of unsuccessful or failed projects that are costing industry billions of dollars a year. Ewusi-Mensah (2003) estimates that one-third of software development projects fail or are abandoned due to cost overruns, delays, and reduced functionality. Furthermore, for every dollar spent on development, five to ten dollars are spent on integration with existing systems. For every $100,000 in an organization's systems development budget, some $50,000 will be spent on modifying existing systems to deal with business change (Gibbs 1994; Raviart 2001; Standish 2003).

These figures are symptomatic of the current situation in systems development and indicate that the most costly and problematic areas are maintenance and integration. In essence, this situation equates to dealing with change in IS. This conclusion is unsurprising, as business organizations are complex systems that constantly need to adapt and change in response to internal and external factors in order to be competitive. Business organizations do not evolve in a stepwise fashion but are best thought of as "emergent" entities whose features are products of continuous social negotiation and consensus building (Truex et al. 1999). Ideally, therefore, IS should be developed in a way that facilitates continuous modifications in face of changing requirements.

IS development approaches, methodologies, and techniques have attempted to tackle the problems of increasing costs and poor quality by focusing on maintenance and integration of IS. Traditionally, applications were developed in a stovepipe fashion. Stovepipe systems were developed to be intrinsically stand-alone and closed to any form of communication, coordination, or collaboration with other systems (e.g., software, business, and physical systems). Such systems were also characterized by nonmodular architectures, making it difficult to localize and set the boundaries of maintenance interventions.

With the growing rate of change of modern organizations and the increasing level of interconnectedness of their business processes (e.g., in e-commerce and virtual organizations), the deficiencies of traditional systems readily emerge.

The practical need of overcoming the problems mentioned above has led IS developers to rethink systems design in terms of independent but collaborating parts, each of which is charged with specific responsibilities. This evolution of development methodologies of the past thirty years has progressed from structured to object-oriented to component-based approaches. The objective was to evolve toward the ideal of developing IS from independent units of software composition (i.e., components).

The idea of component-based development (CBD) was set out by McIlroy (1969). McIlroy coined the term *mass-produced software components* and expressed his vision of the benefits that would derive from component-based systems—benefits such as greater reuse, increased interoperability, and easier software evolution. These advantages echo throughout the software development literature up to today (Brown and Wallnau 1996; Brereton and Budgen 2000; Crnkovic and Larsson 2002).

Among the cited benefits, reuse plays a crucial role in ensuring effective and efficient IS change. In software development, reuse can be defined as further use or the repeated use of an artifact (Jacobson et al. 1997). In a development project, the successful reuse of software artifacts is conditioned by many factors. These include the existence of reusable artifacts (e.g., components), availability of selection and assembly techniques, technological support, and an organizational structure and culture orientated toward reuse. Thus, methodological, technological, and organizational factors are all key to the adoption of reuse strategies within organizations.

In addressing these factors, this chapter is organized as follows. The next section defines the fundamental concepts of component-based development. The presentation of various CBD issues follows, starting with the developmental aspects of component-based systems. These aspects concern the bifaceted nature of CBD, that is, development for reuse (or development of reusable components) and development with reuse (or component assembly). Next, the organizational implications of CBD are considered, followed by a discussion of research methods for component-based information systems. Finally, the chapter presents an overview of the book and some conclusions.

DEFINING COMPONENT-BASED DEVELOPMENT

Component-based development is based on the fundamental concept of composition (Szyperski 1999). This implies that software solutions are developed by assembling independent software

Table 1.1

Definitions of Component

Author	Component definition
Philippe Krutchen, Rational Software	A component is a nontrivial, nearly independent, and replaceable part of a system that fulfills a clear function in the context of a well-defined architecture. A component conforms to and provides the physical realization of a set of interfaces.
Gartner Group	A run-time software component is a dynamically bindable package of one or more programs managed as a unit and accessed through documented interfaces that can be discovered at run-time.
Clemens Szyperski, Microsoft	A software component is a unit of composition with contractually specified interfaces and explicit context dependencies only. A software component can be deployed independently and is subject to composition by third parties.
Wojtek Kozaczynski, SSA	A business component represents the software implementation of an "autonomous" business concept or business process. It consists of all the software artifacts necessary to express, implement, and deploy the concept as a reusable element of a larger business system.

parts and that desired system behavior is achieved through the collaboration of those parts. The notion of components has existed within the software development literature for decades, generally assuming different meanings. At times, the notion has been synonymous with concepts such as function, procedure, module, class, package, and so on. Although a standard, universal definition of the term *component* is not available, in recent years the term has assumed a narrower connotation, defined by specific characteristics. This point was illustrated by a workshop at the Eleventh International Conference on Software Engineering (Brown and Wallnau 1996). Table 1.1 summarizes a few of the proposed definitions.

The third of the definitions in Table 1.1 was originally formulated at the Workshop on Component-Oriented Programming (Szyperski and Pfister 1997) held at the 1996 European Conference on Object-Oriented Programming. This definition was subsequently used by Szyperski (1999). Szyperski's definition is widely referenced throughout the component-based literature. In the context of this definition, the significant characteristics of software components are as follows:

- *Unit of composition and independent deployment.* Composition and independent deployment are relative concepts. First, composition and deployment of software components are dependent on context dependencies. Second, both the literature and anecdotal evidence confirm that a component is not generally adopted as is, but adapted to meet specific requirements (functional, nonfunctional, and architectural) before deployment.
- *Contractually specified interfaces.* A component can support three types of interfaces: provided, required, and configuration (Bosch 2000). Provided interfaces define the services that a component offers. Required interfaces define the services that the component requires from other components. Configuration interfaces provide access to variation points, allowing the component user to configure the component to the instance context. Reflection and introspection provide a candidate for a fourth type of interface, which provides information concerning the component's structure and behavior to other interrogating components and to allow self-adaptive behavior (Maes 1995).

- *Context dependencies.* Required interfaces and a component framework model, providing the "glue" infrastructure, define context dependencies. Microsoft's Component Object Model (COM) and Distributed Component Object Model (DCOM), the Object Management Group's (OMG) Common Object Request Broker Architecture (CORBA), and Sun Microsystems' Java platform provide examples of component frameworks. Cross-platform integration is currently a challenging issue. Work in this area is being undertaken by the Common Component Architecture (CCA) OMG working group (OMG 2001). CCA is a specification for cross-platform portability among components.

Component-Based Development Life Cycles

The current state of the art in component-based development (see Brown and Wallnau 1998; Brereton and Budgen 2000; Crnkovic and Larsson 2002) highlights a number of concerns associated with both components themselves and with assembling sets of commercial off-the-shelf (COTS) components. In the context of component development, these concerns relate to processes, methods, and tools for component generation alongside the management of those components and their respective interfaces. In the assembly context, the concerns are similar but raised to the system level, emphasizing component documentation, assembly mechanisms, adaptation, and customization.

Traditional software development has been primarily concerned with the production and delivery of whole working systems whose functionality is aimed at satisfying the overall requirements of the problem space. Component-based development has produced a significant change in the traditional approach and a shift in the mind-set of the actors involved. Software development has moved from being development-centric to integration-centric (Seacord and Kingsley 1999). A CBD process involves the selection, acquisition, and assembly and integration of components obtained by third parties or previously produced in-house. The difference between component development and system assembly translates into project work in two ways, with the former perspective concentrating on the component development process and the latter perspective concentrating on the solution development process (Allen and Frost 1998). These perspectives represent the two extremes of a value chain encapsulated by management processes ensuring that solution requirements are used to feed component development whose output can be harvested for solution assembly.

As a result, two separate but interdependent processes must be defined: a process for the development of reusable components and a process for the assembly and integration of components into a working software system. The existence of two processes or life cycles presumes the existence of different specialized roles, which together form the software component value chain and at the same time define the component marketplace. A dual life cycle model applied to software development is not new. Foreman (1996) defined a similar model in the area of domain engineering, highlighting the relationships between the two processes (i.e., domain engineering and application engineering), either of which can be outsourced.

The development processes are asynchronous and need not be necessarily carried out within the same organization. The domain is modeled independently of any specific system and the application is subsequently developed on the basis of the system's requirements and the available artifacts (domain models, architectures, and components) for the previously engineered domain. The set of artifacts common to a domain is sometimes referred to as a product family (Deelstra et al. 2005). The fundamental difference between this development model and traditional holistic development is the presence of domain artifacts that influence and can even modify initial user and system requirements.

Component Development

Conventional software development has always recognized the relevance of the development process aimed at producing the overall system, while little attention has been focused on the creation and management of software components. The development of components is essentially centered on the concept of reuse. The primary problem here concerns the identification of reusable components, which can be developed for in-house use or for the marketplace. As a structured process, the development of components is generally part of a broader domain engineering or product line development process.

Several issues surround the development of components for a domain (Brown and Wallnau 1996):

- The identification of the domain to target, its boundary, and stakeholders
- The identification of domain features
- Variation across contexts of use
- The construction of the asset base to allow for classification, retrieval, and query of assets

The typical activities of the domain engineering process include domain analysis, representation of the domain software architecture, and derivation of software components and assets from the domain architectural design.

Domain analysis is often confused with domain engineering. Much of the literature on domain engineering is dedicated to domain analysis, which is defined as the identification, analysis, and specification of common requirements from a specific application domain (Firesmith 1993). Domain analysis was first introduced by Neighbors (1984); various domain analysis methods can currently be found in the literature (Prieto-Diaz 1987; Kang et al. 1990; Lubars 1991). The industrial use of the domain approach, however, can still be considered at an embryonic stage, though it is plausible to predict that the synergies deriving from the combination of domain analysis and component technology will contribute to the maturity of these two merging areas.

Domain analysis derives its tools from diverse disciplines, which include knowledge engineering, library management, the study of taxonomies, and more recently philosophy (Daga et al. 2005). These disciplines are mainly concerned with the extraction of knowledge and its classification, fundamental activities for the engineering of a domain. Sources of domain knowledge include the technical literature, existing applications, customer surveys, expert advice, and current and future requirements (Arango and Prieto-Diaz 1989). Experience must be added to this list. In fact, a typical scenario, which favors the development of a domain model and a corresponding library of assets, is the competence acquired over the years by a software organization in the development of similar systems (e.g., banking systems).

This migration is symptomatic of the fact that traditional software skills, competencies, and expertise are also applicable to the development of reusable assets such as components (see Szyperski 1999). What is required is a shift toward reuse in the mind-set and vision at all levels of the organization (i.e., strategic and tactical management, development teams, and individuals). This change must be preceded or followed by a structural reorganization.

SOLUTION ASSEMBLY

The activities that specifically characterize the life cycle of component-based software systems are (a) component qualification, (b) component adaptation, (c) system assembly, and (d) system evolution. These activities represent the process areas in which traditional software development differs from component-based development (Brown and Wallnau 1996). Organizational, business, cultural, and economic changes dependent on the introduction of CBD within the organization are mostly related to these four activities.

Component qualification refers to the identification and evaluation of components potentially capable of addressing system requirements. This activity is carried out early in the life cycle in conjunction with business and system analysis. A key issue associated with this activity is the semantic characterization of both system requirements and components, covering both functional and nonfunctional capabilities. These capabilities must be evaluated against system requirements in order to determine which component or set of components is best fitted for the purpose. Maiden et al. (1999) propose use cases as a common artifact for eliciting and representing customer requirements and for evaluating software packages. Research in the area of evaluating component specifications against system requirements is, however, limited, and rigorous solutions are not currently available.

In an ideal situation, a component is a black box that can be plugged into a software system as is via its interfaces. More realistically speaking, components may not provide exactly the required capabilities and may have been developed for other contextual situations. A recurring problem is architectural mismatch (Garlan et al. 1995), which originates from mismatched assumptions a reusable part makes about the structure of the system it is to be part of. In these cases, components need to be adapted. Adaptation, which depends on the extent to which a component is internally accessible, takes three forms (Brown and Wallnau 1996; Bosch 2000):

- *White box,* where the internal implementation of a component is accessible. In this case, two adaptation approaches can be applied: copy-paste and inheritance. The copy-paste approach (code scavenging) reuses part of the component's code in a newly developed component. Inheritance is applicable only in the case of components implemented as generalized classes in an object-oriented language. The reuse of all or part of the internal aspects of the generalized class depends on the specific programming language (e.g., attributes and methods can be defined as private, protected, or public in Java).
- *Gray box,* where the internals of components are not accessible, but adaptation can occur at the interface level. This can be achieved by the support of an extension language or Application Programming Interface (API). The most common technique for reuse at the interface level is wrapping. A wrapper encapsulates the adapted component(s) so that all interaction must necessarily pass through the wrapper itself. This approach, however, is noted to have excessive amounts of adaptation code and excessive performance overheads (Holzle 1993). Aggregation also encapsulates adapted component(s) at the interface level, but unlike wrapping aggregation allows for the composition of new functionality.
- *Black box,* where components provide only the binary executable with no support for extending the interface.

Alternative architectural approaches are available for component assembly. These approaches are generally based on the use of more generalized techniques, such as architectural description languages (ADL), protocols, and ontologies, and seek to provide an abstract and technology-independent way of interfacing components.

Traditional (noncomponentized) software evolves as a consequence of change induced by correction, enhancement, and addition of new required functionality. In addition, for a component-based system, evolution can be viewed as the modification, replacement, or addition of new components. More specifically, during corrective maintenance, a faulty component can be replaced with a more correct and reliable one. Conversely, new components can be integrated into the system to either enhance performance or provide additional functionality. In a black box world components would be simply substituted or added. In a white or gray box context, corrective, perfective, or enhancement maintenance could also be achieved by modification of the component internals. Any type of evolution always involves the identification, adaptation, and integration of new or modified components. This is accompanied by all of the problems and issues encountered in first-time development.

Table 1.2 summarizes how the four activities presented above affect the traditional work flows of software development. The second column of the table defines the work flows as traditionally viewed in software development. The third column briefly summarizes the effects of the adoption of a component-based approach. The last column indicates typical CBD activities.

ORGANIZATIONAL IMPLICATIONS OF CBD

To date, research on the organizational implications of component-based development is limited. Drawing attention, however, to the adoption of reuse strategies in the organization, the reuse literature notes that it is generally more expensive to develop reusable components in the short term and makes the following observations. First, the nontechnical issues of reuse are at least as important as the technical issues. Second, changes in organizational structure, process, and culture are required to accommodate reuse. Third, both the scope of reuse and information, communication, and product flows across the process require consideration. Last, the relationship between administrative and technical innovation is emergent, which indicates that the effects of innovation are hard to predict (Apte et al. 1990; Karimi 1990; Kim and Stohr 1998; Fafchamps 1994; Griss and Wosser 1995; Zand and Samadzadeh 1995; Succi and Baruchelli 1997; Ravichandran 1999).

Lycett (2005), in examining CBD within a major systems integrator, notes the following:

- Administrative innovation is a necessary partner to the technical innovation of CBD. The form of innovation explored was structural, implementing a supply-manage-consume model.
- The introduction of CBD increased ambiguity and uncertainty about both what to do and how to do it, in great part caused by inadequate support for terms of process, method, and technique.
- Existing software engineering techniques work well only within the confines of component boundaries (see also Szyperski 1999). Limitations exist both in the applicability and understanding of the life cycle and in the attitudes and skills of development staff.

In relation to such ambiguity, existing research has proposed that (a) communications need a clear, well-defined interface and that (b) synchronization requires commonly defined milestones and clear entry and exit criteria at the principal points of interaction (Hersleb and Moitra 2001). In addition, ambiguity can be decreased by forcing stakeholders to an explicit process of convergence on desired outcomes (Sussman and Guinan 1999). Aspects of concurrent engineering have been developed to deal with some staff issues and suggest collocation as a facilitating condition for the development of norms necessary for concurrent development (Rafi and Perkins 1995). The same literature, however, notes that the attitudes, norms, social structures, and reward and incentive systems need to be developed to support such a process. The design of incentive-compatible reuse programs has been developed to some extent (see Fichman and Kemerer 2001).

Table 1.2

Effects of Component-Based Development on Traditional Development Workflows

Process workflow	Traditional development: definitions	Effects of CBD	CBD activities
Business modeling	Representation of the business organization or one of its subsystems in terms of services provided, their underlying processes, and the overall business architecture.	Business modeling and analysis must take into account the availability of business components and domain artifacts. Modeling decisions may be influenced by the presence of these preexisting artifacts.	Component size qualification
Analysis	Representation of the requirements of the system, both functional and non-functional.		
Design	Representation of the structure and behavior of the solution adopted to realize system requirements.	Selection of components is finalized and adaptation is undertaken. The component-based design represents the architecture connecting and gluing together the selected components.	Component size qualification; component adaptation
Implementation	Realization of the designed solution.	Components are assembled and glue code produced. More realistically, ad hoc components can be implemented if preexisting components do not match required needs.	Component size adaptation; system assembly
Testing	Identification and removal of software errors. Involves unit and integration testing.	Mainly integration testing. Unit testing is carried out for modified white box components.	System assembly
Maintenance	Correction, enhancement, adaptation, and evolution of the software system.	Replacement, addition, and modification of components. Involves identification, adaptation, and integration activities.	System evolution

RESEARCH METHODS FOR COMPONENT-BASED INFORMATION SYSTEMS

Research in component-based information systems (CBIS) is multifaceted and spans several topic areas ranging from organizational to technological issues. This variety of topic areas reflects the high level of diversity also noticeable in information systems research in general. It is interesting to note that explicit studies and discussions of research methods for CBIS are difficult to identify in the literature. This should not be surprising because CBIS is a specialized subject area of IS research and consequently draws upon the same set of research methods, including philosophical stances, investigative techniques, and data sources.

The predominant research method applied throughout this book is design research.

Descriptions of design research and related process guidelines are provided by Nunamaker et al. (1991), Hevner et al. (2004), and Vaishnavi and Kuechler (2004). In design research, "knowledge and understanding of a problem domain and its solution are achieved in the building and application of the designed artifact" (Hevner et al. 2004, 75). Design research is an applied form of research that aims to resolve problems of immediate concern through the development of new solutions in the form of engineered artifacts (Nunamaker et al. 1991). The developed artifacts may take several forms. In CBIS, such artifacts include retrieval algorithms, modeling techniques, software development methodologies, interface specification protocols, and so on (Vaishnavi and Kuechler 2004).

There is a fundamental difference between simple design and design research. While the former applies existing knowledge to solved problems, the latter demonstrates that the designed artifact is capable of addressing effectively either "unresolved problems in unique or innovative ways or solved problems in more effective and efficient ways" (Hevner et al. 2004, 81). Design research also allows for the exploration of new problem areas in order to develop hypotheses or gain further insight (Nunamaker et al. 1991).

As previously stated, design research is primarily concerned with demonstrating the effectiveness of IT artifacts as solutions to well-recognized problems. Unlike other research approaches (e.g., experimental methods) that assume the existence of a truth to discover, design research adheres to the existence of "multiple, contextually situated world-states" that are technologically enabled (Vaishnavi and Kuechler 2004). In this sense, it differentiates itself both from positivist approaches, which recognize the existence of a single reality, and also from interpretive approaches, in which the multiple realities are socially constructed.

In an attempt to identify the research methods most commonly adopted by CBIS researchers, sixteen journal papers have been analyzed. This analysis also serves the purpose of verifying whether the high incidence of research design papers, which characterizes this book, is also significant among the wider CBIS research community. These papers have been specifically studied to understand (1) the theme or topic of research, (2) the outcomes of the work, and, most important, (3) the research methods adopted. The papers analyzed appear in leading IS and software engineering journals. In general, there is a predominance of component-based research conducted within the software engineering community (e.g., research published in *Journal of Systems and Software* and *IEEE Transactions on Software Engineering*). This can be taken as a sign of the issues that CBIS researchers tend to focus on. As in most of the chapters in this book, developmental aspects of component-based systems are dominant. Significantly common in the literature are also papers on the classification and retrieval of components, or, in general, reusable assets. On the other hand, the research on the organizational themes of CBIS is limited. Consequently, CBIS research appears to be an area in which a stronger blend of technical, developmental, and organizational themes is needed. This divide is also noticeable when research methods are considered.

Table 1.3 provides a broad overview of the sixteen journal papers examined. The papers have been chosen in order to encompass a variety of themes. Although some papers did not explicitly mention or describe the research approach used (e.g., Lee and Shirani 2004 and Baster et al. 2000), the papers did contain sufficient information to derive and classify the research method. The key findings of this analysis are as follows:

Table 1.3

Overview of Sixteen CBIS Journal Papers Examined

Journal paper	Topic	Outcomes	Research method
Baster, G., P. Konana, and J.E. Scott. 2000. Business components: A case study of Bankers Trust Australia Limited. *Communications of the ACM* 44, no. 5: 92–98	Business components as a means to lessen the gap between business and technology	Findings show that effective collaboration bridges the gap, resulting in effective implementation of business components	Case study
Jain, H., P. Vitharana, and F.M. Zahedi. 2003. An assessment model for requirements identification in component-based software *DATA BASE for Advances in Information Systems* 34, no. 4: 48–63	Requirements identification in CBD	Assessment model for requirements identification based on information processing theory	Model derived from theory, hence an argumentative approach to its development
Karimi, J. 1990. An asset-based systems development approach to software reusability. *MIS Quarterly* 14, no. 2: 179–198	Reuse; reusable assets	Proposes a long-term organizational strategy for reuse; asset-based systems development method for software reusability (especially at the design level)	Comparative review
Kim, Y.R., and E.A. Stohr. 1998. Software reuse: Survey and research directions. *Journal of Management Information Systems* 14, no. 4 (Spring): 113–149	Software reuse in all aspects relevant to software development in an organization	Survey of the software reuse research. The authors argue that software reuse needs to be viewed in a context of a total systems approach.	Survey by means of review of relevant literature in a topic area
Kunda, D., and L. Brooks. 2000. Assessing organisational obstacles to component-based development: A case study approach. *Information and Software Technology* 42: 715–725	Human, social, and organizational issues affecting the introduction of CBD in organizations	A series of suggestions for developers and managers to consider in order to minimize organizational problems	Case study
Lee, S.C., and A.I. Shirani. 2004. A component-based methodology for Web application development. *Journal of Systems and Software* 71: 177–187	CBD of Web applications	Proposal of a CBD methodology for Web applications	Development example to demonstrate the methodology

Reference	Topic	Findings	Method
Mili, R., A. Mili, and R.T. Mittermeir. 1997. Storing and retrieving software components: A refinement-based system. *IEEE Transactions on Software Engineering*, 23, no. 7: 445–459	Component storage and retrieval	Proposal of a structure for storing and retrieving components from a library	Formal methods and design research through a prototype
Morisio, M., C.B. Seaman, V.R. Basili, A.T. Parra, S.E. Kraft, and S.E. Condon. 2002. COTS-based software development: Processes and open issues. *Journal of Systems and Software* 61: 189–199.	COTS-based software processes	From the interviews the actual process emerged along with insights and issues. The latter were used to propose a new COTS process.	Case study (fifteen projects). Observation study with interviews designed by using the Goal-Question-Metric s (GQM) method
Nazareth, D.L., and M.A. Rithenberger. 2004. Assessing the cost-effectiveness of software reuse: A model for planned reuse. *Journal of Systems and Software* 73, no. 2: 245–255	Evaluation of reuse benefits in software projects	Findings related to the relationships between component size, repository size, and savings	Experimental: design of a mathematical model, application of model to collect data and data analysis
Pighin, M., and G. Brajnik. 2000. A formative evaluation of information retrieval techniques applied to software catalogues. *Journal of Systems and Software* 52: 131–138	Effectiveness of information retrieval techniques from software catalogs	Evaluation of a prototype developed for retrieving information from software catalogs	Prototype and empirical evaluation (experimental method)
Plasil, F., and S. Visnovsky. 2002. Behavior protocols for software components. *IEEE Transactions on Software Engineering* 28, no. 11: 1056–1075	Component description through behavior protocols	Proposal of a means to enhance an architecture description language with a description of component behavior	Formal methods and design research through a proof of concept
Ravichandran, T. 1999. Software reusability as synchronous innovation: A test of four theoretical models. *European Journal of Information Systems* 8, no. 3: 183–199	Administrative change and reuse	Synergies were found to exist between administrative and technological dimensions of reusability to explain variance in systems delivery performance	Postal survey

(continued)

Table 1.3 (continued)

Journal paper	Topic	Outcomes	Research method
Rotheberger, M.A., K.J. Dooley, U.R. Kulkarni, and N. Nada. 2003. Strategies for software reuse: A principal component analysis of reuse practices. *IEEE Transactions on Software Engineering* 29, no. 9: 825–837	Reuse strategies	Consolidation of existing reuse success factors into six dimensions	Survey with statistical analysis of data
Spinellis, D. and K. Raptis. 2000. Component mining: A process and its pattern language. *Information and Software Technology* 42: 609–617	Component mining	Development of a component mining pattern language	Design research through a proof of concept (authors refer to this as a case study)
Sugumaran, V., and V.C. Storey. 2003. A semantic-based approach to component retrieval. *DATA BASE for Advances in Information Systems* 34, no. 3: 8–24	Component retrieval	Development of an approach with a natural language interface for component retrieval that utilizes the domain knowledge embedded in ontologies and domain models	Design research through a prototype
Zhuge, H. 2000. A problem-oriented and rule-based component repository. *Journal of Systems and Software* 50: 201–208	Repository organization and retrieval techniques	Proposal of a problem-oriented component reuse framework that incorporates a problem-solving mechanism into traditional repositories	Simulation

- Design research is the dominant research method applied. This method can be identified in at least five of the papers and is particularly valuable in demonstrating the effectiveness of a particular Information Technology (IT) artifact or solution (Hevner et al. 2004). Examples include a development methodology (Lee and Shirani 2004), techniques for component storage and retrieval (Mili et al. 1997; Sugumaran and Storey 2003), a pattern language for component mining (Spinellis and Raptis 2000) and descriptors for component behaviour (Plasil and Visnovsky 2002).
- As noted earlier, design research is also applied extensively throughout the chapters of this book. The main contributions are in the areas of methodologies for component development and their assembly (see Chapters 2 through 7 and Chapter 9) and techniques for retrieving and selecting commercial off-the-shelf components (see Chapters 10 and 11).
- Case study and survey research is particularly effective for investigating organizational and administrative themes of CBIS (Ravichandran 1999; Kunda and Brooks 2000), and the evaluation of component-based software processes (Morisio et al. 2002). Morisio et al. (2002) collect data through structured interviews formulated with the Goal-Question-Metrics (GQM) technique.
- Case study research has been applied by Bosch in Chapter 8. Bosch proposes alternative organizational structures for software development organizations adopting software product families. His alternatives derive from case study work carried out in several software companies. Case studies are also used as units of analysis, in conjunction with design research, in Chapters 7 and 10. The case studies in these chapters are aimed at demonstrating the effectiveness of the testing and retrieval techniques respectively described.
- Formal methods are mainly applied to themes in which logical rigor is essential, for example in demonstrating the correctness of a solution (Plasil and Visnovsky 2002).
- Comparative literature surveys provide comparative evaluations of the research conducted over time on specific areas. Sometimes the papers develop conceptual frameworks summarizing major issues in the area. For example, Kim and Stohr (1998) survey the research literature on software reuse and develop a comprehensive framework that addresses a broad range of issues (technical, economic, managerial, organizational, and legal) related to reuse in organizations.

VOLUME OVERVIEW

The remaining chapters provide significant detail to the topics summarized in this introduction. All chapters describe research work that has been applied in industrial settings. Thus, the book provides significant contributions to both research and practice. Many case studies are presented as a means to illustrate approaches, methods, and techniques. Several authors use or refer to the Unified Modeling Language (UML) in their work as a means to model the problem or solution domain. At the time of writing of the chapters, a new version of the UML (version 2.0) was released. Therefore, it is important to note that all references to the UML are to versions 1.x.

The book is organized as follows:

- Part I presents six papers (Chapters 2 through 7) related to component-based development methodologies and system architectures.
- Part II presents two papers (Chapters 8 and 9) that analyze different aspects of managing component-based development. The first paper looks into possible organizational structures, while the second is concerned with the developmental aspects of managing CBIS.

• Part III presents two papers (Chapters 10 and 11) on component-based development with commercial off-the-shelf products (COTS). The main topics described in these papers relate to the selection and trade of COTS products.

Brief descriptions of the chapters follow.

In Chapter 2, Stojanovic, Dahanayake, and Sol present an approach that focuses on the analysis and design stages of the development of component-based systems. Effective alignment and balance between business and IT concerns represent the key challenge. In addition, the approach offers a means to enforce bidirectional traceability between the business and system requirements. This is achieved through implementation-independent components, thus raising components' traditional level of abstraction, that is, from the implementation (code) level to the analysis and design level. In terms of platform-independent models (PIM), this approach is in line with the philosophy underpinning Model-Drive Architecture, an initiative of the Object Management Group (OMG).

In Chapter 3, Doğru focuses on the design and implementation phases of component-based systems. In CBD, implementation essentially refers to component integration. The approach proposed by Doğru enforces a "build by integration" paradigm. The approach is supported by conceptual underpinnings as well as a modeling language (COSEML) that provides constructs that overcome the limitations of current modeling languages, such as the UML. Doğru presents a case study in support of the overall approach.

In Chapter 4, Atkinson, Bunse, Kamsties, and Zettel pick up on the challenge of modeling component-based systems and discuss the KobrA method. KobrA supports four well-grounded principles of software development (uniformity, locality, parsimony, and encapsulation). The chapter describes the issues involved in applying these principles to systematic software development. Although, the UML is applied by KobrA, the authors justly point out that in order to model components comprehensively (and in light of the aforementioned principles), it is necessary to use the full power of the UML to create multiple, interrelated views of each component's behavior and properties.

In Chapter 5, Acosta and Madey provide an outline of the technical challenges of building distributed component systems. The chapter initially discusses the basic model of distributed component system architectures and describes the technical aspects of distributed communication. Support for multiple Remote Procedure Call (RPC) mechanisms is specifically considered. The authors emphasize the need to develop distributed architectures with appropriate levels of flexibility and robustness. To achieve this goal, software architects must address various issues (e.g., API syntax, object serialization, protocol compliance, and component usage semantics) that are critical for making decisions concerning not only the overall system architecture, but also the distributed component technology that will be employed. Acosta and Madey describe strategies for addressing these issues and present a Web e-commerce case study. The case study illustrates how decisions were taken during the design of an actual distributed system.

In Chapter 6, O'Callaghan argues that the recent advances achieved in component-based development and integration (CBDi) have had limited impact on the "software crisis." Progress in the area of CBD processes has been insufficient, especially in terms of the skill and experience of development staff. O'Callaghan proposes the use of architectural patterns to address these process issues. The ADAPTOR pattern language is suggested as a means to facilitate and improve the design of software architectures as well as the architectural skills of individuals. The author reviews related work and outlines directions for future work.

In Chapter 7, Kolb and Muthig present testing techniques and strategies for two development paradigms, component-based software and product lines. The chapter describes a test planning framework that guides the systematic definition of an efficient test plan prescribing the usage of test techniques and the scope of testing, for a given reuse context. The authors present case study to illustrate the techniques and strategies presented.

In Chapter 8, Bosch presents four organizational models for software development organizations that apply software product family principles. As Bosch emphasizes, organizational models developed around the technical and process aspects of CBD (and domain engineering) provide only a restricted view of the many alternatives that emerge by observing the way software development organizations structure themselves and naturally evolve. The organizational models described in the chapter derive from work conducted with numerous companies adopting a development approach based on software product families. The chapter presents the situations in which the models are applicable, the advantages and disadvantages of each model, and organizational decision-making factors.

In Chapter 9, Janssen and Wagenaar present a business engineering approach aimed at defining and specifying business processes and mapping the processes to software components. Aligning business and system models is a difficult problem in information systems development in general and presents specific problems in the context of component-based development in which business requirements may sometimes be modified in order to align with available components. The authors present the advantages and disadvantages of the approach and illustrate its application through a case study.

In Chapter 10, Leung compares selection methods for COTS products. Mainly two types of methods for assessing components are analyzed. (1) Direct assessment methods assess all components from a source. The selection is based on a comparison and evaluation of all characteristics describing the components. (2) Indirect assessment methods make use of a domain model to narrow down the number of components to assess and select from. The comparison takes into account the steps and efficiency of the respective processes. Leung presents a case study to illustrate one of the methods analyzed.

In Chapter 11, Iribarne, Troya, and Vallecillo investigate the issues surrounding the selection of COTS components and their subsequent assembly. A trading-based development method (TBDM) is described. TBDM relates to three areas: (1) the documentation and specification of COTS components, (2) the description of software architectures with COTS components, and (3) the trading processes for COTS components. The trading process is automated in TBDM. Automation relies on two functions. First, the COTStrader function is used to search for COTS components. Second, the COTSconfig function generates combinations of components that are considered suitable to fulfill the architectural requirements. After presenting the method, the authors present related work and future development of the method.

CONCLUSION

This chapter has provided an overview of the fundamental concepts of CBIS and presented the main problem areas surrounding the subject. Three lines of research have emerged. First, the organization of CBIS was described. This area relates to the administrative mechanisms and organizational structures to put in place in order to implement CBD within the business effectively. Second, the chapter described the problems and issues related to methodological support for both component development and solution assembly, including techniques for the identification and retrieval of stored components and their integration. Last, the third area of CBIS research identified was the technological infrastructure supporting the distribution and communication between components and their execution. This volume presents research work conducted in all three areas, with significant implications for both theory and practice.

This chapter has also presented an analysis of research methods for CBIS. Given the diverse research topics that CBIS covers, various research methods have emerged, with a significant predominance of design research. This finding is a result of the high frequency of papers published on CBIS development and technology as opposed to its organizational aspects. The main conclusion that can be drawn from this analysis is the presence of a dichotomy in CBIS research between the soft (organizational, administrative, and social) aspects of CBIS versus its technical aspects, with a predominance of the latter. This finding identifies a gap to bridge in CBIS research represented by the need for a stronger integration between organizational, developmental, and technological aspects.

REFERENCES

Allen, P., and S. Frost. 1998. *Component-Based Development for Enterprise Systems: Applying the SE-LECT Perspective.* Cambridge: Cambridge University Press.

Apte, U., C.S. Sankar, M. Thakur, and J.E. Turner. 1990. Reusability-based strategy for development of information systems: Implementation experience of a bank. *MIS Quarterly* 14, no. 4: 421–434.

Arango, G., and R. Prieto-Diaz. 1989. Domain analysis concepts and research directions. In *Domain Analysis: Acquisition of Reusable Information for Software Construction,* ed. G. Arango and R. Prieto-Diaz. Los Alamitos, CA: IEEE Computer Society Press.

Baster, G., P. Konana, and J.E. Scott. 2000. Business components: A case study of Bankers Trust Australia Limited. *Communications of the ACM* 44, no. 5: 92–98.

Bosch, J. 2000. *Design and Use of Software Architectures.* New York: Addison-Wesley.

Brereton, P., and D. Budgen. 2000. Component-based systems: A classification of issues. *IEEE Computer* 33, no. 11: 54–62.

Brown, A.W., and K.C. Wallnau. 1996. Engineering of component-based systems. In *Component-Based Software Engineering: Selected Papers from the Software Engineering Institute.* Los Alamitos, CA: IEEE Computer Society Press, 1996.

———. 1998. The current state of CBSE. *IEEE Software* 15, no. 5: 37–46.

Crnkovic, I., and M. Larsson. 2002. Challenges of component-based development. *Journal of Systems and Software* 61, no. 3: 201–212.

Daga, A., S. de Cesare, M. Lycett, and C. Partridge. 2005. An ontological approach for recovering legacy business content. Proceedings of the 38th Hawaii International Conference on System Sciences. Los Alamitos, CA: IEEE Computer Society Press.

Deelstra, S., M. Sinnema, and J. Bosch. 2005. Product derivation in software product families: A case study. *Journal of Systems and Software* 74: 173–194.

Ewusi-Mensah, K. 2003. *Software Development Failures.* Cambridge, MA: MIT Press.

Fafchamps, D. 1994. Organisational factors and reuse. *IEEE Software* 11, no. 5: 31–41.

Fichman, R.G., and C.F. Kemerer. 2001. Incentive Compatibility and Systematic Software Reuse. *Journal of Systems and Software* 57, no. 1: 45–60.

Firesmith, D.G. 1993. *Object-Oriented Requirements Analysis and Logical Design.* New York: Wiley.

Fitzgerald, B., N.L.Russo, and E. Stolterman. 2002. *Information Systems Development.* London: McGraw-Hill.

Foreman, J. 1996. Product line based software development: Significant results, future challenges. Presented at the *Software Technology Conference.* Salt Lake City.

Garlan, D., R. Allen, and J. Ockerbloom. 1995. Architectural mismatch: Why reuse is so hard. *IEEE Software* 12, no. 6: 17–26.

Gibbs, W.W. 1994. Software's chronic crisis. *Scientific American* 271, no. 3 September: 72–81.

Griss, M.L., and M. Wosser. 1995. Making reuse work at Hewlett-Packard. *IEEE Software* 12, no. 1: 105–107.

Hersleb, J.D., and D. Moitra. 2001. Global software development. *IEEE Software* 18, no. 2: 16–20.

Hevner, A.R., S.T. March, J. Park, and S. Ram. 2004. Design science in information systems research. *MIS Quarterly* 28, no. 2: 74–105.

Holzle, U. 1993. Integrating independently developed components in object-oriented languages. In *Proceedings of European Conference on Object-Oriented Programming (ECOOP '93)*. Kaiserlautern, Germany: 36–56.

Jacobson, I., M. Griss, and P. Jonsson. 1997. *Software Reuse: Architecture, Process and Organization for Business Success*. New York: ACM Press Addison-Wesley.

Jain, H., P. Vitharana, and F.M. Zahedi. 2003. An assessment model for requirements identification in component-based software development. *DATA BASE for Advances in Information Systems* 34, no. 4: 48–63.

Kang, K.C., S.G. Cohen, J.A. Hess, W.E. Novak, and A.S. Peterson. 1990. *Feature-Oriented Domain Analysis (FODA) Feasibility Study*, Special Report CMU/SEI-90-TR-21. Pittsburgh, PA: Software Engineering Institute, Carnegie Mellon University.

Karimi, J. 1990. An asset-based systems development approach to software reusability. *MIS Quarterly* 14, no. 2: 179–198.

Kim, Y.R., and E.A. Stohr. 1998. Software reuse: Survey and research directions. *Journal of Management Information Systems* 14, no. 4 (Spring): 113–149.

Kunda, D., and L. Brooks. 2000. Assessing organisational obstacles to component-based development: A case study approach. *Information and Software Technology* 42: 715–725.

Lee, S.C., and A.I. Shirani. 2004. A component based methodology for Web application development. *Journal of Systems and Software* 71: 177–187.

Lubars, M. 1991. Domain analysis and domain engineering in IDeA. In *Domain Analysis and Software Systems Modelling*. Los Alamitos, CA: IEEE Computer Society Press.

Lycett, M. 2005. Administrative innovation in component-based development: A clinical fieldwork perspective. Submitted to the *Journal of Management Information Systems*.

Maes, P. 1995. Modeling adaptive autonomous agents. In *Artificial Life, An Overview*, ed. Christopher G. Langton. Cambridge, MA: MIT Press.

Maiden, N.A.M., L. James, and C. Ncube. 1999. Evaluating large COTS software packages: Why requirements and use cases are important. Presented at *Workshop on Ensuring Successful COTS Development, International Conference on Software Engineering (ICSE)*, Los Angeles.

McIlroy, M.D. 1968. Mass produced software components. In *Proceedings of NATO Conference on Software Engineering*, Garmisch, Germany.

Mili, R., A. Mili, and R.T. Mittermeir. 1997. Storing and retrieving software components: A refinement based system. *IEEE Transactions on Software Engineering* 23, no. 7: 445–459.

Morisio, M., C.B. Seaman, V.R. Basili, A.T. Parra, S.E. Kraft, and S.E. Condon. 2002. COTS-based software development: Processes and open issues. *Journal of Systems and Software* 61: 189–199.

Nazareth, D.L., and M.A. Rithenberger. 2004. Assessing the cost-effectiveness of software reuse: A model for planned reuse. *Journal of Systems and Software* 73, no. 2: 245–255.

Neighbors, J. 1984. The Draco approach to constructing software from reusable components. *IEEE Transactions of Software Engineering* 10, no. 5: 564–574.

Nunamaker, J., M. Chen, and T. Purdin. 1991. System Development in Information Systems Research. *Journal of Management Information Systems* 7, no. 3: 89–106.

OMG. 2001. *The Common Component Architecture Technical Specification*.

Pighin, M., and G. Brajnik. 2000. A formative evaluation of information retrieval techniques applied to software catalogues. *Journal of Systems and Software* 52: 131–138.

Plasil, F., and S. Visnovsky. 2002. Behavior protocols for software components. *IEEE Transactions on Software Engineering* 28, no. 11: 1056–1075.

Prieto-Diaz, R. 1987. Domain analysis for reusability. In *Proceedings of 11th Annual International Computer Software and Application Conference*. Los Alamitos: IEEE Computer Society Press.

Rafi, F., and S. Perkins. 1995. Internationalising software with concurrent engineering. *IEEE Software* 12, no. 5: 39–46.

Raviart, D. 2001. *System Integration and Custom Application Development: A Market Forecast and the Leading Players*. Framingham, MA: International Data Corporation.

Ravichandran, T. 1999. Software reusability as synchronous innovation: A test of four theoretical models. *European Journal of Information Systems* 8, no. 3: 183–199.

Rotheberger, M.A., K.J. Dooley, U.R. Kulkarni, and N. Nada. 2003. Strategies for software reuse: A principal component analysis of reuse practices. *IEEE Transactions on Software Engineering* 29, no. 9: 825–837.

Seacord, R.C., and C.N. Kingsley. 1999. Life cycle activity areas for component-based software engineering processes. In *Proceedings of Technology of Object-Oriented Languages and Systems (TOOLS)*. Los Alamitos, CA: IEEE Computer Society Press.

Spinellis, D., and K. Raptis. 2000. Component mining: A process and its pattern language. *Information and Software Technology,* 42: 609–617.

Standish Group. 2003. *CHAOS Chronicles v3.0.* West Yarmouth, MA: Standish Group.

Succi, G., and F. Baruchelli. 1997. The cost of standardising components for software reuse. *StandardView* 5, no. 2: 61–65.

Sugumaran, V., and V.C. Storey. 2003. A semantic-based approach to component retrieval. *DATA BASE for Advances in Information Systems* 34, no. 3: 8–24.

Sussman, S.W., and P.J. Guinan. 1999. Antidotes for high complexity and ambiguity in software development. *Information & Management* 36, no. 1: 23–35.

Szyperski, C. 1999. *Component Software.* New York: Addison-Wesley.

Szyperski, C., and C. Pfister. 1997. Workshop on component-oriented programming, summary. In *Special Issues in Object-Oriented Programming: ECOOP96 Workshop Reader,* ed. M. Muhlhauser. Heidelberg: Springer-Verlag.

Truex, D.P., R. Baskerville, and H. Klein. 1999. Growing systems in emergent organisations. *Communications of the ACM* 42, no. 8: 117–123.

Vaishnavi, V., and B. Kuechler. 2004. Design research in information systems, www.isworld.org/Researchdesign/drisISworld.htm.

Zand, M., and M. Samadzadeh. 1995. Software Reuse: Current Status and Trends. *Journal of Systems and Software* 30, no. 3: 167–170.

Zhuge, H. 2000. A problem-oriented and rule-based component repository. *Journal of Systems and Software,* 50, no. 3: 201–208.

PART I

COMPONENT-BASED DEVELOPMENT METHODOLOGIES AND SYSTEMS ARCHITECTURES

PART I

CHAPTER 2

AN APPROACH TO COMPONENT-BASED AND SERVICE-ORIENTED SYSTEM ARCHITECTURE DESIGN

ZORAN STOJANOVIC, AJANTHA DAHANAYAKE, AND HENK SOL

Abstract: *Although component-based middleware technologies, such as Common Object Request Broker Architecture (CORBA), COM+/.NET, and Enterprise JavaBeans (EJB), are now de facto standards for implementation and deployment of complex enterprise distributed systems, the full benefit of the component way of thinking has not been gained yet. Current component-based development theory and practice treat and use components mainly as binary or source-code implementation artifacts that can be deployed over network nodes. The component concept is rarely used during system analysis and design, and when it is, components are mainly defined as closely matching the underlying business entities and represented as corresponding business objects. Little attention so far has been paid to components as architectural building blocks that provide real-world, value-added business services that in collaboration support the goal of the system in the business context. This chapter presents an approach to component-based design that uses service-based components as first-class citizens in mapping the requirements into software code. By using the set of implementation-independent component concepts, the approach creates a multilevel, platform-independent system architecture that provides an effective way of balancing business and IT concerns, as well as bi-directional traceability between business needs and software implementation.*

Keywords: *Service-Oriented Component Architecture, Analysis and Design, Separation of Concerns, Business Architecture, Component and Service Modeling*

INTRODUCTION

The main challenges enterprises face today are how to manage the complexity of systems being developed, effectively utilize the power of the Internet, and rapidly adapt to changes in both technology and business. New, highly changeable demands in the business environment require an immediate support of the corresponding information technology (IT) solutions. At the same time, new IT opportunities must be rapidly adopted through the new way of conducting business. Therefore, today more than ever it is important to provide a seamless integration between the business and IT as well as a flexible, agile way of building software systems in order to achieve the high flexibility and quality of the solution within the short time-to-market.

The paradigm of component-based development (CBD) has been introduced as an excellent solution for building complex enterprise-scale information systems (Brown and Wallnau 1998; Szyperski 1998). CBD provides organizations with a method for building flexible, enterprise-scale solutions that are able to accommodate ever-changing requirements in a cost-effective, timely manner. Following the CBD approach, system development becomes the selection, reconfiguration, adaptation, assembling, and deployment of encapsulated, replaceable, and reusable building blocks called components, rather than building the whole system from scratch. CBD provides higher productivity in system development through reusability, more effective system maintenance, higher quality of solutions, and the possibility for parallel work. Moreover, it provides better system adaptability through the replaceability of parts, localization and better control of changes, system scalability, and possibility of using legacy assets.

The CBD paradigm has often been presented as a new silver bullet for complex, enterprise-scale system development in the Internet age (Udell 1994). However, CBD is more an evolutionary than revolutionary approach, since it inherits many concepts and ideas from the earlier encapsulation and modularization, divide-and-conquer initiatives in computer science. The Garmisch NATO Conference on software engineering in 1968 recognized that producing software should be treated as an engineering discipline in the sense that software systems should be made by assembling software components (McIlroy 1969). Parnas (1972) defines concepts and requirements for decomposing the system into modules. These principles of separation of concerns, encapsulation, and plug-and-play building blocks have been applied in different ways through the concepts of functions, subroutines, modules, units, packages, subsystems, objects, and now components. Recently, the new paradigm of Web services has been introduced, representing the further convergence of business and technology issues. The concept of Web service is a natural extension of the component concept in building loosely coupled systems according to the service-oriented architecture. A number of industry standards for utilizing Web services have been proposed (Web Services Description Language (WSDL); Simple Object Access Protocol (SOAP); Universal Description, Discovery, and Integration (UDDI), etc.) (Curbera et al. 2002).

The CBD paradigm was first introduced at the level of implementation and deployment. CBD middleware technologies, such as CORBA Components (Siegel 2000), Enterprise JavaBeans (developed by Sun Microsystems), and COM+/.NET (developed by Microsoft), are now used as standards for the development of complex enterprise distributed systems. On the other hand, several CBD methods and approaches have been proposed so far. Since these approaches mainly follow object-oriented methodology practice and the standard Unified Modeling Language (UML) (Booch et al. 1999), they treat components as implementation artifacts, that is, packages of binary or source code that can be deployed over network nodes. At the levels of architectural modeling, system analysis, and design, components are commonly represented as data-driven business classes and objects, encapsulating business entity data and providing methods to access and manipulate that data.

Numerous definitions of a component proposed so far show that everybody still sees components differently. The clear distinction between components and concepts such as objects and classes, packages, subsystems, and modules has not been made yet. As a consequence, the significance of the new component mind-set in system development and specially the potential of the component concept in providing a common ground between business and technology concerns have not been truly recognized yet. Therefore, the component mind-set must be adopted and applied in earlier phases of the development life cycle, as a way to organize business requirements, specify the system architecture, and provide an effective mapping to the component middleware code.

Components must be defined in a more behavior-driven, service-based way in order to provide easy mapping of business processes and services into the service-oriented system architecture, where the collaboration and coordination of services and components represent the core of the system. Therefore, a clear set of uniform and implementation-independent component models must be defined so that it can be applied throughout the development process, providing the point of consistency among different viewpoints on the system.

Furthermore, proposed CBD approaches are often very complex and heavyweight, making them difficult and time-consuming to understand and apply. In the current, fast-changing world of business and IT, more flexible, adaptable, agile, and easy-to-use approaches are needed, in order to shorten time to market and produce high-quality, easily adaptable solutions. More precisely components and services, as mechanisms for raising the level of abstraction in system development and equally understandable for both business and IT, should be the cornerstones and prerequisites of the new, agile development practice.

This chapter proposes a service-based approach to components that provides a consistent and integrated view of components as the central concept of model-driven system development. The approach defines the set of technology-independent and consistent component concepts and applies the same component way of thinking to different aspects of enterprise systems development, from autonomous business services to implementation artifacts. Components are defined as managers of business and/or technical services and the main building blocks of the business-driven system architecture. This architecture represents a way of balancing business and technology issues. It provides ability to model business services and requirements at a higher level, in a domain-specific, but implementation-independent way. On the other hand, the specification component architecture can be easily mapped into complete implementation based on particular component technology. As a consequence, the clear connection between particular business requirements and software artifacts that realize them is provided in both directions. The approach presented here can be effectively applied for modeling, analysis, and design of systems that are realized using Web services (Curbera et al. 2002). By using this approach, Web services become just one way of realizing a component-based architecture specification. The approach provides a paradigm shift from components as objects to components as services. The approach presented here can be defined as a service-based, agile approach for designing component architecture, since it provides an effective and agile manner of specifying components and component-based solutions that can be easily adapted to changes in the business and technology environment.

In the remainder of this chapter, we first present the state of the art of CBD and outline various approaches to components and component-based design and development proposed so far. In describing the most relevant CBD approaches, we mainly focus on the way they define, identify, and use component concepts. In the next section, we define essential component concepts that represent the very nature of components, as well as component specification concepts that represent the contractual interface of the component to the context. Various types of components in terms of scope and granularity are identified.

Following that, we propose a component-oriented design approach that maps business requirements into flexible multilayer architecture. This architecture can serve as a point of negotiation between different actors in the component-based development process. The example of a location-based geographic information application shows how defined component concepts and the design approach can be applied in practice. The chapter ends with a discussion and conclusion.

THE STATE OF THE ART OF COMPONENT-BASED DEVELOPMENT

Component technologies are now widely used in the development of complex distributed information systems. First, VBX controls, DCOM/COM, CORBA, and JavaBeans, and now COM+/.NET, CORBA components, and Enterprise JavaBeans (EJB) represent the standard component-based implementation solutions. Based on them, component-based frameworks and architectures have been developed to speed up the application development—for example, the IBM San Francisco framework based on EJB (Carey et al. 2000) and the TINA architecture for building telecommunication systems based on CORBA (TINA 1997).

The physical perspective on components as binary packages of software is still predominant. UML treats components as packages of binary code and uses them in describing system implementation through component and deployment diagrams (Booch et al. 1999). Components in UML represent physical things that can be deployed over network nodes. The Catalysis approach defines a component as a package of software code as well as other software artifacts (D'Souza and Wills 1999). According to Szyperski, a software component is a unit of composition with contractually specified interfaces and explicit context dependencies (Szyperski 1998). A software component can be deployed independently and is subject to composition by third parties. Herzum and Sims (2000) define business component as the software implementation of an autonomous business concept or business process. Business components represent a means for modeling real-world concepts in the business domain. When introducing components, the question about similarities and differences between objects and components naturally arises. According to Udell (1994), components represent a new silver bullet for system development in the Internet age, while objects have failed to provide higher level of reusability. In the UML, components are nothing else than larger-grained objects deployed on network nodes (OMG 2003a). According to Szyperski (1998), a component comes to life through objects and, therefore, it would normally contain one or more classes, as well as traditional procedures and even global variables. In a debate over this topic, granularity has been seen as the main issue in distinguishing components and objects (Henderson-Sellers et al. 1999). In Catalysis, components are often larger-grained than traditional objects and can be implemented as multiple objects of different classes. Components can use persistent storage, while objects typically work only within the main memory.

Academia and industry have just started to recognize the importance of new CBD methods, processes, techniques, and guidelines. The methods and approaches are often greatly influenced by the object-oriented concepts, constructs, and principles dictated by the use of the standard UML. The Rational Unified Process (RUP) (Jacobson et al. 1999), Catalysis, and the Select Perspective (Allen and Frost 1998) can be considered the first generation of the CBD methods as presented in Dahanayake et al. (2003). The RUP does not specifically target at component-based development. It rather offers a general framework for object-oriented design and construction. Components are implementation units that package other software artifacts and are deployed over network nodes. The Select Perspective was originally an object-oriented method with the later addition of component modeling principles. It defines a component as a service or implementation package. The method is not that sophisticated; it rather combines best of breed techniques and tools. The Catalysis approach originates from several Object Oriented (OO) methods and approaches, with the component concepts added afterward. Therefore, object and component concepts are interleaved in Catalysis to some extent. Catalysis provides a remarkable CBD support and many valuable concepts and principles for understanding components, but not a systematic road map or ease of use.

The Business Component Factory (BCF) (Herzum and Sims 2000), the UML Components approach (Cheesman and Daniels 2000), and the KobrA approach (Atkinson et al. 2001) represent the second generation of the CBD methods. These methods are more focused on components concepts than previous ones. They provide comprehensive support to CBD throughout the system life cycle, and they represent remarkable achievements in the field. On the other hand, there are certain shortcomings. The BCF approach defines business components as representation of autonomous business concepts and business processes in the domain. By separating entities and behavior, this approach does not provide a uniform view of components. On the other hand, the role and importance of service-based interfaces are diminished. The UML components approach does not take into account potential different levels of component granularity and the importance of using the separation of concerns in defining them. The approach proposes mainly a data-driven way of identifying components that does not fit well into the advanced service-driven computing initiatives. The KobrA method describes components by using UML class and object diagrams. A KobrA component has at the same time properties of a class and a package. On the other hand, the role of component interface is not emphasized enough. The composition of components is defined mainly through containment trees, instead of collaboration between component interfaces.

One of the most important activities in practicing component-oriented development is how to start with components, that is, how to identify components and place them properly in the development life cycle. The way of identifying components is very closely related to how components are defined and treated. According to the UML guide, components are identified during the implementation and deployment phases as a way of packaging and deploying software code artifacts (Booch et al. 1999). In the Business Component Factory, business components are identified as important business concepts that are relatively autonomous in the problem space. In the UML components approach, components are identified through the core business types. These core types result in business component interfaces to manage instances of those types. In addition, system interfaces interacting with those components are derived from use cases. In RUP, components are represented as subsystems in component-based design, but without further details about their identification. There is no strict prescription for identifying components in Catalysis. The emphasis in Catalysis is on component collaboration in the form of the framework, and components are represented through type analysis. The KobrA approach does not offer strict rules about how to identify components (Atkinson et al. 2001). The approach rather treats important business domain concepts as components and follows OO analysis and design on them. In Jain et al. (2001), an algorithmic approach is proposed that treats components as containers of classes. It uses a clustering algorithm on the domain model that represents significant domain classes, together with the sets of managerial and technical goals in component-based system design.

THE COMPONENT WAY OF THINKING

Little attention has been paid so far to applying the component concepts and component way of thinking in earlier phases of the system life cycle, that is, system analysis and design. In our opinion, the component concept becomes most useful when used as an architectural-level artifact to model the logical architecture of the technical or business and domain infrastructures. In this chapter we are interested in how components can help in the effective building of flexible, business-driven system architecture. After the complete distributed system architecture is precisely specified in a component-oriented manner, we can decide on concrete realizations of specified components in one of the technologies mentioned above. In this way, the precise system specification is a durable result that can be implemented afterward in different ways, using different algorithms, platforms, and technologies. This strategy is now the mainstream of the Object Management Group's (OMG) Model-Driven Architecture (MDA) (OMG 2003b). MDA proposes first designing a Platform Independent Model (PIM) using modeling standards such as the UML, the Meta Object Facility (MOF), and the Common Warehouse Metamodel (CWM), then specifying the Platform Specific Model (PSM) of the system using, for example, the UML Profiles for EJB or CORBA (OMG 2003), and, finally, implementing the system in the target middleware technology.

Our main goal is to propose an approach to define a business-driven, truly component-

Figure 2.1 **Basic Component Concepts**

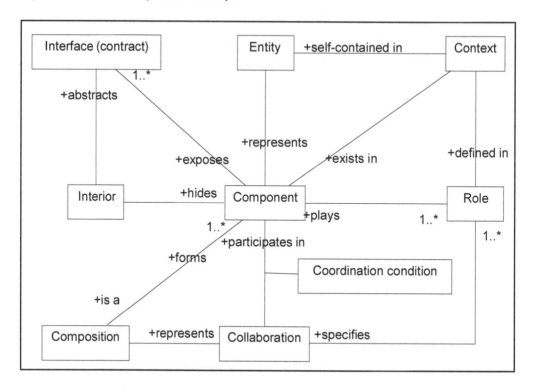

oriented Platform Independent Model that flexibly adopts changes in the business environment and at the same time can be easily transferable to code and middleware. The component concept is the focus and the main artifact of this PIM. In this way, the component architecture specified by the PIM can provide a bridge between business and implementation issues.

Basic Component Concepts

In order to use the consistent component way of thinking at different levels of abstraction, from business concepts to system distribution, we propose a general, implementation-independent concept of a component. In our opinion, a component defined mainly as an autonomous provider of necessary services to its environment represents the point of integration of business and system concerns (Stojanovic and Dahanayake 2002). Regardless of the context of usage, the essence of the component is the explicit separation between the outside and the inside of the concepts being addressed. This means that only the question "What?" is considered (what useful services are provided by the particular building block to the context of its existence), not the "How?" (how these services are actually implemented). The concept of services is equally useful and precise in both business and technical terms. Instead of providing a one-size-fits-all definition of a component, we will define a set of essential component concepts and properties uniformly applicable for component variants. A component is a representation of an entity, which means something that exists as a distinct, independent, or self-contained unit with a clear purpose of existence. A component does not exist in isolation; it fulfils a particular role in a given context and actively communicates with that context. A component encapsulates its content (interior) by exposing its interface (contract) to the context. The context can rely only on the component's interface and not on its interior. So the very basic elements of the component are interior (content), interface (contract), and context (environment). A component participates in a composition with other components to form a higher-level component. At the same time, every component can be represented as a composition of lower-level components. A component must collaborate and coordinate its activities with other components in a composition in order to achieve a higher-level goal of its supercomponent. Well-defined behavioral dependencies and coordination in time between components are extremely important in achieving the common goal. The basic component concepts are shown in Figure 2.1.

Component Specification Concepts

Component specification concepts represent the complete information about the component necessary for its consumer to use it without knowing the component interior. These concepts represent important elements of the contract between the component and its context (Figure 2.2). The following are the main specification concepts of a component:

Component identification—A component is identified in the context by its unique name in the naming space and/or a unique identifier. The name of the component should clearly indicate its purpose in the context and the goal of its existence.

Component behavior—A component is a behavioral unit representing a manager or provider of services. According to the role(s) a component plays in the given context, it exposes corresponding behavior by providing and requiring services to and from its context or emitting and receiving events. The services a component provides and requires are the basic part of its contract. Services can be of different types, such as performing computation, providing information, and communicating with the user. They are fully specified in a contract-based manner using preconditions, postconditions, and other types of constraints. The component with its services collaborates with other components in the context to provide some richer, higher-level behavior. It is important to provide a proper coordination among services participating in the collaboration in order to reach the goal. Coordination of component services can be defined at two levels:

- Coordination among provided and required services of a component, which is basically how the component services are coordinated with the services of other components to reach a higher-level goal.
- Coordination among services of a component's subcomponents in order to produce the expected behavior of the component (i.e., its provided services).

Component information—A component must handle, use, create, or simply be aware of certain information resources in order to provide its services properly. The component contract defines what types of information are of interest to the component, as well as constraints and rules on them. This does not necessarily mean that the component owns or contains that information; the contract defines what information the component needs for exposing the proper behavior. In its simplest form, that information can be considered as parameters of component services.

Context-aware configuration parameters—A component is often dependent on the context of its existence. In order to be used in different contexts or to be adaptable to the changes in its context, a component possesses so-called configuration parameters that can adapt the component contract to fit into possibly new requirements coming from the outside. In this way, the compo-

Figure 2.2 **Component Specification Concepts**

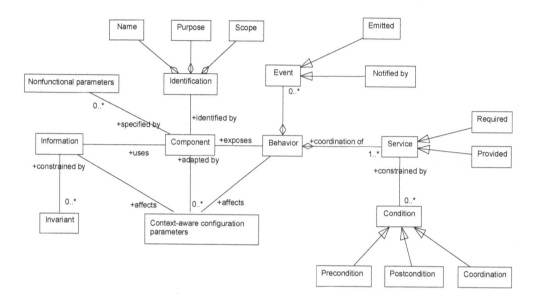

nent can be effectively used in different circumstances and "survive" the possibly frequent changes in the context. Examples of configuration parameters are required quality-of-service (QoS), different profiles of component consumers, and different component locations in time and space.

Nonfunctional (quality) parameters—A component can have defined a set of so-called nonfunctional parameters that characterizes the "quality" of its behavior in the context. Nonfunctional parameters are, for example, performance, reliability, fault tolerance, priority, and security.

All defined component properties must be fully and precisely defined using the concepts of the contract-based theory (Meyer 1997). Precise and formal contract-like specifications of the component and its interface are used to properly assemble and integrate the component into an overall solution for a given problem, to substitute the component by a compatible component if necessary, to browse the component catalog in order to find a component that matches the needed specification, or to reuse the component in a different context. The basic component contract can be extended with the elements of coordination and synchronization of component activities, as well as nonfunctional and configuration parameters. A fully specified component at a specification architecture level is normally implemented by one or many components at the implementation level (using, e.g., CORBA, COM+ components, or EJB) (Figure 2.3).

Component Types

Although many variants of components can be defined at different levels of granularity and/or abstraction, the two basic component design types are business components and application components (Figure 2.4). The main difference between them is that business components provide services that have meaningful, perceivable, and measurable value for the business user, while application components provide lower-level services that in collaboration with other components form a business value for the user. Business components provide business and/or business-

Figure 2.3 **Specification and Implementation of the Component**

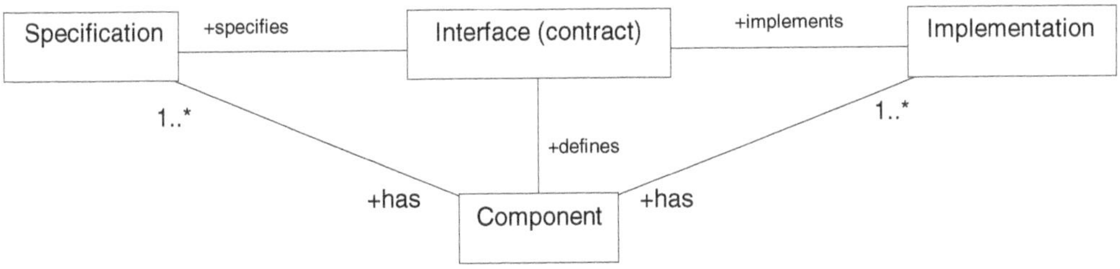

oriented technical services for the business processes in which the system participates. Application components provide finer-grained services, which have more technical than business meaning. Both business and application components can be of different granularity. Therefore, a business component can contain other business components and application components. Application components can contain other application components and lower-level constructs such as object-oriented objects and classes. On the opposite side of the hierarchy, a coarse-grained business component containing lower-level business components that can exist autonomously in the enterprise and that asynchronously communicate with other elements of the enterprise (people, IT systems, other automated systems) is called an enterprise component.

Regarding implementation, application components are normally implemented using one or many implementation components, language classes, or other programming constructs (COM+/.NET components, CORBA components, or EJB). Business components are implemented as a composition of software constructs that realize their subcomponents or can be used as already built third-party software units, such as wrapped legacy assets, Web services, or commercial off-the-shelf (COTS) components.

DESIGNING THE SERVICE-ORIENTED COMPONENT ARCHITECTURE

In this section, we will focus on modeling and specifying complete component-oriented system architectures based on the given business requirements. Enterprise distributed systems being developed are potentially very complex and demanding. That raises the need for applying separation of concerns in specifying system architecture as an effective general strategy for managing the problem complexity. Furthermore, the way of working of our approach is organized in a different manner than in the case of previous object-oriented methods and CBD methods derived from them. So far, the system has been developed from the requirements specification through the set of analysis-level, design-level, and implementation-level class and object diagrams, while behavioral diagrams (sequence or collaboration) have been used to define methods of those classes at different levels of detail. Then, components have been introduced as the way of grouping, packaging, and deploying those classes and objects over the application tiers. Our approach defines the component concept as the focus of the whole development process. The approach identifies components, specifies them, composes them, and decomposes them if necessary until the complete service-based component architecture is fully specified. After that, the black-box components are "opened" and their interiors are specified in terms of classes and objects and their collaboration as the object-oriented implementation has been naturally chosen. If not, the interior of a component can be realized in any other way (e.g., procedural).

Figure 2.4 **Types of Components**

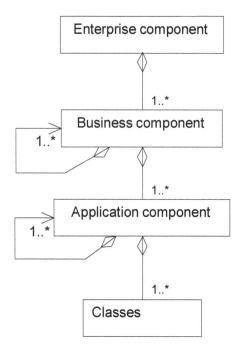

Separation of Concerns

In order to manage complexity and ensure the completeness of the specification of components and component-oriented system architectures, we use the International Standard Organization (ISO) standard Reference Model of Open Distributed Processing (RM-ODP) as an underlying idea (ODP 1996). RM-ODP defines a framework for specifying architectures for distribution, interoperability, and portability of applications based on object-oriented technology. It is widely recognized as offering the most complete and internally consistent specification framework. The RM-ODP specification of a system consists of five different specifications, corresponding to five separate but related and consistent viewpoints—enterprise, information, computation, engineering, and technology.

- The *enterprise viewpoint* specification of the system defines the purpose, scope, and policies of the system in the context of the enterprise it belongs to. The specification defines the set of business rules, constraints, and policies applied to the system as a means of automating the business processes of the enterprise.
- The *information viewpoint* specification of the system defines the types, constraints, and semantics of information handled by the system, as well as the possible ways of information processing. The information specification of the system is a model and dynamics of the information that the system holds, uses, or remembers.
- The *computation viewpoint* specification of the system specifies the components and services inside the system and how they collaborate to produce a cohesive set of functionalities provided by the system.

- The *engineering viewpoint* specification of the system specifies in detail how components and services of the system are deployed on the network tiers when distribution aspects are taken into account, as well as how that distribution is organized.
- The *technology viewpoint* specification of the system defines particular technology aspects, requirements, and constraints of the future implementation of the system.

We use the RM-ODP as an underlying framework for the specification of the system architecture in a component- and service-oriented manner (Stojanovic et al. 2000; Stojanovic et al. 2001). Based on the ODP viewpoints, we propose the following three architectural models that represent logical layers of our service-oriented component architecture:

- Business Architecture Model (BAM)—a model of the system as collaboration of components and services that offer business value.
- Application Architecture Model (AAM)—a model of the system that shows how business components and services are realized by the collaboration of finer-grained components.
- Implementation Architecture Model (IAM)—a model of the system that shows how business and application components and services can be realized using a particular implementation platform.

The BAM roughly corresponds to the ODP Enterprise Viewpoint, the AAM to the Computation Viewpoint, and the IAM to the Technology Viewpoint. Distribution concerns described by the ODP Engineering Viewpoint, and information semantics and dynamics described by the ODP Information Viewpoint, are integrated throughout all three architectural models. Thus, distribution can be considered as business components distribution (virtual enterprises, legacy assets, Web services), application distribution (logical distribution tiers), and implementation distribution (support by the particular middleware). Similarly, in the BAM a conceptual information model is defined, in the AAM a specification information model is fully specified, and in the IAM the ways of data organization and storage are considered. Our main idea is to incorporate the component concept into each of the RM-ODP viewpoints (Stojanovic et al. 2000). In this way, we can define component-oriented viewpoints on the system, completely focused on the component concept and organized around it, as a powerful means for specifying the component architecture. The same consistent set of component concepts used in different viewpoints represents the point of consistency and integration between them (Stojanovic et al. 2001). The same is true for the architectural models in the sense that the central artifact of each model is a component of a particular type. The BAM and AAM actually represent two levels of abstraction of a component-oriented platform independent model (PIM), while the IAM describes a component-oriented platform specific model (PSM) for a particular technology platform. By defining all three models in a consistent manner, the whole system is specified and ready for implementation. Completing the models is not done in a sequential order, although it is natural to start in a top-down manner. The best result is achieved using an incremental and iterative approach that represents the de facto standard in systems development, in both traditional and agile methodologies. Figure 2.5 shows our architectural modeling and design framework.

Business Architecture Model

The starting point for the business architecture model (BAM) is information about the business context and processes in which the system participates, services offered by the system to fulfill

Figure 2.5   **Architectural Modeling and Design Framework**

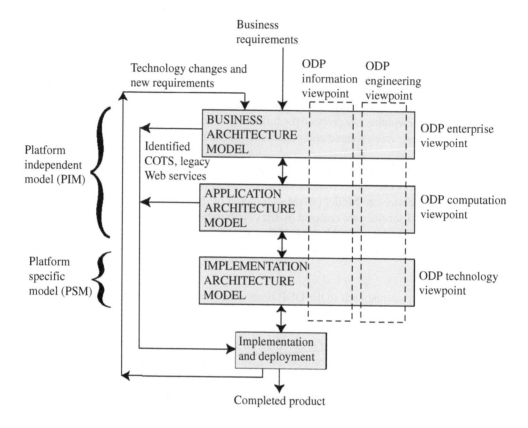

business goals, business domain information supported by the system, business rules fulfilled by the system, and business events handled by the system. The main goal of the BAM is to specify the behavior of the system in the context of the business for which it is implemented in terms of collaborating and coordinating chunks of business functionality represented using the concepts of components and services.

Two models should be created at the beginning: the domain object model and the model that defines the flow of activities in the system. The domain object model represents business domain entities handled by the system, their main attributes, and the relationships among them. This model represents a high-level domain vocabulary of the system being developed. Next to it, the activity diagram is defined to show the flow of business processes and activities that the system should support. The specified activity diagram assists in identifying and defining use cases of the system. Furthermore, the activity diagram helps in determining the way of coordination between defined use cases in terms of what use case precedes, follows, or is done in parallel to the given one, as well as how their preconditions and postconditions match each other. For example, the use case *Find a product* precedes the use case *Send an order,* which precedes the use case *Pay a bill,* and the postconditions of the preceeding use case must match the preconditions of the following one (Figure 2.6).

Use case analysis is an effective mechanism for defining cohesive sets of features and services

Figure 2.6 **Relation <<precede>> Between Use Cases**

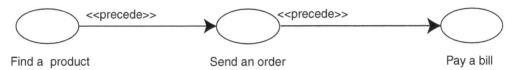

Find a product   Send an order   Pay a bill

on the system boundary since it captures the intended behavior of the system without having to specify how that behavior is implemented (Jacobson et al. 1992). We use here the goal-oriented approach to use cases defined by Cockburn (2001), by which a use case is described as a goal-oriented sequence of business or work steps. Both the goals and the interactions in a use case scenario can be unfolded into finer- and finer-grained goals and interactions. Three types of use cases as three named goal levels are defined: summary goals, user goals, and subfunction goals. We focus here on user-goal use cases since they correspond to so-called elementary business processes (EBPs). An EBP is a task performed by one person in one place at one time, which adds measurable business value and leaves the data in a consistent state. Besides specifying the requirements on the system, use cases can be used for the specification of functional features offered by the system as a response to user activities. Based on defined use cases, we define the set of business services of the system as responsible for supporting the realization of defined use cases, which means user business goals. In identifying system services in this business goal-driven manner, we consider only the first two categories of use cases (summary-goal and user-goal) that represent a particular business value for the user. In this way, we avoid ending up in functional decomposition, which is one of the critical points in performing use case–driven architecture design. So-called change cases as potential changing requirements on the system in the future can be included as well to provide higher adaptability of the system solution in the future.

Use cases can be specified in detail according to the use case template that includes name, description, involved actors, goal in the context, scope, level, preconditions, postconditions, triggers, main success scenario, extensions, subscenarios, priority, frequency, performance, and so on (Cockburn 2001). This use case specification can be extended with the information about the role of the use case in the wider context of a business process that the system participates in. Therefore, for each use case, the use cases that precede it, follow it, perform in parallel with it, or are synchronized in other ways with it should be defined. Furthermore, for each use case, its superordinate and subordinate use cases should be defined, providing a composite hierarchy of use cases, that is, corresponding business goals. Finally, information types from the defined domain object model are cross-referenced with the use cases. In this way, for each use case, the type and structure of information that are needed for its performance are defined. Finally, the first-cut business components (BCs) are defined as providing operations that support the realization of one or several cohesive business goal–level use cases (Figure 2.7).

The business component provides services to support a cohesive set of use cases, and it requires services that are required by these use cases. Next, domain data objects used by particular services of the business component in order to support and realize corresponding use cases should be considered. These data objects represent information about the domain that the component should obtain in order to expose required behavior; they can be considered parameters of component services. This does not mean that the business component owns these domain data objects locally. The component handles and uses particular data objects to provide its services, and it is able to find and use them when necessary. By defining the component in this way, it still represents a unity of data and behavior as in the case of classes and objects, but now in a different

Figure 2.7 **Relations Between Use Cases, Services, and Business Components**

Business component		Service		Use case
	+provides 1..*		+supports 1..*	

order. In the case of a component, its behavior and the services that it provides and requires are defined first, and then information that should be handled (not necessarily owned) by the component in order to perform its role is specified based on the domain object model.

In order to decide what use cases are under the responsibility of a particular BC and how to group use cases into distinct BC, a number of business and technical criteria can be defined:

- Use cases that handle the same domain information objects by creating, updating, or deleting them should be under the responsibility of a single BC.
- Use cases that are expected to change at the same rate and under the same circumstances should be under the responsibility of a single BC.
- Use cases already supported by an existing solution (legacy, COTS, or Web service) used in the project should "belong" to a single BC that models the given solution.
- Use cases that belong to physically distributed parts of the system cannot "belong" to the same BC that basically represents a unit of collocated services.
- Use cases that belong to the same business transaction or correlated transactions required or performed together should be under the responsibility of a single BC.
- Use cases that coherently represent a known marketable and attractive unit of business functionality and, therefore, can be successfully exposed as a Web service product should "belong" to a single BC.

By limiting the scope of the defined system use cases to the business-goal level, we ensure that our BCs provide value-added real business services, and not low-level technical operations such as *get* and *set* methods. Moreover, by clustering use cases in business components based on the information objects they handle (the first item of the list above), we provide a balance between process-based and entity-based decomposition of the system.

For the purpose of detailed component specification, all component concepts (component identifier, component behavior, component information, configuration parameters, and nonfunctional parameters) must be fully specified using, for example, the elements of contract-based theory. Initial collaboration and coordination of business components as business component architecture can be represented using the component collaboration and sequence diagrams as component-based variants of the corresponding UML diagrams. Distribution aspects of the business components must be considered as well, for example, in the cases of architecting systems for virtual enterprises, using legacy assets or Web services. The initial set of business components and the business component architecture represent the result of the business architectural model and, at the same time, the input for the application architectural model.

According to the discussion so far, the semantics of the business component represented using the UML concepts can be defined as subtypes of both *subsystem* and *collaboration* metaclasses, as shown in Figure 2.8 (OMG 2003a).

The UML specifies a subsystem as both package and classifier, meaning that a subsystem is a grouping mechanism that encapsulates its interior and defines a name for its content, and at the same

Figure 2.8 **Business Component as a Subtype of Both Subsystem and Collaboration**

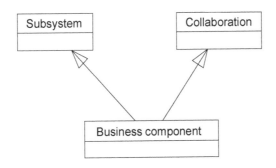

time it is a unit that provides both structural and behavioral features. The subsystem offers interfaces and has operations. It is defined through the specification of its operations and their realizations. On the other hand, the collaboration in UML is defined as "a society of classes, interfaces, and other elements that work together to provide some cooperative behavior that is bigger than the sum of all its parts." Collaboration represents a realization of a use case or operation by a set of lower-level classifiers and associations among them that are defined inside the collaboration. Collaboration has two aspects: a structural part that specifies the elements of the collaboration and a behavioral part that specifies the dynamics of how those elements interact. Since our business component represents a realization of one or several cohesive use cases, it is well represented by the collaboration concept. Similar to collaboration, our business component does not necessarily own its structural elements (for example, information objects), but it "knows" how and where to find them when it needs them. These mechanisms are further considered in the application architecture model.

Application Architecture Model

The goal of the application architecture model (AAM) is to define how business components are realized in terms of collaboration of lower-level application components (ACs) that do not provide a direct business value. For the purpose of identifying application components inside a given business component, we apply the analysis similar to robustness analysis as defined by Jacobson in his objectory method (Jacobson et al. 1992). The robustness analysis is an intermediate level of design, between the "use cases and domain classes" level and the detailed software design level, which identifies user interface, control, and entity objects for each use case. We use a similar strategy for each business component in order to define boundary, control, and entity services of the component. This analysis of a business component defines its services that support the interaction of the component with the consumer (boundary), the services that capture business logic (control), and the services that manage information necessary for the component to fulfill its role in the context. The result is the following list of possible types of application components:

- Consumer interface AC—provides services necessary for communication with the consumer of the BC by transforming the consumer's input into a form understandable by the service logic, and the service output into a form understandable by the consumer. This AC makes the service logic available to different types of consumers. If a consumer is a human user, corresponding presentation logic is added to the AC.

- Data access AC—provides services for accessing data stored in a permanent storage. The role of this AC is to protect the BC logic from peculiarities and possible changes of the underlying database structure. Depending on characteristics of the data storage, this AC can be enriched with proper access methods (indexing structures) that speed up information retrieval, as well as with mechanisms for data mining.
- Business logic AC—provides the services that determine the logic of the BC. These ACs can be further divided into two basic types based on the type of services they provide (query or update):

  - ACs that mainly provide information about particular business entities, that is, represent the so-called contact point for that information.
  - ACs, that encapsulate computational logic, control logic, or data transformation logic, are not parts of any business entity object and can possibly handle several business entity objects. Since a BC is defined as a realization support for one or several cohesive use cases, the ACs that realize included and/or extended use cases of those business-level use cases can be identified as well.

One of the necessary elements of each BC is the Coordination Manager component. The main role of this component is to manage and control how the ACs interact to produce a higher-level business goal specified by the contract of the BC that encapsulates them. A Coordination Manager can be realized by using a combination of the Mediator and Façade design patterns as defined in Gamma et al. (1995). In this way, the collaboration aspects and flows of control and activities between ACs inside the given BC are encapsulated and managed by this manager component. This mechanism hides the complexity of internal collaboration and coordination of the BC and at the same time provides better flexibility of the solutions and replaceability of particular ACs. Next to it, the Event Manager and Rule Manager application components can be defined inside a BC as well. The Event Manager handles mechanisms for publishing and subscribing events important for the given BC component and defines their coordination with provided and required services in terms of trigger and response patterns. The Rule Manager organizes the business rules encapsulated by the given component and provides references to the mechanisms for their fulfillment, such as invariants on information objects, pre- and postconditions on services, as well as the ways of coordination and triggering sequences of services and events.

The collaboration and coordination of application components to form the business component can be represented using component sequence and collaboration diagrams. The distribution aspects should be taken into account so that the place of application components in the logical multitier architecture is determined. The potential problems, such as data and computation redundancy and referential integrity, must be solved at this level. The result of the AAM is a complete, fully specified, component-oriented, platform-independent model that should be further considered for implementation on a particular technology platform.

Implementation Architecture Model

The implementation architecture model (IAM) model uses the complete, business-driven, component-based, distributed system architecture specified through the previous models to give some hints and guidelines about the implementation of this architecture. The IAM can introduce particular technology-dependent concepts and mechanisms to provide a blueprint for future implementation. The concepts defined so far are now translated into more technology-oriented vocabulary, using the mechanisms of distributed component platforms, such as CORBA,

Table 2.1

Mapping Logical Architecture Concepts to Implementation Constructs

Application components	EJB constructs
Consumer interface ACs	Servlets, message-driven beans, Java plug-ins
Data access ACs	Database APIs, JDBC
Computation logic ACs	Session beans, message-driven beans
Information provider ACs	Entity beans
Data types	Java classes

COM+/.NET or Enterprise JavaBeans. If the component architecture has been modeled using the UML, then the UML models of the components that are built in-house should be first transformed into platform-specific models using the corresponding UML profile and finally implemented in the target technology platform. These PIM-to-PSM and model-to-code mappings can be performed by using today's advanced tools for model transformation, code generation, and round-trip engineering. Provisional mapping of different types of application components presented here into corresponding Enterprise JavaBeans constructs is shown in Table 2.1. Further details are beyond the scope of this chapter.

COMPONENT MODELING AND SPECIFICATION NOTATION

For the purpose of architecture modeling, design, and specification as a basis for implementation, it is necessary to define appropriate modeling notation and specification mechanisms. Various representational forms can be used to represent components: a graphical modeling notation such as the UML, a human-understandable textual notation that has Java-like grammar, or a machine-readable notation (e.g., Extensible Markup Language-like grammar).

For the purpose of high-level business component modeling in an agile way, we propose Component-Responsibility-Collaborator (CRC) cards and Service-Responsibility-Coordination (SRC) cards, shown in Figure 2.9, that represent variants of well-known Class-Responsibility-Collaborator cards (Wirfs-Brock et al. 1990). Using the cards, the basic properties of a business component or a business service are specified without going into detail, which is an effective solution for communication with business users (analysts) of the system.

For the purpose of modeling components in a semiformal, graphical way, the natural approach is to use the UML as a standard, object-oriented modeling notation. The UML provides component notation only at the physical level through implementation and deployment diagrams and does not provide support for various component concepts at the analysis and design level. The solution is to use UML extension mechanisms, such as stereotypes and tagged values, in order to represent component concepts. Component-based design and development methods that strictly follow the UML use its notation for components as implementation artifacts (Booch et al. 1999). Approaches more focused to the component way of thinking use semantically more proper ways to represent components. Some authors use a corresponding <<component>> stereotype of the class (Cheesman and Daniels 2000) for modeling components, while others use the UML packages or subsystems (Atkinson et al. 2001) or even some provisional notation (Herzum and Sims 2000) for that purpose.

Since the component concept as defined here is semantically similar to the UML concept of subsystem as a stereotype of package, we think that the appropriate way for representing compo-

Figure 2.9 **The CRC and SRC Cards**

Component (Name)	
Responsibility	Collaborator

Service (Name)	
Responsibility	Coordination

nents is using the package icon with the stereotype representing the type of the component (business or application). For a more detailed representation of a component, its provided and required operation signatures together with the list of parameters are listed. They can be placed inside the component (then, the standard lollipop notation is used for representing the component interface) or listed in the interface icon through the <<interface>> stereotype of a class. Coordination and time dependency of these operations can be represented using an attached activity or component sequence diagram. Preconditions and postconditions of operations are represented using the Object Constraint Language (OCL) constructs (Warmer and Kleppe 1999).

Component context-aware configuration parameters and nonfunctional parameters can be listed in two new compartments of the component icon. The logical information model of the component is represented using the class icon with listed attributes and without methods, and it can be placed inside the component or attached as a class diagram representing data types and their associations. Particular stereotypes of a class can be used for representing these data types, for example <<Business Entity>>. Dynamics of data objects attached to the component can be represented in a separate state-chart diagram. For the purpose of representing a component as a composition of its subcomponents, the interior of the component icon can be filled with the collaboration of its subcomponents. What services of these subcomponents are exposed through the interface of the component (and can be used from the outside of the component), and what services are internal and used only for collaboration among the subcomponents, must be defined. Collaboration and coordination of components and their services are represented using component sequence and collaboration diagrams as variants of corresponding UML diagrams. Other, less important concepts can be represented using the current UML version. We hope that the next major version of the UML 2.0 will provide significant improvements in supporting components as analysis and design-level concepts as well (OMG 2003a). Some elements of the proposed UML notation for representing components will be shown in the next section through the description of a location-based service system case study.

For the purpose of defining a human-understandable textual notation for representing components, the existing definition languages, Interface Definition Language (IDL) (Siegel 2000) and Object Definition Language (ODL) (Cattell et al. 2000), can be used as a basis. They should be extended with the constructs in a Java-like grammar to express the specification elements of a component defined in this chapter. The IDL can be used for specifying services and functions, while the ODL serves for specifying information object types. Constructs and mechanisms that represent the coordination of component operations, configuration and nonfunctional parameters, and other important component elements need to be defined in the same fashion.

For the purpose of defining a machine-readable notation for representing components, the standard Extensible Markup Language (XML) can be used (W3C 2003). The component specification elements should be defined using appropriate XML tags. An XML-based specification

Figure 2.10 **The Use Case Diagram of the System**

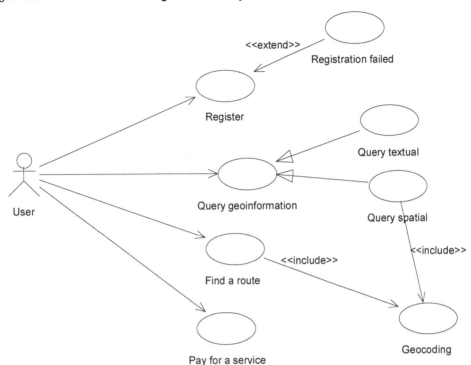

language, such as Web Services Description Language (WSDL) (W3C 2003), can be used as a basis and then extended with the necessary higher-level constructs for representing components, such as coordination and choreography of services, and context-aware configuration parameters.

It should be possible to easily transfer the component specification from one form to the other, depending on the particular needs, using appropriate transformation tools and parsers. New, advanced modeling and development tools provide mechanisms for translating, for example, UML models to software code or to XML-based grammar, which can be extended and customized to fit into our particular purpose and the proposed component definition. Further details about component specification notations are beyond the scope of this chapter.

LOCATION-BASED SERVICE SYSTEM EXMPLE

The approach for identifying and defining components of different granularity will be illustrated in this section through the example of the Location-Based Service Geographic Information System (LBS-GIS). Users can access the LBS-GIS to request and get information about geographic entities of interest (EOI) remotely using browser-enabled smart phones and Personal Digital Assistants (PDAs) in a secure environment. The LBS-GIS provides users with services needed to browse, query, and analyze real-time information in a consistent and secure manner. Posed queries can be related to alphanumeric or geographic properties of the entities. Users can create and maintain their own profiles in order to personalize their usage of the system. The system allows users to determine the shortest or fastest route between two points in a geographical space. Both

Figure 2.11 **Domain Object Model**

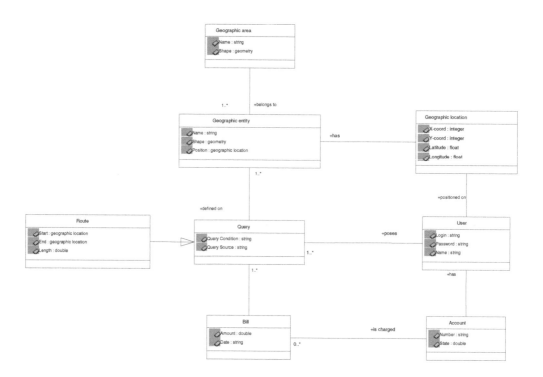

Query Spatial Data and *Find a Route* use cases utilize the mechanism of geocoding, which translates street names into geographic coordinates and vice versa. Users can pay via the system for location-based services that they have used, for example, in the pay-per-use manner. Based on the given problem description and the typical scenario of system usage, the use case diagram (Figure 2.10) can be defined.

The domain object model of the system is shown in Figure 2.11. This model contains the main types of information that represent the concepts of the business domain that should be handled by the system. Each information type has the list of attributes and constraints and invariants defined on it.

Following the algorithm for identifying components based on the use case analysis presented above, we can define the first-cut business services and components of the system. These components are responsible for supporting the realization of the main use cases of the system. They are as follows:

- *Registration Manager*—to control login and password information, enable the creation and modification of user profiles, and ensure security.
- *Query Manager*—to handle requests for information about the geographic entities of interest based on different criteria.
- *Route Finder*—to manage activities related to determining the shortest or fastest route between two points in the given geographical space.
- *Payment Manager*—to support the user payments.

Figure 2.12   **The Specification of the *Query Manager* Component**

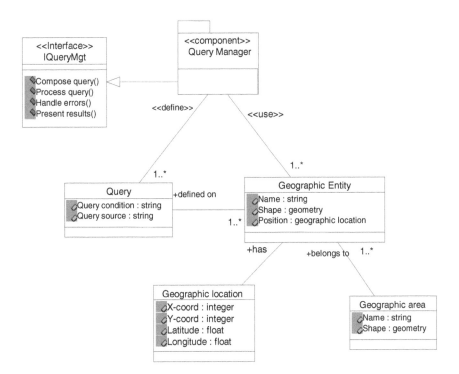

Some of these components can be further specialized into more concrete components. For example, the *Query Manager* component can be specialized into *Spatial Query Manager* and *Textual Query Manager* components. Similarly, the *Payment Manager* component can be further specialized into the *Payment Per-Use Manager* and the *Payment through Subscription Manager* components, depending on the types of payment. On the other hand, the application component *Geocoder* can be defined to provide important mechanisms for business-oriented services, such as *Querying* and *Route Finding*.

Business services defined for each business component now cross-reference the given information model to decide what information types are needed by a particular component to provide its services and how these services are defined with regard to information types. By following given business rules, services that each component should offer are precisely specified using preconditions and postconditions and defined constraints on information types. These services correspond to steps in use cases that are previously used for identifying higher-level business components. Each step suggested by Cockburn (2001) has its own lower-level goal. The goals of application components are to provide realization of these lower-level use case goals. The provisional specification of two components of the system—*Query Manager* and *Registration Manager*—together with information types they should handle, is shown in Figures 2.12 and 2.13, respectively.

Services of business components are actually realized by particular application components (or in the case of a large-scale application with several component recursive levels, by lower-level business components). Again, the main characteristic of a business component that distin-

Figure 2.13 **The Specification of the *Registration Manager* Component**

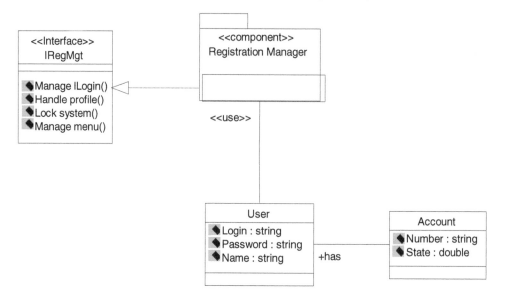

guishes it from an application component is that a business component provides some business-meaningful services, that is, it adds some value to the user of the system. In the case of the *Query Manager* component, we can define the following lower-level business components: *Query Composer, Query Processor, Error Handler,* and *Result Presenter.* Similarly, in the case of the component *Registration Manager,* we can define the following application components that belong to it: *Login & Password Manager, Profile Handler, Locking Handler,* and *Menu Manager.* Application components use or are simply aware of the same types of information (or their subset) as the business components they belong to.

The collaboration between application components in providing higher-level business services of the *Query Manager* component is shown in Figure 2.14.

When system distribution and multitier system architecture are taken into account, defined application components can be transferred to corresponding distributed components. Some applications are related to the user interface (UI) tier, some to the business logic tier, and some to the data storage tier. For example, *Query Composer* and *Result Presenter* are attached to the UI tier, while *Query Processor* is attached to the business logic tier, communicating with the *Data Handler* that resides in the data storage tier, as shown in Figure 2.15.

The initial business component-oriented architecture of the LBS-GIS system representing the main business components of the system and dependencies between them is shown in Figure 2.16. Further steps of the approach include precise specification of all business, application, distributed, and implementation components of the system. The complete system architecture specification can then be realized using a particular component implementation.

DISCUSSION AND CONCLUSION

Although component-based platforms and technologies such as CORBA, COM+/.NET, and EJB are widely used as a standard for implementation and deployment of complex systems, the com-

Figure 2.14 **The Sequence Diagram Showing the Collaboration of Application Components**

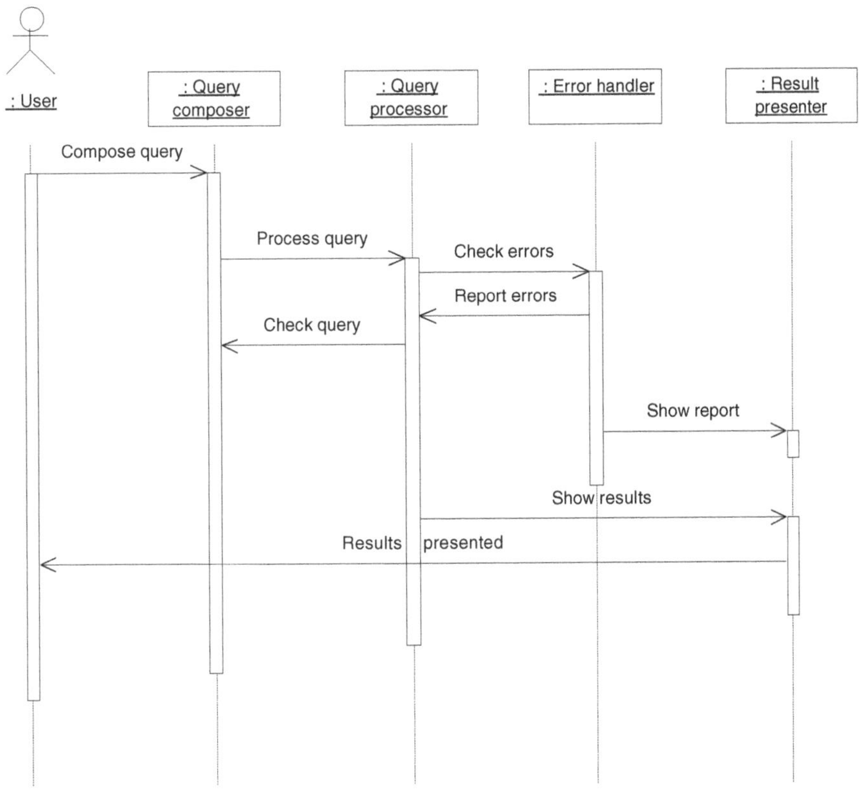

ponent way of thinking has not yet become a driving force in the system development process. Current CBD best practices, approaches, and methods do not fully support various component concepts and, therefore, are not able to provide the full benefit of the CBD approach. Handling components mainly at the implementation level and treating them as binary code packages actually limits the usefulness of the component paradigm. At the design level, components are mainly defined in the form of larger-grained classes and objects that are rather data-driven than behavior-driven. The real power of using the service-based component way of thinking as a bridge between business and technology concerns has not been truly recognized yet.

The main goal of this chapter has been to define a component- and service-based design approach that provides comprehensive support to the model-driven development of complex enterprise-scale systems. The approach applies the same component way of thinking and the same consistent set of technology-independent component concepts in different aspects and phases of enterprise systems development, from autonomous business services to distributed artifacts. Defined service-based components provide greater ability to model business services and requirements at a higher level, in a domain-specific, but implementation-independent way. On the other hand, the application developers retain control over how business-driven system models are turned into complete applications using advanced component-based technology infrastructures.

In this way, component architecture is flexible enough to be easily adapted according to frequent changes in the business. On the other hand, the architecture is minimally affected by the underlying

Figure 2.15 **The Application Components Distributed Over the Tiers**

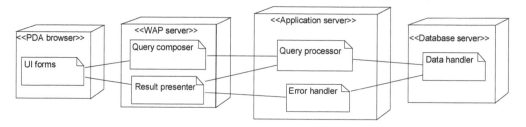

Figure 2.16 **The Initial Business Component-Oriented System Architecture**

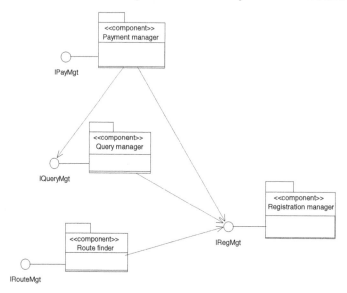

technology choices, providing a durable solution that can survive the changes in technology. Thus, the presented component architecture represents a point of negotiation between different actors in a development process: the user, assembler, and provider or implementer of component services.

The approach presented in this chapter is in line with the current OMG strategy in establishing Model Driven Architecture. MDA suggests first creating a high-level UML description of how applications will be structured and integrated, independently of any implementation details (PIM), then moving toward more constrained UML design according to a chosen platform (PSM), and, finally, converting into language code for a specific platform. Our service-based component approach actually aims at a fully specified component-oriented PIM that can be easily mapped first to a component-oriented PSM and then to a particular component middleware. In this way, components are not only implementation units but also the main artifacts in system analysis and design. The component concept is the focus of the whole development process and the point of integration and consistency between different perspectives, viewpoints, and abstraction levels of the system.

The approach presented here represents a paradigm shift from components as objects to components as services. Defining components as basically service managers provides both business and IT people with a powerful and easily understandable concept for representing their views on the enterprise distributed system. Thus, a business analyst represents a system through the set of collaborating business-oriented services, a system architect specifies this service assembly in the form of the component system architecture, and a software developer provides a realization of these services using lower-level software artifacts. The approach can be effectively applied for modeling, analysis, and design of systems using the new paradigm of Web services. Web services are self-contained, self-describing, modular units providing a location-independent business or technical service that can be published, located, and invoked across the Web. From a technical perspective, of course, the Web service is essentially an extended and enhanced component interface construct. Web services represent a natural extension to component thinking and a further convergence of business and technology. In the approach presented here, Web services become just one possible realization of a service-based component specification. In this way, the approach provides a smooth transition from the standard object-oriented way of thinking to the advanced Web-service one.

In recent years, eXtreme Programming (XP) and Agile Software Development (ASD) have started to gain considerable interest in the IT community (Ambler and Jeffries 2002; Cockburn 2002). They have been proposed as a quick way to build quality software systems that can adapt easily to rapidly and frequently changing requirements in the environment. Agile processes are focused on early, fast, and frequent production of working code through fast iterations and small increments. They are characterized by intensive communication between participants, rapid feedback, simple design, and frequent testing. On the other hand, current CBD methods and processes, such as RUP (Jacobson et al. 1999), Catalysis (D'Souza and Wills 1999), and Business Component Factory (Herzum and Sims 2000), are rather heavyweight and often difficult to apply in practice, especially when time and flexibility are critical factors in the success of a project.

Our strong opinion is that the component concepts presented here can be naturally integrated in agile methodology practice, resulting in a truly agile component-oriented development process. Using the component way of thinking as proposed here can provide and further strengthen the values, principles, and practices of XP and ASD in general, making them easier to achieve and follow. Components as business-driven architectural artifacts can help overcome the limitations and shortcomings of ASD, such as the lack of support for large projects and teams and for distributed development environments. On the other hand, ASD concepts and principles can strengthen current component- and service-based development practice, making current enterprise-scale systems more flexible and agile in satisfying ever-changing business needs.

REFERENCES

Allen, P., and S. Frost. 1998. *Component-Based Development for Enterprise Systems: Applying the Select Perspective.* Cambridge, UK: Cambridge University Press.

Ambler, S.W., and R. Jeffries. 2002. *Agile Modeling: Effective Practices for Extreme Programming and the Unified Process.* New York: Wiley.

Atkinson, C., J. Bayer, B. Christian, E. Kamsties, O. Laitenberger, R. Laqua, D. Mutig, B. Paech, J. Wust, and J. Zettel. 2001. *Component-Based Product Line Engineering with UML.* Boston: Addison-Wesley.

Booch, G., J. Rumbaugh, and I. Jacobson. 1999. *The Unified Modeling Language User Guide.* Boston: Addison-Wesley.

Brown, A.W., and K.C. Wallnau. 1998. The current state of component-based software engineering. *IEEE Software* 15, no. 5: 37–47.

Carey, J., B. Carlson, and T. Graser. 2000. *San Francisco Design Patterns: Blueprints for Business Software.* Boston: Addison-Wesley.

Cattell, R., et al. 2000. *The Object Data Standard: ODMG 3.0.* San Francisco: Morgan Kaufmann.

Cheesman, J., and J. Daniels. 2000. *UML Components: A Simple Process for Specifying Component-Based Software.* Boston: Addison-Wesley.

Cockburn, A. 2001. *Writing Effective Use Cases.* Boston: Addison-Wesley.

————. 2002. *Agile Software Development.* Boston: Addison-Wesley.

Curbera, F., M. Duftler, R. Khalaf, W. Nagy, N. Mukhi, S. Weerawarana. 2002. Unraveling the Web services Web: An introduction to SOAP, WSDL, and UDDI. *IEEE Internet Computing* 6, no. 2: 86–93.

Dahanayake, A., H. Sol, and Z. Stojanovic. 2003. Methodology evaluation framework for component-based system development. *Journal of Database Management (JDM)* 14, no. 1: 1–26.

D'Souza, D.F., and A.C. Wills. 1999. *Objects, Components, and Frameworks with UML: The Catalysis Approach.* Boston: Addison-Wesley.

Gamma, E., R. Helm, R. Johnson, and J. Vlissides. 1995. *Design Patterns: Elements of Reusable Object-Oriented Software.* Boston: Addison-Wesley.

Henderson-Sellers, B., C. Szyperski, A. Taivalsaari, and A. Wills. 1999. Are components objects? In Proceedings of the 14th ACM SIG Plan Conference on *Object-Oriented Programming, Systems, Languages, and Applications,* Panel Discussion. New York: ACM Press.

Herzum, P., and O. Sims. 2000. *Business Component Factory: A Comprehensive Overview of Business Component Development for the Enterprise.* New York: Wiley.

Jacobson, I., M. Christerson, P. Jonsson, and G. Overgaard. 1992. *Object-Oriented Software Engineering: A Use Case Driven Approach.* Boston: Addison-Wesley.

Jacobson, I., G. Booch, and J. Rumbaugh. 1999. *The Unified Software Development Process.* Boston: Addison-Wesley.

Jain, H., N. Chalimeda, N. Ivaturi, and B. Reddy. 2001. Business component identification—A formal approach. In *Proceedings, Fifth IEEE International Enterprise Distributed Object Computing Conference.* Los Alamitos, CA: *IEEE Computer Society.*

McIlroy, M.D. 1969. Mass produced software components. In *Software Engineering,* ed. F.L. Bauer, L. Bolliet, and H.J. Helms. Garmisch, Germany: NATO Science Committee.

Meyer, B. 1997. *Object-Oriented Software Construction.* Upper Saddle River, NJ: Prentice Hall.

ODP. International Standard Organization (ISO). 1996. *Reference Model of Open Distributed Processing: Overview, Foundation, Architecture and Architecture Semantics.* ISO/IEC JTC1/SC07. 10746–1 to 4. ITU-T Recommendations X.901 to 904.

OMG. 2003a. OMG Unified Modeling Language Specification, March, www.omg.org/docs/formal/03-03-01.pdf.

————. 2003b. Object Management Group, June 12. MDA Guide Version 1.01, www.omg.org/docs/omg/03-06-01.pdf.

Parnas, D.L. 1972. On the criteria to be used in decomposing systems into modules. *Communication of the ACM* 15: 1053–1058.

Siegel, J. 2000. *CORBA 3: Fundamentals and Programming.* New York: Wiley.

Stojanovic, Z., and A.N.W. Dahanayake. 2002. A new approach to components. In *Issues and Trends of Information Technology Management in Contemporary Organizations,* ed. M. Khosrow-Pour. Hershey, PA: IRM Press.

Stojanovic, Z., A.N.W. Dahanayake, and H.G. Sol. 2000. *Integrated Component-Based Framework for Effective and Flexible Telematics Application Development.* Technical Report. Delft, Netherlands: Delft University of Technology.

————. 2001. Integration of component-based development concepts and RM-ODP viewpoints. In *Open Distribute Processing Enterprise, Computation, Knowledge, Engineering and Realisation,* ed. J.A.M. Cordeiro and H. Kilov. Setúbal, Portugal: ICEIS Press.

Szyperski, C. 1998. *Component Software: Beyond Object-Oriented Programming.* Boston: ACM Press, Addison-Wesley.

TINA. Telecommunications Information Networking Architecture. 1997. TINA Consortium. *Service Architecture 5.0,* www.tinac.com.

Udell, J. 1994. Cover story: Componentware. *Byte Magazine,* May.

Warmer, J.B., and A.G. Kleppe. 1999. *The Object Constraint Language: Precise Modeling with UML.* Reading, MA: Addison-Wesley.

W3C. World-Wide-Web Consortium. 2003. *Extensible Markup Language (XML),* www.w3c.org/xml.

Wirfs-Brock, R., B. Wilkerson, and L. Wiener. 1990. *Designing Object-Oriented Software.* Upper Saddle River, NJ: Prentice Hall.

CHAPTER 3

TOWARD A COMPONENT-ORIENTED METHODOLOGY TO BUILD-BY-INTEGRATION

ALI DOĞRU

Abstract: *This chapter presents the foundations of a software development approach that promotes the "build-by-integration" paradigm. So far, both the traditional and the object-oriented methodologies have offered sophisticated processes oriented toward defining the final development activity as "code writing." In contrast to such established practices, we propose to orient the entire development toward composing complex software systems using already implemented components. This concern is consistently maintained throughout the development, starting with requirements modeling. A graphical language is utilized to represent components in both abstract and physical levels within the main modeling view, that is, structural breakdown. This chapter relates the new notions to the existing concepts. The proposed approach is introduced and partially demonstrated through examples represented with graphical models.*

Keywords: *Component-Oriented Methodology, Build-by-Integration, COSEML*

INTRODUCTION

The emergence of component technologies (Krieger and Adler 1998) has started a new era in information systems development. Extensive research and technological work on component-based development have been carried out in recent years, and contributions to the area are constantly reported. However, limited work has contributed to significantly increasing the efficiency of systems development. The bulk of the work has focused on wiring-level issues and the representation of components in object-oriented (OO) platforms. It would be useful to capitalize on those features of components that can lead to and enable the paradigm shift from "code development" to "integration" (Tanik and Ertas 1997).

The ever-growing demand for more complex software cannot be satisfied by linear gains in the one-line-at-a-time production of code. Sizes in excess of 10 million lines are a practical reality. Such systems require development periods comparable to a decade. And such durations bring together the problems of changing requirements and changing arrays of different parameters, causing critical risks. It is not feasible to create huge systems from scratch. In fact, a lot of code has been developed and tested before, with the potential of being (re)utilized in new systems. Component technologies offer ease of utilization of code modules.

New engineering approaches should facilitate the formulation of problems in a decomposable manner. The system definition should be decomposed into logical modules. Starting with higher abstraction-level modules, the system specification should be decomposed at lower levels. Interface specifications would facilitate integration efforts, especially within the context of a component-based environment.

This chapter outlines the basics of a new approach that targets an enactment of the "build-by-integration" paradigm. This goal has been studied before (Tanik and Ertas 1997) and only can be realized after the commercialization of enabling component technologies. The fundamental ideas and a supporting process model were introduced by Doğru and Tanik (2003). For the approach to be adopted by the industry, a practical methodology is required. The description of a complete methodology is well beyond the limits of this chapter; however, a broad overview is provided along with a discussion of the associated techniques.

RECENT TRENDS

Most OO languages have been available since the 1980s, while others even predate this period. However, OO development methodologies appeared later. Currently, component technologies (Szyperski 1998) are maturing, and attempts to engineer their utilization address issues starting from lower levels. This is essentially why the literature tends to refer to these approaches as component-*based* (Heineman and Councill 2001) rather than component-oriented. In the early days of object orientation, some environments could not incorporate any OO features except for encapsulation and hence were referred to as object-*based.* It is time for the component era to shift from a component-based start to a total component orientation. Initially, ways of connecting components together were studied. At a later stage, design modeling was addressed to accommodate components in OO representations. It has been reported that the engineering approaches to utilize these technologies are still missing (Herzum and Sims 2000; Wallnau et al. 2002).

To obtain the desired leverage increase, component-oriented software engineering (Doğru and Tanik 2003) must evolve, implementing the build-by-integration paradigm. The orientation guides the process toward a future composition of components, from the requirements specification stage onward. The alternative offered through OO platforms carries the intention to develop code.

Components, often regarded as an extension to OO techniques, need to be viewed from this revolutionary perspective. They may resemble objects, but the real component concept goes beyond objects. Components obey a protocol that includes structured interfaces and the commitment to provide the services declared in the interfaces. Therefore, whether a component is developed through OO or through other approaches is not important.

Development, wiring, and protocols for components are important; they constitute the enabling technologies. Although improvements will still be welcomed, the fundamental problems defining the "software crisis" are not related to technology-level issues. There is enough know-how to make components connect and work. Also, there is an abundance of previously coded algorithms, and creating new components or converting existing code to comply with component standards does not seem to constitute the main challenge nowadays. The new focus should be on locating and integrating *existing* components to satisfy a given set of requirements.

COMPONENT ORIENTATION AND EXISTING APPROACHES

To orient the developers toward components, a paradigm shift is required. Treating components as units of code with a defined protocol, for easier reuse within an OO development, is insufficient. From a static perspective, object orientation tends to emphasize the "data" aspects, whereas component orientation emphasizes the "structural" dimensions. In the earliest stages of modeling, the developers should regard the elements of their system as possible chunks of code ready for integration, rather than as data-oriented entities. The initial chunks in the model should nevertheless be as logical as possible. The logical decomposition, after locating candidate components,

Figure 3.1 **Levels for Software Development Terminology**

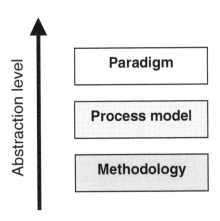

should later be mapped to a physical composition. In this regard, the units of integration could be components or any other kind of code modules. Components, however, transform the idea to a practical approach. (For the reader interested in the theoretical foundations behind these notions, Doğru and Tanik [2003] and Tanik and Chan [1991] are recommended.) The fact that a component is a structural element is very important in the orientation. Any unit in the model (whether logical or physical, large- or small-grained) corresponds to a structural element.

After commitment to a paradigm, a set of activities should be adopted. This fundamentally constitutes the process model. For the purposes of this chapter, a detailed process model supported with modeling formalisms represents a methodology. Figure 3.1 depicts the abstraction levels of the process-related terminology.

Existing component-based approaches have made contributions toward process models and methodologies; however, coverage of the component-oriented paradigm is usually not complete. Major component-based methodologies and techniques are briefly described in the remainder of this section.

UML and Components

The Unified Modeling Language (UML) provides a set of diagrams (Booch et al. 1998). Most of the UML concepts are so general and powerful that almost any diagram type can be used for any purpose. This strength also points to a methodological weakness. Given a project, how and when to use each diagram type is not defined in sufficient detail; there is too much freedom and not enough guidance. The notational building blocks of a development process are offered by the UML. The process dimension is fortified by methodologies such as the Rational Unified Process (RUP). This applies for OO development. Recently, the component diagrams and symbols used in UML were supported with the "interface" element derived as a "stereotype" of a class, and all these aspects were used in representing component-based (CB) models.

In addition to providing limited support for CB methodologies, UML does not specifically facilitate a top-down decomposition. Component and deployment diagrams are provided to address the structural dimension. However, a hierarchical organization is not considered. The elements that could be used to represent structural chunks in higher levels of a hierarchy are subsystems, packages, and, maybe, even classes. Component symbols could also be used although they are more appropriate for representing physical entities. Currently, the way to represent decomposition is by drawing one subsystem symbol inside another. From the perspective of model visualization as applied in practice, it is problematic to define many composition levels in the UML.

Other Approaches

Catalysis (D'Souza and Wills 1998) is probably the earliest work with substantial detail in methodology. Here, components are accepted as recursive units of composition and decomposition. Catalysis presents an elegant way to develop intermediate levels of a CB system. Actually, a set of collaborating components is at the heart of this approach, with appropriate relations to use cases, design patterns (Gamma et al. 1995), and frameworks (Fayad 2000). The KobrA approach (Atkinson et al. 2001) is an approach toward component orientation that also considers domain orientation and product line architectures. It is philosophically closer to the views incorporated in this chapter. Domain engineering facilitates component-oriented development. The product line view further specifies scope, while at the same time reduces the level of generality. Within a domain framework, the solution is sought holistically and within a hierarchical structure.

The Business Component Factory methodology (Herzum and Sims 2000) also provides a substantial process-related contribution. The business-level concept is a definite advantage of this approach. Also, a limited hierarchy notion is provided through the layering of components within process, entity, and utility levels.

Other important contributions are presented by Wallnau et al. (2002). The distinguishing feature of this approach is a design effort supported with a blackboard utility. The methods aid the developers with intermediate abstraction-level issues such as the collaboration of a small set of components. Finally, a similar collection of valuable work, also providing intermediate mechanisms, can be found in Crnkovic and Larsson (2002).

The Difference

There are two issues that have not been substantially addressed in the literature: (1) support for hierarchical decomposition and (2) abstract as well as physical component representation. There are two main categories for CB development activities: component development and component composition. The concept presented in this chapter belongs exclusively to the latter category. Having handled decomposition, component and interface specifications can possibly utilize techniques covered in the existing literature. Component development, maintenance, and other lifecycle tasks are not within the scope of this chapter. An inclusive methodology would preferably include some of these activities.

The commitment to OO conceptions of some CB approaches needs to be reconsidered. Software engineering is mature enough to devise the next generation of methodologies based on how they should be ideally, rather than how technologies dictate. Fundamental modeling elements of data, function, control, and structure are taken and enhanced toward physical components in the proposed approach called component-oriented software engineering (COSE). Components happen to be in line with correct design foundations (Simon 1969); consequently, the build-by-integration paradigm and the COSE approach are enabled by component technologies.

Figure 3.2 **Component-Oriented Development Process**

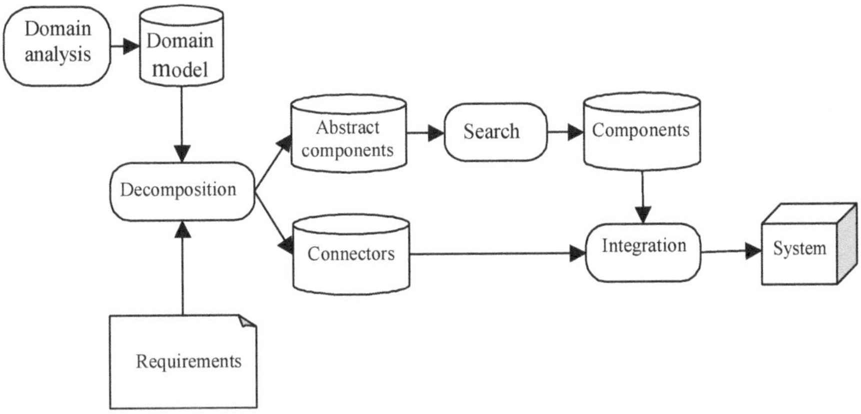

BUILDING BLOCKS

Although in its infancy, some constituents of COSE have been applied while the approach was under development. The approach proposed in this chapter is supported by fundamental definitions (Doğru and Tanik 2003), a graphical modeling language, COSEML (Doğru and Altintas 2000), and supporting methodological research work (Bayar 2001; Salman 2002).

The Process Model

As this chapter will show, the concepts and the process model introduced in Doğru and Tanik (2003) can be improved by domain analysis (Itoh et al. 2003). A typical process should decompose the system into a set of abstract components that communicate. This results in a defined set of abstract components and a set of connectors. Connectors model the communication among the components. The defined abstract components then provide the specification to be used in the search for implemented components. Once all the needed components are gathered, their integration will be conducted, guided by the specifications contained in the connectors. Figure 3.2 presents the component-oriented development process model.

Existing practices of other methodologies can be incorporated. The critical issue is to comply with the build-by-integration principle. A graphical model supporting the structure view is fundamental in a designer's decomposition and, consequently, significant are also composition decisions. COSEML provides such support. The inspiration from UML is accommodated where suitable. Established practices, such as use case analysis, are also adopted. The ovals in a UML use case diagram can be mapped to high-level COSEML elements. Collaboration modeling in UML also has a counterpart in a COSEML representation; ordering the messages in a COSEML model represents similar information. Messages represent the lowest abstraction level connectors in COSEML.

The idea is to partition the system into modules in such a way that those pieces can be matched by existing components. The system development then reduces to decompose-find-integrate rather than define and develop from scratch. To be effective, decomposition should consider existing components. On the other hand, implementation-level issues should not be considered while defining the requirements. Even at its early stages, the design should try to stick with logical definitions. In other words, questions of what to build and how to build should clearly separate the requirements activity from design. Also, overspecification in early design tends to limit the chances for better or more efficient designs.

In component orientation, a paradox may be observed, that is, the initial definition of a system is immediately matched to implemented components during decomposition. There is an explanation, however. The "What? How?" question is carried to an earlier stage boundary: Domain analysis is where the "What?" question is explicitly addressed. Also, it should be noted that a component-based understanding works better in defined domains rather than for general software development. Consequently, partial solutions are easier to determine, implement, and recognize in a limited domain. Some inefficiency is inevitable, but in return, reliability, speed of development, and predictability are gained. The "hard" engineering disciplines discovered this long ago and are currently benefiting from it.

Another explanation of the paradox is that it is not really a paradox at all: consideration of the implemented components during the definition phase is not actually about the "implementation" issues of components, but about their definitions. Nevertheless, a revolutionary shift is required for component orientation.

The Modeling Language

COSEML is an adaptation of earlier structure-based and decomposition-oriented specifications (Tanik and Chan 1991). This earlier research defined a framework for decomposition and abstract design. COSEML adapted the notations, replacing some with UML counterparts where they existed, and added physical component and interface symbols. As a result, abstract design was integrated with current component technologies, enabling aid for the modeling conception spectrum from abstractions to implementation, based on components.

Hierarchy, which is a key concept in design cognition (Simon 1969), is not supported effectively in UML and other languages. The goal is to provide the human developer with the natural divide-and-conquer discipline based on *structure*. UML could possibly be enhanced to provide a top-down, well-aligned, tree-shaped hierarchy diagram. Although there are no exact counterparts for data, function, and control abstractions, class or subsystem stereotypes can be used in the hierarchy diagram. For the lower levels, UML is already equipped with the component symbol, and the interface concept is later introduced as a class stereotype. Likewise, Architecture Description Languages (ADL) can be enhanced with visual versions that support hierarchy. Such languages incorporate component and connector constructs not present in UML. Some have implicit mechanisms to represent a recursive composition, usually not through specific structural abstractions. Also, the higher-level data, function, and control abstractions may need more support through specific language primitives.

COSEML addresses both abstract and physical components. The higher-level elements represent the abstractions for package, data, function, and control. Lower-level elements correspond to components and interfaces. Figure 3.3 depicts the abstract elements of COSEML. There are also connectors to represent communications among components, both in abstract and physical levels. In abstraction, a connector represents many message or event connections between two components. There are also structural links to indicate a composition relation. A typical model is made of abstract elements starting with the system as the root of a tree, drawn at the top. Composition links connect a higher-level element to lower-level elements as its constituents. Finally, a special kind of link associates an abstraction to a physical component. This is the "represents" link engaging a component to commit to the specifications in the abstract element.

Figure 3.3 **Abstractions in COSEML**

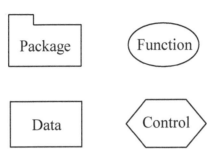

Package is a structural tool that groups related elements in an encapsulation and defines the scope of the abstractions contained within. A package can contain further packages, function, data, and control abstractions. There is no limit to what any of those abstractions could contain. Limitations such as "not to allow a data abstraction to be composed of packages or functions" can be imposed by the methodology. Package is the fundamental structural element used in the definition of whole-part relations. Decomposition is conducted naturally through the use of packages.

Any process (e.g., computer program) can be represented by the primitive abstractions of data, function, and control. Therefore, in addition to the decomposition ability of packages, the modeling language provides such primitive abstractions in order to have the ability to represent the functional requirements of the system under development.

Data abstractions relate to data structures. In the requirements model, they can model high-level entities. Internal operations are included. Function abstractions are meant to represent high-level system functions. They can have local data. Control abstractions are basically state machines, accepting messages that cause state changes and outgoing messages. State changes can trigger the execution of function abstractions or of operations inside data abstractions.

Implementation Level

The abstraction elements provide the decomposition so that matching components can be found to build the system. Physical components should also be presented in a model to indicate how they communicate to execute system functionality and how they correspond to the overall system specification. Communication is through messages, and specifications are traced by virtue of "represents" links connecting a component to an abstraction.

Components and their interfaces are represented with symbols as the lowest-level elements. Figure 3.4 shows the graphical representation of low-level elements of COSEML. A connector between two components is still an abstract element. It represents at least one, but possibly more than one message (or event) link. A message link represents a function call (local or remote) originating in one component and terminating at the interface of another. Events are similar to messages but semantically they stand for calls initiated by external causes in contrast to calls made under program control. Other than this categorization, messages or events are similar in the way they are represented.

Figure 3.4 **Physical Level Elements in COSEML**

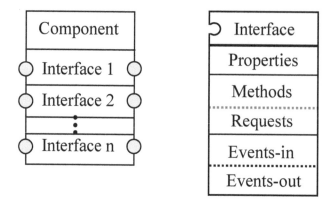

Figure 3.5 **Connectors in COSEML**

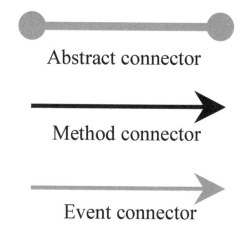

Connectors

An abstract connector can be repeated in a model at various levels. Connectors can be drawn between two abstractions, between the interface ports of two components, between the headers of two interfaces, and finally as a set of method or event links connecting the method or event slots of two interfaces. Figure 3.5 shows the different kinds of connectors.

The events have explicitly defined origins and destinations. Most component protocols allow components to specify the events they want to subscribe to as their inputs and the events they can deliver as their outputs. Corresponding slots have been allocated in an interface representation of COSEML. However, the same cannot be said for methods. Some literature prefers to list only the input methods for interfaces, meaning that the method names listed are for the services a component can offer. Since components will be integrated to form systems, it would be convenient to know what external services they require, as well as what services they offer. This problem of presenting request or response kinds of dependencies has been solved in two different approaches by the compiler technologies. C language programming suggests that only input functions be listed in the header (.h) files. FORTRAN programs used to list the required external services only, by using the word "EXTERNAL" with the name of a function. For a linker, dependencies indicated in one direction are sufficient; however, for components, it is more helpful to know both kinds of information before a designer decides to use them in a configuration. It should be noted that the interfaces act as a specification of a component.

If output methods are not specified, a method connection has to originate from a component rather than from a specific outgoing method slot in an interface. COSEML allows this but also there is no restriction on interpreting a method slot as a requesting method.

DEVELOPMENT

The key stages displaying specific features of component orientation are requirements specification, design, and implementation. "Requirements" is basically conducted through decomposition: a system is defined by dividing it into abstract components and by specifying the relations among them. Design corresponds to mapping abstract components to real ones and specifying connection details. Implementation is integration and modification of components. As previously discussed, traditional boundaries between requirements and design cannot be observed here exactly. Also, the implementation phase almost loses its meaning in component orientation and is therefore not covered in this chapter.

Requirements Specification

Requirements work is finalized with the development of a hierarchy of abstract components. Other techniques can also be utilized during the requirements activity. Widely accepted use case analysis can provide the necessary first step and also a visual language to communicate with the customer.

A use case diagram should be drawn per system capability as the highest level of system functions. Every oval in these diagrams corresponds to system functions, as perceived by the users, and should be described through scenarios. The scenarios are formalized by a sequence of messages to enact them. This simulates the collaboration idea borrowed from the UML. In COSEML, messages are not explicitly modeled but they can be described in the specification of the connectors. It is after representing the abstractions by components that actual messages are drawn.

Any use case should be associated with an abstraction in the COSEML hierarchy. If no other element is suitable, at least a package should be dedicated for a use case oval. After presenting the use case diagram to the user, it can be replaced by another version where the oval shapes are replaced by the package, data, function, or control elements. Figure 3.6 represents a simple demonstrative case where system capabilities correspond to different types of elements. This means the assignment of system capabilities and functions to abstract components of COSEML. The main view is the hierarchy, displaying the composition relations and forming a tree for the abstractions. Even if some of those abstractions also take place in a use case diagram, they still keep their positions in the hierarchy view.

Specification continues with lower-level abstractions appended to the existing hierarchy. In

Figure 3.6 **COSEML Elements in a Use Case Diagram**

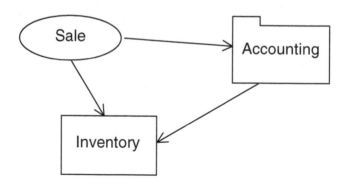

most cases, the use case–level elements correspond to user requirements along with any others added afterward to the system requirements as defined by the development team. It is important to pause after the inclusion of every new element in order to investigate the need for new connectors and update the existing connectors. The best time to explain how parts will connect is when they are being separated from the whole.

Utilization of the Domain Model

What if parts of the system definition are already available as partial models in a repository? It would definitely be beneficial to reuse the partial specification rather than reinventing the wheel. This means a subtree can be retrieved and pasted into the model under construction. Modification to the imported subsolution, and revision of all the connection probabilities, may be necessary.

Requirements, implemented components, know-how, and a dictionary can be maintained in domain models. Locating a requirements cluster implies the completion of considerable amounts of design and implementation. A matured domain suggests that the definition of a subproblem comes with a readily available solution. The subproblem could be as small as an abstraction that is directly represented by a component, or it could be as big as to assume a system capability such as in the case of some commercial off-the-shelf (COTS) components. For example, the accounting capability of a business automation software system could be handled by a large-grained component.

Collaboration Analysis

To visualize the collaborating parties executing a scenario in terms of a sequence of messages, a separate diagram can be drawn. As in use case analysis, this diagram copies some of the abstract elements from the COSEML hierarchy. Messages can now be drawn among the elements which are not allowed in the main hierarchy diagram. The reason messages are not allowed is that they are too detailed for abstractions and are represented by an embedding connector. For some simple cases, a collaboration model can be traced in the abstract hierarchy assuming that messages are hidden inside the connectors. Rather than requirements, a collaboration model corresponding to

Figure 3.7   **Logical-Level Collaboration Example for Sale Operation**

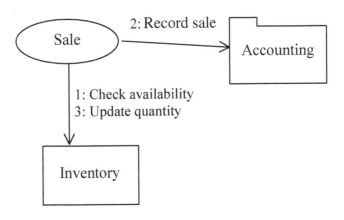

Figure 3.8   **Run-Time Collaboration Diagram**

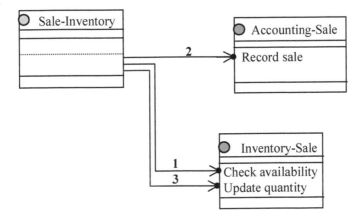

run time can utilize physical messages that take place among physical components. Figure 3.7 displays an abstract collaboration diagram that models a sale scenario: a sale request triggers a check for the availability of the item in the inventory. The corresponding run-time collaboration diagram is shown in Figure 3.8. The sale should then be recorded by accounting, for bookkeeping and inventory are updated to reflect the after-sale values for the item quantities.

Having confirmed that the system functions can be achieved using decomposition and messages, the developers are ready for the product definition. This will be achieved by making abstract elements correspond to existing components. However, there is no guarantee that specified abstractions will be matched by components. This matching includes a match for the messages—the methods a component commits to serve through its interfaces.

Design and Implementation

The information contained in the abstract components will be used as a specification in locating candidate components. If there is a complete match for any component, it is placed in the graphical model and connected to the abstraction it matches via a "represents" link. If there is no complete match, the designer has some options to overcome this problem. A minimal modification to an existing component or a minimal revision in the abstraction hierarchy may solve the difficulty. Otherwise, the options increase in complexity up to a point where it becomes feasible to create a new component.

Revision of the hierarchy is basically on the abstract level. The other option would be to place it on the components side where a component will be made by combining other components. This solution implies code writing, even if it is only for combining existing code. Any combined component should act like a single component, meaning that it should obey the protocol and exert interfaces. For the optimistic case, this means copying the method definitions from the contained components and placing them in the interfaces of the newly generated supercomponent. What is more suitable for a component-oriented approach is a revision in the abstract levels rather than code-level development. The required integration can be carried to this higher level, by splitting an abstraction into two and defining a connector in between. Then each of the two abstractions can be represented by a single component.

Component Acquisition

In the future, all components are expected to be available for the majority of projects. For a well-modeled domain, the components will be available in the framework and they will be imported into the design by a drag-and-drop kind of operation. Some cases may require the locating of a component outside the company. There will be component marketplaces on the Internet and also widely available established search methods for individual components. For a successful search, the complex issue of semantic description for components must mature. For younger domains, there will be a need to decide between two alternatives: either to develop a component in house or subcontract it externally. Meanwhile, mixed development will continue for mixing legacy code with existing components and even newly developed object-oriented modules.

Interface definitions should be supported by textual specifications about the component. Denotational semantics will aid the automatic search in the future. After the matching of required functional specifications to component descriptions, determination of efficiency and other quality factors will remain as problematic issues for some time. This problem has been solved to a considerable extent, though, in the digital electronics field by transistor-transistor logic technology. Different families of components are offered for different speed and power consumption requirements.

Customization

Adapting an existing component to specifications on the abstract levels in the composition is regarded as an implementation-level activity. Some code may be required for modification or development. Modification mechanisms accompanying the component (Heineman 1999) are desirable. Such mechanisms should be capable of satisfying the different requirements. If such a mechanism is not sufficient, the redecomposition alternatives discussed in the previous section should be resorted to. If all fails, then customization needs to be conducted; any technique in the CB literature can be employed as this activity will not affect the main COSE-compliant development.

Some Guidelines

The observations of Bayar (2001) suggest some rules in the utilization of COSEML for development. These may be revised after evaluating the industrial use of the approach. As the trend settles, more guidelines are expected to surface. The suggestions below outline the fundamentals of a methodological approach:

- Abstraction level

  - No connectors are allowed among the components inside a package.
  - Only packages should decompose to lower-level components.
  - Allow only one control abstraction per package.
  - One abstraction cannot be represented by more than one component.
  - Avoid a central control as much as possible.

- Implementation level

  - Try to dedicate one interface per connection for every component.
  - One component can represent more than one abstraction.
  - Abstract connectors may require some code writing.
  - Complexity in a connector may lead to the introduction of a new component.
  - Declare outgoing methods in interfaces for each outgoing message.
  - Try to represent packages only by components (avoid mapping data, function, or control elements to components).
  - Try not to have noncomponent modules.

This early work (Bayar 2001) is based on a declarative approach and relies on the existence of components that match the abstract definitions. New components can be created or existing components can be modified if there is no direct match. However, it is anticipated that some of the development cases will not meet a set of ready components and developing new ones is a deviation from the develop-by-integration paradigm. The COSE approach is advantageous when a domain is matured with a good set of components that satisfy most of the requirements. Otherwise, developing modules for the specific system is much cheaper than developing modules for reuse (components), rendering the nonmatured domains expensive for the approach.

Some creation or modification may be inevitable, especially during the early days of a component domain. Nevertheless, the process should try to refine the model with respect to the existing components, rather than creating them wherever necessary. The following additional suggestions are crucial for the efficiency of a COSE practice:

- Employ domain analysis techniques

  - Developers should be intimately familiar with the domain model.
  - Efficiently mapping abstractions to components is a valuable talent and should be acquired.

- Refine the model with respect to the component set.

  - Be familiar with previous practice of using decomposition.
  - For unmatched abstractions, take a bottom-up approach.
  - Find a set of components that represent the closest solution for those abstractions.
  - Declare a hierarchy of abstractions above the selected components.
  - Revise the model to accommodate the modification.

- Maintain models with different levels of information hiding.

  - Include internals of supercomponents for understanding the local functionalities in "detail models."
  - Maintain a model that hides any subcomponent and displays a corresponding abstraction hierarchy.

Finally, it should be noted that abuse of any kind of modeling orientation is possible, like writing procedural codes in C++ and avoiding object orientation. It is easy to bypass the philosophy of this approach, especially if no mature set of components is to be considered. The suggestions provided in this section can be followed to support the development-by-integration paradigm. The rest of this chapter is dedicated to a case study, followed by concluding remarks.

A BUS RESERVATION SYSTEM

This section presents a case study of the modeling of a bus reservation system. Trips are defined between origin and destination locations for a specific date and time. A bus is also assigned to a trip. Customers select a trip and then a seat for that trip to define a reservation.

After the initial definition of the system, the developers try to decompose the system definition, bearing in mind that any partition should yield modules that could lead to matching with existing components. At this point, the candidate packages are named

- Customer
- Reservation
- Office
- Bus

The articulation considers the generality of the components that could be used, preferably by any kind of business, then particularly for travel domain. At this highest level of partitioning, success for the future locating of a component increases for more general-purpose modules. Figure 3.9 displays the first-level decomposition in the definition of the system. Also defined are the connections among the packages. The office package is connected to every other package, due to the minimum need for office personnel to change the configuration of the system. The reservation packages assumed to contain the trip information and requires the seat numbers from the buses, thus proposing a connector between the reservation and the bus packages.

Normally development continues with further decomposition and review of the current specification. The office package includes a personnel list and accounting operations. The reservation package should maintain lists for locations (origin and destination for trips), trips, and reservation records. The sale of a ticket requires a reservation operation. Returning a ticket should also be

Figure 3.9 **First-Level Decomposition for the Bus Reservation System**

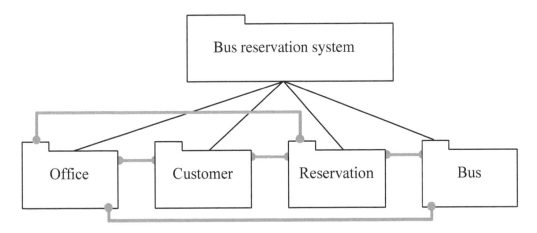

handled in the same package as it will affect a reservation record. The bus package should maintain a list of buses with every bus capable of drawing its own seat layout. A driver listed in the personnel list of the office package should be assigned to a bus.

The partitioning takes the modularity principles of coupling and cohesion into account. Also, encapsulation as a strong concept borrowed from object orientation is important. Following these rules, the proposed decomposition should dictate that the reservation package carries the responsibility to record the seat status information of every trip. At the same time, it is the duty of a bus to draw its layout. Although the drawing depends on the reservation status (different colors for free and sold seats), status information belongs to the reservation package, and the bus package must utilize this information while painting a seat layout. With this information, the next step of decomposition can define the abstract components within the defined packages, as shown in Figure 3.10.

So far, a static description has been made. To satisfy the principle of finding errors early, we should try what we have specified, to observe its compliance with the requirements. Also, the newly introduced principle of defining connections during decomposition suggests introducing connectors and enacting a logical collaboration scenario. The most involved operation seems to be the reservation of a seat for a trip; therefore, for various levels of dynamic modeling the reservation operation will be used. Figure 3.11 presents the logical-level collaboration diagram for a reservation operation. The connections among elements within a package can be used in this diagram for its understandability. They do not have to be shown in the main structural view.

This case study could easily grow out of the limits for a chapter. Instead of introducing further detail to the reservation scenario or providing collaboration models for other system functions, the next demonstrated step is the inclusion of the components.

Implementation by Components

In the bus reservation system example, it is assumed that there are existing components with the same names as the packages shown in Figures 3.9 and 3.10. Also assumed to exist are separate interfaces for each connection and methods to satisfy the collaboration example. Figure 3.11 depicts the components corresponding to the packages.

Figure 3.10   **Refinement After the Initial Decomposition**

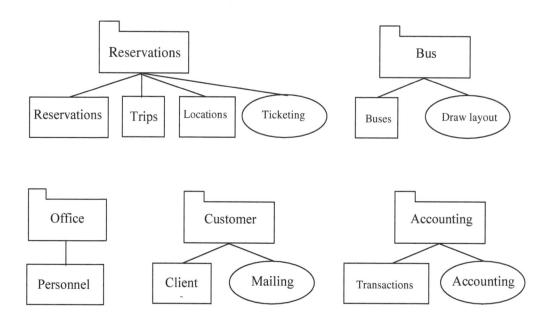

Figure 3.11   **Logical-Level Collaboration Model for the Reservation Operation**

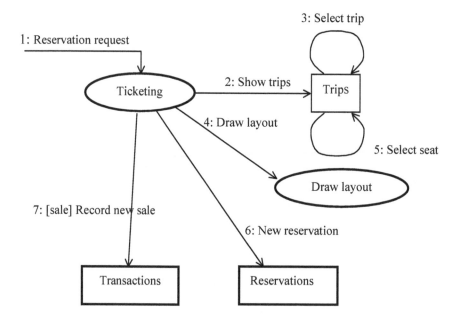

Figure 3.12 **Components Representing the Abstractions**

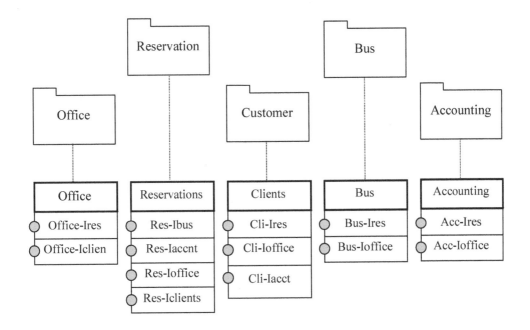

The assumptions made above, however, transform the case study to a rather simplistic one. A complex model could include many levels of decomposition, and anticipated components may be not available. The office package for example, could be further specified to have subcomponents. Later included inside the office package, the accounting package could also be composed of different components.

Components are not complete without their interfaces. One interface per connection is assumed and declared with specific names to suit the example. Interface names are introduced in Figure 3.12 and their details are shown in Figure 3.13. The interfaces present "requesting methods" as well as "service methods." In Figure 3.13, the real messages appear as connections between a requesting method and a service method. These connections can be numbered to represent a collaboration model corresponding to the run-time behavior. Figure 3.12 does not include all the interfaces. A demonstrative subset is selected that is critical for the reservation operation.

Information hiding is one of the principles that can be utilized in any kind of modeling approach. In any model, the level of detail and types included need to be determined. There are two parameters affecting the decision on what to include, namely completeness and modularity. While drawing a run-time collaboration diagram for the reservation operation, messages internal to a component are the target items for such a consideration. To follow the reservation process completely, the internal messages in a component may be necessary. On the other hand, to observe the composition of components, only intercomponent messages are important. For the latter case, messages connecting the interfaces that are the external connection ports are important and the others should be omitted according to guidance from the information hiding principle.

Figure 3.13 emphasizes the composition of components, so intracomponent messages are not shown. Actually, they cannot be shown other than as reflexive messages if they do not take place among any included subcomponents. To demonstrate the complete sequence of actions, the re-

Figure 3.13   **Run-Time Collaboration Diagram for the Reservation Operation**

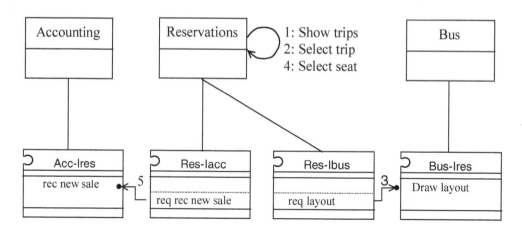

flexive messages on a component also can be included. Reflexive messages leave a component and arrive at the same component. If the component contains further components, messages can be shown to leave a subcomponent (or its interface) and arrive at another subcomponent (or its interface). *Show trips, select trip,* and *select seat* are reflexive messages for the reservation component if the "ticketing" functional abstraction and the "trips" data abstraction belong to the same component. None of these messages crosses the boundary of the reservation component. However, a component-only version of the same model shown in Figure 3.13 would be useful for information hiding during the composition activity.

Interfaces and their connections are the lowest level of a COSEML model. Actually, there is a single model that contains all the structural pieces and their connections. For different views, parts of the model should be omitted in submodels throughout the development process. The submodels could be selected with respect to abstraction levels, types of elements, or a group of elements such as in collaboration analyses.

It is frequently desirable to observe the complete picture at some place and some time. Usually, the teams paste sheets on a wall and draw connections across the sheets, for various structured or object-oriented models. Figure 3.14 provides such a complete view of the case study. It is as complete as it can be with the information supplied so far. When the model information itself is complete, this figure could get overcrowded.

In the documentation, a complete model will not fit onto standard page sizes. The picture distributed across many pages can be linked with connectors discontinuing at the page boundaries. Different graphical techniques can be applied to link information at such discontinuity locations.

CONCLUSION

This chapter has introduced an approach to support the build-by-integration paradigm. This is different from traditional software development approaches, in that code writing is not the target activity. Of course, we are still far from applying the paradigm as a common practice. However, despite the difficulties emanating from the infancy of component orientation, there is sufficient experimental practice. Besides academic projects (Altintas 2001), the approach was tried out on

Figure 3.14 **Including All the Existing Information in the Model**

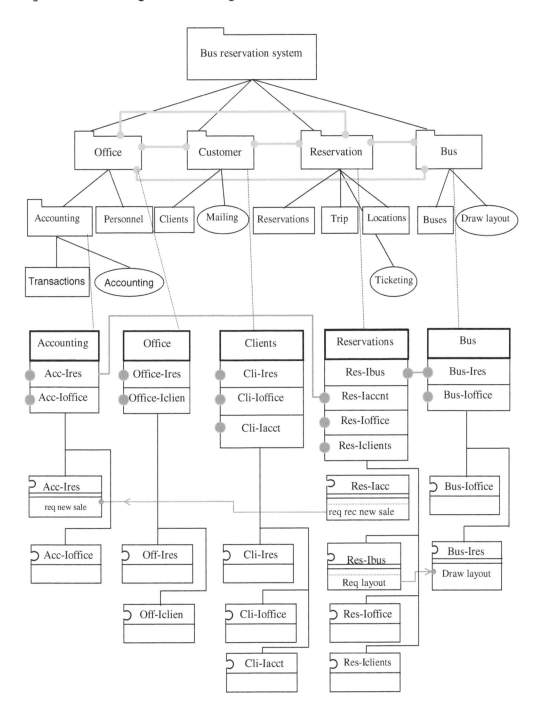

two commercial systems, yielding alternative design models to their existing object-oriented models.

Component-oriented software engineering provides the tools to conduct specification in a top-down process. This is a desired property for many developers. Until the component domains mature, the approach may be partially used to guide any development project with or without code writing. After the top-down decomposition of the model constructs in abstraction, it is also possible to implement the low-level elements as "objects" instead of "components." This method will introduce component orientation to an OO environment, despite the absence of "components" as they are defined today. It would be wise to create "interface" objects in this case. Code writing for the implementation of the specified objects will still be necessary. However, if such objects are intended for reuse, more investment will be required for their development. The ultimate reuse consideration will lead to complying with a component protocol, either for marketing the components or for future development without code writing.

Some peculiar issues will be interesting to watch as they yield rules for the engineers. One new problem is the separation of definition from implementation. After moving most of the definition to the domain analysis activity, the development will inevitably have to consider (implemented) components during the decomposition (specification).

To consolidate a top-town specification approach with a composition that is the destiny of the components and that is naturally bottom-up, special experience will develop. A developer could specify abstractions according to a logical view of the system, but the outcome might assume components that are different from the existing set. Some iteration with respect to different optimization parameters will result in modifying the logical view or the component set so that the specifications meet the readily available building blocks.

The ultimate expectations from this approach will be the automatic search and integration of the components, once a specification is made. Before then, we can still benefit from component orientations, with or without existing components.

REFERENCES

Altintas, I. 2001. A Comparative Study for Component-Oriented Design Modeling. MS thesis, Middle East Technical University, Ankara, Turkey.

Atkinson, C., J. Bayer, B. Christian, E. Kamsties, O. Laitenberger, R. Laqua, D. Muthig, B. Paech, J. Wust, and J. Zettel. 2001. *Component-Based Product Line Engineering with UML.* Reading, MA: Addison-Wesley.

Bayar, V. 2001. A Component Oriented Process Model. MS thesis, Middle East Technical University, Ankara, Turkey.

Booch, G., J. Rumbaugh, and I. Jacobson. 1998. *The Unified Modeling Language User Guide.* Reading, MA: Addison-Wesley.

Crnkovic, I., and M. Larsson, eds. 2002. *Building Reliable Component-Based Software Systems.* Norwood, MA: Artech House.

Doğru, A., and I. Altintas. 2000. Modeling language for component oriented software engineering: COSEML. In *Proceedings of the 5th World Conference on Integrated Design and Process Technologies.* Austin, TX: Addison-Wesley.

Doğru, A., and M.M. Tanik. 2003. A process model for component-oriented software engineering. *IEEE Software* 20, no. 2: 34–41.

D'Souza, D.F., and A.C. Wills. 1998. *Objects, Components, and Frameworks with UML: The Catalysis Approach.* Reading, MA: Addison-Wesley.

Fayad, M.E. 2000. Introduction to the *Computing Surveys'* electronic symposium on object-oriented application frameworks. *ACM Computing Surveys* 32, no. 1: 1–11.

Gamma, E., R. Helm, R. Johnson, and J. Vlissides. 1995. *Design Patterns: Elements of Reusable Object-Oriented Software.* Reading, MA: Addison-Wesley.

Heineman, G.T. 1999. An evaluation of component adaptation techniques. Paper presented at *International*

Workshop on Component-Based Software Engineering: The 21st International Conference on Software Engineering. Los Angeles, California.

Heineman, G.T., and W.T. Councill. 2001. *Component-Based Software Engineering.* Reading, MA: Addison-Wesley.

Herzum, P., and O. Sims. 2000. *Business Component Factory.* New York: Wiley.

Itoh, K., T. Hirota, S. Kumagai, and H. Yoshida, eds. 2003. *Domain Oriented Systems Development: Principles and Approaches.* New York: Taylor and Francis.

Krieger, D., and R.M. Adler. 1998. The emergence of distributed component platforms. *IEEE Computer* 31, no. 3: 43–53.

Salman, N. 2002. Extending object oriented metrics to components. In *Proceedings of the 6th World Conference on Integrated Design and Process Technology.* Austin, TX: Addison-Wesley.

Simon, H.A. 1969. *Sciences of the Artificial.* Cambridge, MA: MIT Press.

Szyperski, C. 1998. *Component Software: Beyond Object-Oriented Programming.* New York: Addison-Wesley.

Tanik, M.M., and E.S. Chan. 1991. *Fundamentals of Computing for Software Engineers.* New York: Van Nostrand Reinhold.

Tanik, M.M., and A. Ertas. 1997. Interdisciplinary design and process science: A discourse on scientific method for the integration age. *Journal of Integrated Design and Process Science* 1, no. 1: 76–94.

Wallnau, K., C. Hissam, A. Scott, and R.C. Seacord. 2002. *Building Systems from Commercial Components.* Boston, MA: Addison-Wesley.

CHAPTER 4

PRINCIPLES OF UML-BASED
COMPONENT MODELING

COLIN ATKINSON, CHRISTIAN BUNSE, ERIK KAMSTIES, AND JÖRG ZETTEL

Abstract: *With the proliferation of middleware technologies and component infrastructures, there is a growing need to support high-level, platform-independent ways of modeling components and component-based systems. This need is reflected in the model-driven architecture vision of the Object-Management Group (OMG). However, component modeling involves much more than merely depicting physical deployment units using the Unified Modeling Language's (UML) component notation. On the contrary, since components are often large, highly complex subsystems of an application, they can be fully described only by using the full range of the UML's modeling portfolio. This chapter explains how this can be done. It suggests four basic principles by which the UML should be used to document components and component-based system in a rigorous, engineering-based manner. These principles essentially clarify how the core principles of software engineering (information hiding, separation of concerns, etc.) can be applied at the model level in terms of suites of interrelated UML diagrams.*

Keywords: *Component Modeling, UML, Uniformity, Locality, Parsimony, Encapsulation, KobrA Method*

INTRODUCTION

As the software industry moves toward more model-driven and reuse-oriented ways of developing software, there is a growing interest in using the UML for modeling components and component-based systems. The UML already contains a rudimentary component modeling capability, but this is rather limited and focuses exclusively on modeling components at the level of physical implementation technologies such as COM+/.NET and Java 2 Enterprise Edition/Enterprise Java Beans (J2EE/EJB). In other words, the current UML view of components (as supported in component and deployment diagrams) corresponds to the "binary module" notion of components as "physical, replaceable part[s] of a system that packages implementation" (OMG 2001).

At higher levels of abstraction, however, a more abstract, architectural concept of components is needed, more akin to the notion of (sub)systems or services than to low-level physical components. Complex, large-grained components of this form cannot be adequately modeled using the simple "box" notation supported in component and deployment diagrams. To model such components comprehensively, it is necessary to use the full power of the UML to create multiple, interrelated views of each component's behavior and properties. In this chapter, we present four fundamental modeling principles by which we believe this goal can be best achieved. We describe how these principles relate to well-known foundations of software engineering and discuss the issues involved in applying them in systematic software development. We then use a small case study to explain how they are supported in the KobrA (Komponentenbasierte Anwendungsentwicklung—German for component-based application development) method (Atkinson et al. 2001) Finally, in the last part of the chapter, we examine other approaches to component-based software development and evaluate to what extent they support these basic principles.

PRINCIPLES OF COMPONENT MODELING

Component diagrams of the form currently offered in the UML focus on the final stages of development when a design is mapped into an executable representation. To describe logical, architectural components in the earlier phases of development, it is necessary to use a more general modeling approach in which a component is treated more like a system (or subsystem) than a physical component. This, in turn, is best achieved by modeling a component systematically from several interrelated viewpoints. We believe there are four fundamental principles that govern what diagrams should be created, what these diagrams should contain, and how they should be related:

1. the principle of uniformity,
2. the principle of locality,
3. the principle of parsimony, and
4. the principle of encapsulation.

In the following subsections, we discuss each of these principles in turn and explain why they contribute toward a component-oriented way of system decomposition and modeling.

The Principle of Uniformity

Many contemporary methods change the way in which they represent a particular kind of abstraction or concept during the development process. Moreover, the choice of representation is often based solely on the level of granularity, or phase of development, in which the abstraction is used rather than on the properties of the artifact being described. A prime example is the different ways in which procedural abstractions are handled in leading object-oriented methods (Jacobson et al. 1999; D'Souza and Wills 1998; Coleman et al. 1994). In the early phases of development, procedural abstraction is typically captured in the form of use cases, whereas in later phases of development the same basic concept is represented in the form of collaborations, object interactions, and/or operation or method invocations. The modeling concepts, terminology, and techniques differ significantly, although the basic ideas expressed are the same.

To avoid this unnecessary redundancy, the principle of uniformity requires that (wherever possible) a given fundamental concept should be represented and manipulated in the same way in all phases of a project. The principle of uniformity also requires that all components be modeled in the same basic way regardless of their level of granularity or position in a development project. In other words, the nature of the models describing a component should be dictated only by its properties.

Following this principle not only simplifies the task of the developers, since it reduces the number of concepts and associated processes that they have to learn and differentiate, but also inherently supports scalability, since big components are treated in the same way as small ones. Furthermore, the principle enhances reusability, since a uniform representation approach simplifies the task of incorporating existing components into new applications.

The Principle of Locality

The idea of building systems by the stepwise and hierarchic refinement of large building blocks into smaller building blocks has existed since the days of structured analysis and design. However, when each building block (i.e., component) is described by its own suite of diagrams, it is important that each diagram fits into the overall hierarchical organization scheme and focuses on the component it is intended to describe. This is the purpose of the principle of locality.

The principle of locality requires that every development artifact, including every UML model and diagram, be oriented toward the description of a single architectural component. In other words, there should be no truly global models. Instead, every model or diagram should focus on the description of a single component: that is, it should be "local" to that component. This view of the organization of the development-time artifacts is depicted in Figure 4.1. The left side of this figure shows the component instances deployed within a system. The right side shows that the development artifacts (i.e., the diagrams and documents that describe these components) are also organized in a component-oriented (i.e., modularized) way and that this modularization is aligned with the run-time organization of the system. Modularization has the great advantage that information about a given component is localized (i.e., decoupled from any global information) and thus can easily be reused within different applications. Having a concise, focused description of an individual component also simplifies the task of the development teams charged with implementing the component.

The Principle of Parsimony

A potential disadvantage of the principles of uniformity and locality is the unnecessary duplication of information, since separate views of an artifact (i.e., separate UML diagrams) necessarily overlap to some degree, and since each diagram describes a specific piece of information from its own viewpoint. This is particularly so for class diagrams, which have a tendency to become overly complex and cluttered with an unlimited number of artificial associations. To avoid this problem, the aforementioned principles are complemented by the principle of parsimony, which requires that every diagram contain the minimum information needed to describe the component's behavior. This principle implies the need for concrete guidelines to determine when a diagram has enough information.

The Principle of Encapsulation

A long established principle of software engineering is the separation of the description of *what* a software unit does (e.g., "specification," "interface," and "signature") from the description of *how* it does it (e.g., "realization," "design," "architecture," "body," and "implementation"). This separation facilitates a divide-and-conquer approach to modeling in which a software unit can be developed independently. It also allows new versions of a unit to be interchanged with old versions provided that they do the same thing.

This principle is as important when modeling architectural components as it is when implementing them (Daniels and Cheesman 2000). A component modeled according to this principle is essentially described at two levels of detail—one representing a component's interface (what it does) and the other representing its body (i.e., how it fulfills the specified interface). These levels are shown in Figure 4.2. This separation allows developers who want to use an existing component or to replace one component with another to concentrate on the interface, neglecting the details of the body.

Figure 4.1   **Organization of Development Artifacts**

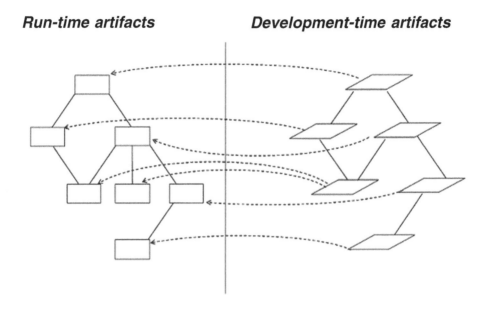

Figure 4.2   **Levels of Component Descriptions**

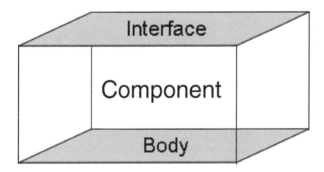

THE KOBRA METHOD

The previous section introduced our four key principles for modeling components using the UML. In this section, we introduce the KobrA method and explain how the aforementioned principles are implemented within this method.

General Overview

The KobrA method (Atkinson et al. 2001), developed at the Fraunhofer Institut Experimentelles Software Engineering, Germany (IESE), represents a synthesis of well-known software engineering technologies, including product-line development, component-based development, frameworks, architecture-centric inspections, quality modeling, and process modeling. By integrating these technologies, the method aims to provide a systematic approach to the development of high-quality, component-based frameworks.

In KobrA, the architecture of a system is organized as a tree of components, each described by a set of models (i.e., UML diagrams). Thus, all KobrA artifacts are organized around, and oriented toward, the description of individual components. Although the different diagrams belonging to an individual component are well defined, the method does not require the creation of every diagram for each component. The method provides guidelines on which diagrams to create and when (i.e., KobrA is scalable).

In addition to the central component tree, the KobrA method provides a systematic approach for ensuring that the system under development is of high quality. It provides an integrated strategy for quality assurance by combining construction and analytical aspects of quality assurance—that is, construction guidelines and techniques for efficiently identifying and removing defects (Bunse 2001; Laitenberger 2000). The strategy is specifically adapted to the needs of component-based and object-oriented systems and intertwined with the individual process steps. In short, quality assurance is an integral part of the method and not a simple add-on as in more traditional approaches.

Application of Principles

The four principles identified in the previous section play a fundamental role in the KobrA approach.

Implementing the Principle of Uniformity

The principle of uniformity requires that a given concept be represented and manipulated in the same way in all phases of development. The fundamental development artifact to which this applies in KobrA is the component. KobrA views the overall system under development, as well as any subsystems it may contain, as components and models them all in the same basic way. The distinction between what constitutes a system and what constitutes a part of a system (i.e., a subsystem) is therefore blurred in KobrA. Every component potentially can be a system in its own right or can be used as part of a larger component (through composition).

In principle, this implies a top-down approach based on the decomposition of a system (i.e., a component) into several smaller subsystems (i.e., components), where every component is described by the same set of models. KobrA therefore uses the same basic strategy to describe a system (i.e., a component) and its environment. This means that the KobrA description of a system in some ways resembles a fractal, since the products (and the accompanying processes) are identical at all levels of granularity. It also promotes reuse because any component, anywhere in the system, can be made into an application if it satisfies the needs of some customer.

Implementing the Principle of Locality

The principle of locality requires that every development artifact be oriented toward the description of a single component. The basic idea is to capture how coarse-grained components (e.g., a system) are "made up of" more fine-grained components, in a recursive manner, down to the level of small, primitive components. However, the concept of being "made up of" generally has a

Figure 4.3 **Component Trees**

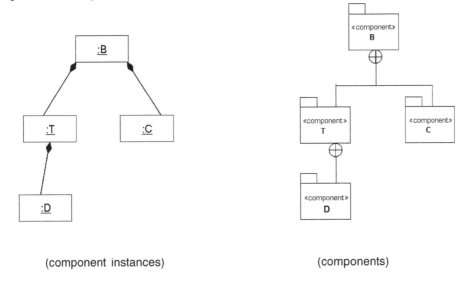

(component instances)   (components)

different interpretation at run time than at development time. Being precise about the differences and relationships between the two interpretations is essential for systematic development and the fulfillment of the principle of locality.

At run time, the notion of one component instance being "made up of" other instances is captured by the concept of composition. KobrA adopts UML's concept of composition, which is viewed as a variant of aggregation, in which a part is private to, and created by, the composite. At development time, however, the notion of one component being "made up of" other components is captured by module containment (a variant of UML ownership).

Since composition and containment both define tree structures, one principle of KobrA is that the run-time and development-time organization of components and their instances should be "aligned." In other words, the shape of the development-time containment tree should be driven by the nature of the run-time composition tree. In this case the principle of locality is satisfied. Aligning the two trees provides a systematic way of ensuring high cohesion and low coupling of components.

Figure 4.3 shows a simple example of aligned composition and containment trees described using the UML notation. The left side represents the run-time composition tree of the deployed component instances, while the right represents the development-time containment tree of components types. The basic goal is to ensure that the latter is "aligned" with the former, which in this example can be achieved by giving the trees the same shape and organization. However, in general, aligning the trees is usually more difficult. One problem is that a system of component instances does not always have a single composition tree. Often a system can contain multiple, dispersed containment trees, or it may contain none at all. Moreover, the shape of these trees may change over time. For these reasons, a different run-time tree is used as the starting point for alignment—the so-called creation tree. The creation relationship exists between two component instances when one creates the other. Since a component must be created by exactly one other component instance, the creation relationship traces out a tree structure. Once established, the creation tree is fixed and subsumes any start-up composition tree that may exist.

Implementing the Principle of Parsimony

The principal of parsimony is essentially an application of Occam's razor. It addresses the problem raised by having multiple diagrams describing a single entity. In essence, it requires that each diagram contain the minimum amount of information needed to describe the component fully. In other words, it requires that a model should contain just enough information, no more and no less. To fulfill this principle, KobrA precisely defines the relationships between the single components within the tree, as well as the overlap between the diagrams of a component's specification and realization.

Implementing the Principle of Encapsulation

The principle of encapsulation is based on the decoupling of the "what?" and the "how?" of a software unit. This principle also applies naturally to components. In KobrA, a component is described by:

1. a *specification,* which describes what a component's instances do and what they need from their surroundings,
2. a *realization,* which describes how a component instance realizes its specification by means of interactions with other component instances, and
3. an *implementation,* which describes the component's realization at a level of abstraction that can be automatically translated into an executable form.

The realization of a component therefore represents a description of how the component works, but at a lower level of abstraction than the specification, while the implementation describes how the abstract realization is mapped into a tool-comprehensible form. A given version of a component has one specification and at most one realization, but can have multiple implementations. In some situations, it is possible for a component specification to have no associated realization or implementations.

To reinforce the distinction between component specifications, realizations, and implementations, it is helpful to think of a component as a cube, as illustrated in Figure 4.4. The top surface of the cube can be thought of as the specification that describes what a component does and what it needs. It therefore represents the interface to the component. The bottom surface can be thought of as the realization of the component that describes how it realizes the specification using other components. It therefore represents the body of the component. Finally, the implementations can be thought of as separate artifacts, each providing an alternative description of the realization, but at a more concrete level of abstraction akin to a program. The realization and implementation of a component therefore elaborate upon how it works but in different dimensions.

The specification of a component describes all the properties of its instances that are visible to other component instances, including the set of services that the instances make available to others (commonly called the supplied, or server interface), the information supplied by or needed by the component, and the set of server instances that the component instances need to acquire (commonly called imported, supplied, or used interfaces). The specification also defines the behavior of the component instances over time, including the different states that they may exhibit.

The realization of a component describes the private design by which its instances realize the properties defined in the specification. This includes a description of any server creations performed by the instances, and the identification of any subcomponents. The realization also de-

Figure 4.4 **Levels of Component Descriptions in KobrA**

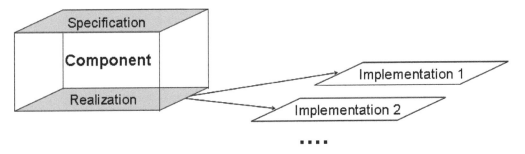

Figure 4.5 **A KobrA Component**

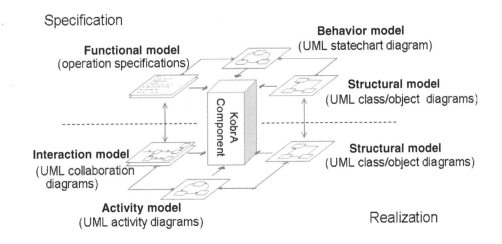

scribes how the various server instances (created and acquired) are linked together within the component's instances. In other words, it describes the architecture (design) of the component.

Following the principle of uniformity and the principle of encapsulation, every component has a specification and a realization that are described with a standard set of models (see Figure 4.5). The principle of locality then describes how these components can be put together to define a tree, in which every component is uniformly described. This tree structure is shown in Figure 4.6.

Finally, a component realization describes how a component works, but at a level of abstraction akin to design. In order to attain an executable version of a component, it is first necessary to create a description of how the component works in a form that can be processed by automated compilation tools. This is the role of the component implementation.

An important decision to be made when implementing components is to decide how the *logical* components in the component tree are to be mapped to physical components that are *deployable* in the final execution environment. A logical component can be mapped individually into a single physical component or can be grouped together with its children and/or parent into a combined physical component. Instances of physical components represent the smallest granularity of deployment and replacement in the run-time system.

Figure 4.6   **A KobrA Component Tree**

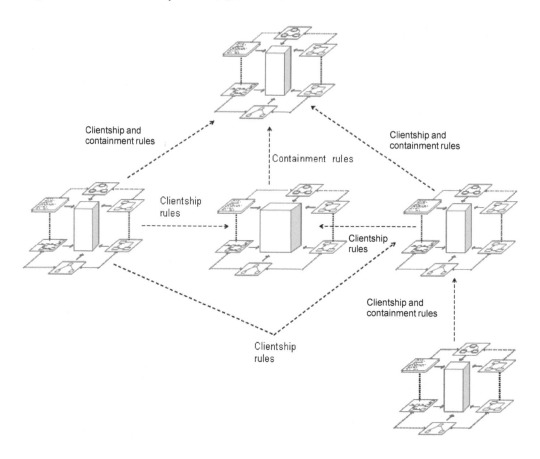

Since the UML is not an executable language, a component implementation cannot consist of UML diagrams alone. It must contain some form of program in an executable programming language. However, a component implementation can also contain supplementary UML diagrams to explain how the program works. In principle, any programming language or general-purpose implementation vehicle can be used to implement a component. In practice, however, the implementation process is significantly easier with a programming language that is at least object-oriented, such as Java, C++, or ADA. The ideal implementation vehicle for a physical component is the implementation-level component technologies such as an Enterprise JavaBean, a .NET object, or a Common Object Request Broker Architecture (CORBA) object. When physical components are implemented using one of these technologies, the advantages of component-based development at the analysis and design levels are combined with the advantage of components at the implementation and deployment levels.

Recursive Decomposition

An important characteristic of the overall KobrA development process is that it is highly recursive. Every component specification is defined in the context of a component realization and vice versa. In practice, a component specification represents a subset of the diagrams of its supercomponent's realization, and this subset contains only the information relevant to the component under consideration. In turn, the realization of a component is essentially a refinement of its specification. This means that the diagrams of a component specification define the core of its realization, which is then refined in order to obtain the final version.

This recursive approach raises one major question—what realization serves as the context for the specification of the system (i.e., the root component)? To address this question, we introduce the concept of the context realization. The purpose of the context realization is to define a top-level realization without the benefit of an associated specification. Although it bears the name "realization," it actually leans heavily on front-end development techniques. The basic goal of the context realization is to describe the properties of the environments of the system to be constructed. This is achieved by looking in detail at the business context and the usage context.

A SIMPLE CASE STUDY

To explain how these principles work, a small case study, known as the simple banking system (SBS), is presented in this section. The banking system enables customers to open accounts in some specified currency and to deposit money into or withdraw money from the account in any currency. To facilitate the necessary currency conversions, the system maintains a set of exchange rates between euros and other currencies. Clerks working for the bank can change a particular rate at any time. Customers can also request that an amount in a foreign currency be converted to and from euros. Finally, an account can have an associated limit specifying to what extent a customer can overdraw money from the account.

SIB Context Realization

As illustrated in Figure 4.7, the simple banking system's context realization is composed of three closely interrelated models, each providing a distinct view of the overall set of properties of the context. The structural model is composed of a class diagram and conveys information about the actors with which the bank interacts and the externally visible data that it manipulates (in this case only accounts). The interaction model is composed of multiple interaction diagrams (customarily sequence diagrams) that describe the interactions involved in the various system usage scenarios. These are very similar to the sequence diagrams commonly created to describe use case instances in modern object-oriented methods. The activity model is composed of multiple activity diagrams, which describe the interactions in which the system is involved in a flow chart style rather than an interaction-oriented style.

SIB Specification

As illustrated in Figure 4.8, the specification of the bank component (i.e., the system) is also composed of three main models. The structural model defines the information (i.e., the types) that the system utilizes in order to fulfill its contract. As well as data entities, this can in general also include other components that the component being specified (i.e., the subject) needs to "acquire" at run time. Notice that this model contains some information already contained in the context realization. However, according to the principle of locality, the model presents this information from the perspective of the bank, the "subject" of this specification.

The functional model is composed of multiple textual operation specifications, each declara-

Figure 4.7 **Context Realization of the Bank Component**

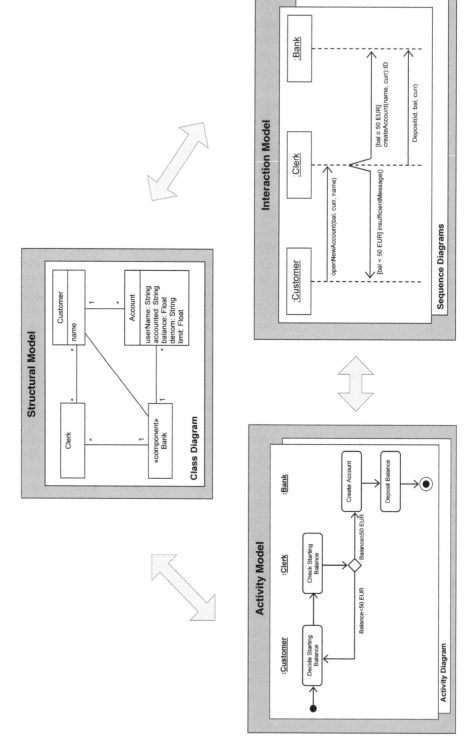

Figure 4.8 **Specification of the Bank Component**

Structural Model

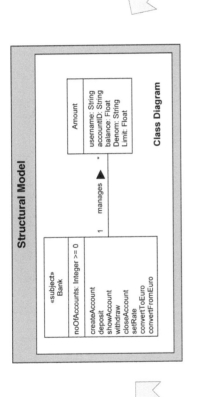

Class Diagram

Behavioral Model

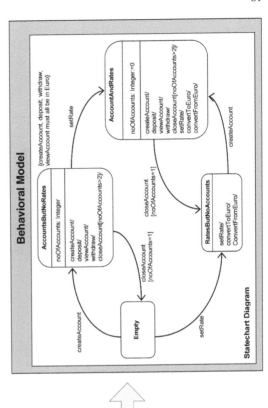

Statechart Diagram

Functional Model

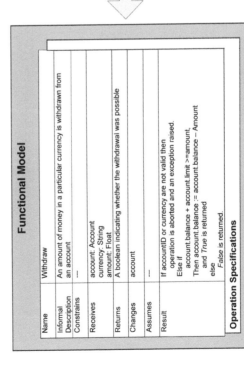

Operation Specifications

82

Figure 4.9 **Realization of the Bank Component**

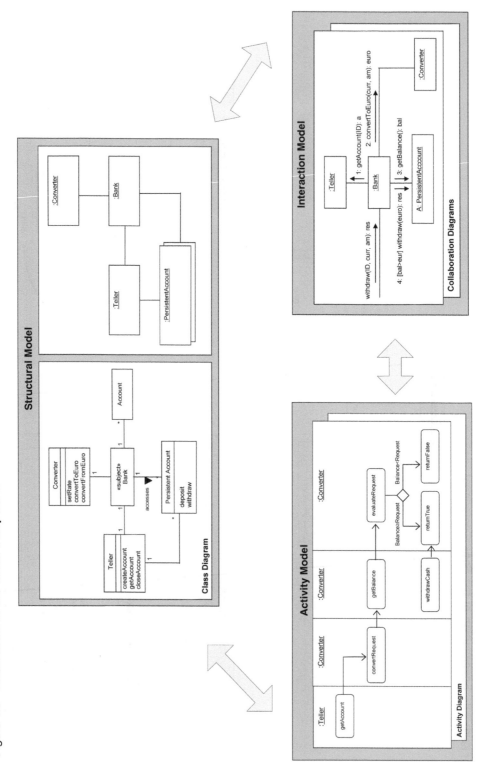

tively describing the effects of one of the component's operations. These effects are captured in terms of the concepts defined in the class diagram and thus provide a concrete way of ensuring that the structural model conforms to the principle of parsimony and does not present unnecessary concepts. The behavioral model is a state chart diagram that captures the externally visible states of the component as they relate to its operations and logical attributes.

SBS Realization

The realization of a component defines how it works. Therefore, the realization describes a component's private design. As illustrated in Figure 4.9, a component realization is composed of the same kinds of models as a context realization. This time, however, the diagrams making up the realization must be consistent with the corresponding diagrams in the component's specification.

The class diagram in the structural model constitutes a refinement of the class diagram in the specification. It includes the model elements from the specification class diagram but contains more information related to the component's realization (e.g., additional classes or components, and the full set of attributes and methods that each model element needs to provide). As can be seen in Figure 4.9, the class diagram can be complemented by an object diagram, which illustrates the linkage of instances.

As in a context realization, the interaction model is composed of interaction diagrams, describing how an operation is realized through interactions with other component instances and classes. The activity model is composed of a set of activity diagrams, each providing a flowchart-oriented view of the algorithm used to implement an operation, as opposed to an interaction-oriented view.

Following the principles introduced by this chapter, the realization of the bank component is then used to identify lower level components (e.g., teller or converter), which are then described in the same way, following the same guidelines and principles as for the Bank component.

RELATED WORK

Several methods have been devised in recent years to support component-based development. One of the first and most well-known methods is Catalysis, created by D'Souza and Wills (1998).

Most of the principles outlined in the previous sections have their roots in the Catalysis method, at least implicitly, if not explicitly. The ideas of recursive development and fractal-like products are a core theme in the Catalysis approach, although the process is only loosely defined in the form of patterns. Moreover, the idea that components can exist at all levels of granularity also plays a central role in Catalysis, although the method does not make it clear whether a system as a whole can be treated and modeled as a component.

The principle of locality is manifest in Catalysis in several ways. Type models, which play a similar role to the specification structural model in KobrA, are perhaps the most visible application of this principle, but other diagrams, such as operation pre- and postconditions, collaboration diagrams, and statechart diagrams, are also inherently localized. The method also emphasizes the organization of model elements and diagrams within packages. The principle of parsimony is not explicitly highlighted in Catalysis, but is implicitly applied to many of the models thanks to the method's adoption of the Fusion (Coleman et al. 1994) strategy for specifying operation pre- and postconditions in terms of class diagrams (i.e., type models).

The principle of encapsulation is also present in Catalysis, but not at the level of UML models. The method does separate the implementation of a component from its specification, but the implementation is viewed as a representation at the source code level of a component, not something represented at the UML level. The idea of creating models to describe the realization of a component separately from the specification is not present in Catalysis.

A more recently published component-oriented development method is the UML Components method created by Daniels and Cheesman (2000). Fewer of the principles outlined in chapter are evident in UML Components than in Catalysis. The component specification and interface models developed during the component specification workflow apply the principle of locality to create type models for interfaces and components. However, other models, such as component architectures, are very much based on the concept of a global description of a system's configuration. The UML Components method is also explicitly a flat method and therefore does not apply the principle of uniformity to create a hierarchy of nested components or to treat systems in the same way as their components. The principle of parsimony is implicitly adopted in the method, again due to its use of pre- and postconditions to document the effects of operations in terms of the type models.

SUMMARY AND CONCLUSION

The component paradigm holds the potential to improve significantly the way in which software is developed and used. However, because of the binary-module view of components that currently prevails in the UML and contemporary component technologies such as COM+/.NET and J2EE/EJB, many of their potential advantages are lost in the earlier phases of development.

This chapter has outlined the UML modeling practices that we believe are needed to fully leverage the component paradigm in the earlier stages of software development. Four basic principles capture the essence of component-oriented modeling: the principle of uniformity, the principle of locality, the principle of parsimony, and the principle of encapsulation. In one form or other, these are all detectable in leading component-oriented development methods, but not always explicitly or coherently.

The KobrA method, presented in the second part of this chapter, was developed specifically to support the application of these principles in the development and organization of UML models. To this end, the method cleanly separates the specification of a component from its realization (both modeled at the level of the UML) and further separates these from the implementation (primarily represented in a tool-comprehensible form such as source code). Organizing the UML description of components in terms of a hierarchical containment tree and treating the component embodiment activities as a separation dimension of concern allows the KobrA method to support a recursive approach to system development that is compatible with all major development methods and results in high-quality components.

By identifying and explaining the key principles upon which UML-based modeling of components should be established, the ideas presented in this chapter may help the current process standardization effort of the Object Management Group (OMG 2001) and may also point to potential improvements in future versions of the UML.

REFERENCES

Atkinson, C., J. Bayer, C. Bunse, E. Kamsties, O. Laitenberger, R. Laqua, D. Muthig, B. Paech, J. Wuest, and J. Zettel. 2001. *Component-Based Product Line Engineering with the UML.* Reading, MA: Addison-Wesley.

Bunse, C. 2001. *Pattern-Based Refinement and Translation of Object-Oriented Models to Code.* PhD Thesis., Fraunhofer IRB Verlag.

Coleman, D. et al. 1994. *Object-Oriented Development: The Fusion Method.* Englewood Cliffs, NJ: Prentice Hall.

D'Souza, D., and A.C. Wills. 1998. *Catalysis: Objects, Frameworks, and Components in UM.* Reading, MA: Addison-Wesley.

Daniels, J., and J. Cheesman. 2000. *UML Components: A Simple Process for Specifying Component-Based Software.* London: Addison-Wesley.

Jacobson, I., G. Booch, and J. Rumbaugh. 1999. *The Unified Software Development Process.* Boston, MA: Addison-Wesley.

Laitenberger, O. 2000. *Cost-effective Detection of Software Defects Through Perspective-based Inspections.* PhD Thesis., Fraunhofer IRB Verlag.

Object Management Group (OMG). 2001. *Unified Modeling Language Specification,* Version 1.4, www.omg.org/docs/formal/01-09-67.pdf (September 2001).

Selic, B., G. Gullekson, and P.T. Ward. 1994. *Real-Time Object-Oriented Modeling.* New York: Wiley.

CHAPTER 5

DESIGNING FLEXIBLE DISTRIBUTED COMPONENT SYSTEMS

WILLIAM F. ACOSTA AND GREGORY MADEY

Abstract: Recent advances in software and networking technologies have enabled developers to create increasingly complex and robust distributed applications. The technologies used in these applications must address issues specific to the distributed realm and largely absent in traditional, nondistributed component applications. In this chapter, we discuss the central issues encountered when designing component systems for distributed applications. In particular, we discuss the problems faced in locating and accessing remote components as well as communication protocols for and usage semantics of distributed components. We proceed to illustrate the concepts presented in this chapter by describing the design of an e-commerce application and examining the approach taken by the application designers to solve the issues specific to distributed components that arose during the development process.

Keywords: Distributed Components, Design, Architecture, Flexible Component Systems

INTRODUCTION

Advances in software development tools have enabled developers to create increasingly sophisticated software applications. Technologies such as Java Remote Method Invocation/Enterprise JavaBeans (RMI/EJB) and Microsoft .NET have introduced the ability to create distributed, component-based applications. However, the idea for building distributed functionality is not new. Java's RMI mechanism is an object-oriented evolution of Unix's Remote Procedure Call (RPC) mechanism.

Although traditional RPC provided limited flexibility in communications and data types, it did introduce a few key concepts that served as the foundation for the design of modern distributed component technologies. Because an application can interact with a remote component only via the published interface, the application can make no assumptions about the underlying implementation. This separation of interface from implementation allows the distributed functionality to exist on a remote server that runs a different operating system from that of the calling application. In this way, RPC forms a bridge for facilitating heterogeneous systems to interoperate at the application level.

This model for RPC was very successful with procedural languages. However, the lack of higher-level features such as type safety and polymorphism limit the applicability of traditional RPC to the object-oriented domain. As a result, technologies like Object Management Group's (OMG) Common Object Request Broker Architecture (CORBA) emerged as a natural object-oriented extension to the traditional RPC model. CORBA represented a significant leap forward in the development of distributed applications. Although heavily biased toward C/C++ syntactically, CORBA can be used with many programming languages, such as Java, Smalltalk, Eiffel, and FORTRAN. This was another important evolutionary step for distributed component systems as it addressed the issue of multiple programming languages and not just multiple operating systems.

The need to create distributed applications for the World Wide Web has served as a catalyst in the development of technologies that address the issues of multiplatform distributed component systems. Web Services Description Language (WSDL) and Universal Description, Discovery, and Integration (UDDI) of Web Services address the issue of describing and locating business components for distributed Web-based applications. In addition, Simple Object Access Protocol (SOAP) emerged as a technology to support cross-platform RPC by providing a mechanism for encoding structured and typed data using Extensible Markup Language (XML). By combining these technologies with Java, CORBA, and .NET, developers have a robust set of tools at their disposal for creating distributed component-based systems.

The goal of this chapter is to outline some of the technical challenges in building distributed component systems as well as to explain the basic model of a distributed component system architecture. Although the flexibility of the information technology (IT) infrastructure of an organization greatly influences the deployment success of a distributed application (Duncan, 1995), in this chapter we will examine distributed component architectures only as they are key technologies that are affected by and influence the broader IT infrastructure. The rest of this chapter is organized as follows. The second section provides a brief history and motivation for distributed components. The basic model of a distributed component system is described in the third section, while the fourth section describes the technical aspects of distributed component communication. The fifth section discusses some of the technical issues that must be addressed when designing a distributed system and choosing or designing a distributed component technology. The sixth section describes design strategies for addressing some of these issues. The seventh section provides a case study of an actual Web e-commerce application that was designed as a distributed system, and the eighth section provides some discussion on future directions for distributed component research. The last section offers concluding remarks.

MOTIVATION FOR DISTRIBUTED COMPONENTS

Although there is certainly a wide range of applications and trends that have contributed to the current breed of distributed component technologies, it is important to understand the historical context in which these technologies were created. Rather than trying to enumerate the impact of every type of application on the design of current distributed technologies, we will instead focus on observing the evolution of these technologies and, in particular, how that evolution relates to the evolution of e-commerce applications. E-commerce, or, more generally, Web-based applications, represent a broad class of applications with an equally broad spectrum for functional requirements. Web applications, therefore, lend themselves well to the examination of both the evolution and motivation for distributed component technologies.

Electronic commerce was one of the first and most successful Web-based applications. It was a natural extension of the early Web sites created by companies to promote their products. These early Web sites were little more than advertisements with either an e-mail address or a phone number for customers to use to place their orders. As the technologies evolved, it became feasible for companies to accept orders online. The ability to handle orders online required a great improvement in the underlying technology's ability to generate dynamic content. This ability is necessary in order to do even the routine operations of displaying products from the inventory database and the customer's shopping cart. However, dynamic content is only half the story. The technology that powers the Web site must operate correctly when a user performs an action such as clicking on a button to add the current product to the shopping cart. To handle this user input, Web sites required a great deal of code, thus demanding that they be designed with software engineering principles in mind.

The next step in the evolution from Web site to e-commerce application came about in order to address performance and scalability issues. It became clear very early that to handle a large volume of user traffic, the different functional elements of a Web site should not reside on a single server. The goal was to limit performance bottlenecks and provide some measure of load balancing and fault tolerance. By splitting the functionality of the application across several tiers, Web application developers were able to provide better performance and fault tolerance for their Web applications. The earliest models used two-tier architectures with the back-end database on one tier and the Web application itself on another.

As e-commerce and Web applications in general became more complex, the two-tier model became difficult to manage. The main difficulty was that the application tier became very complex and difficult to maintain as new functionality was added to the Web site. One of the main culprits in this problem was the fact that most of the business logic for the application was tightly coupled with the code to handle user input and generate the dynamic HyperText Markup Language (HTML), making it extremely difficult to reuse business logic functionality in different parts of the application. The solution was to create so-called three-tier architectures (see Figure 5.1) that separated the business logic and the presentation layer of the application into two separate layers.

In this way, the business logic for these e-commerce systems evolved into what we know today as components. The transition from tightly coupled application code to business logic components required an additional factor: the ability to access the components from remote applications. The split did not require that the presentation layer software and the business logic software reside on separate machines. It simply created a layer of abstraction between the two functional entities of the application. Nevertheless, it became apparent that just as the e-commerce application itself benefited from refactoring the business logic into components, other applications related to the Web site could benefit from having access to the same business-logic components. For example, consider a typical situation in an e-commerce site in which a customer is having trouble with an account and calls the customer service line. The customer's information is located in a central database that is accessible to the customer service representative. Ideally, the customer service representative would have some software application giving access to the customer's information, product information, and any other information needed to assist the customer. However, the e-commerce site is its own application and it needs to access much of the same information to allow customers to, for example, update their own information via the Web site. This implies that the component required to access customer information could be shared between the e-commerce application and the customer service application.

A naive approach would be to have both applications share a common code base for their components. Such a model would simply treat components as code libraries that are distributed with the application. However, more opportunities exist to exploit reusability if a component instance itself, as opposed to only its source code, is shared. More specifically, because a component instance has to exist in some location for at least one of those applications, it makes sense to leverage that fact by having all applications that use the component simply communicate with one instance instead of having many copies of the same component in multiple locations. By creating components as entities of a distributed system, we not only reuse the component's code,

Figure 5.1 **Basic Three-Tier Architecture**

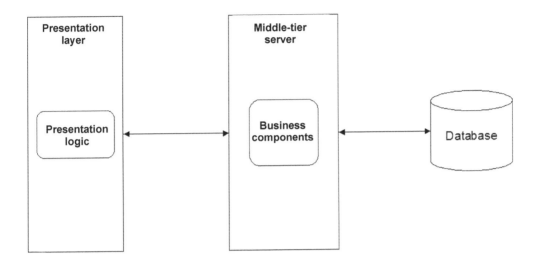

Figure 5.2 **Component Instance Reuse**

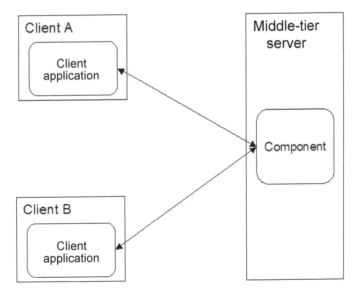

but we also reuse the component itself as a deployed resource. Figure 5.2 shows a diagram of two separate client applications using the same component instance.

Sharing a component instance across applications has many advantages over the more simplistic code reuse model. To understand these advantages, we must consider what a component "looks like" to external applications that use it. A component has an interface that defines how an appli-

Figure 5.3 **Basic Component Model**

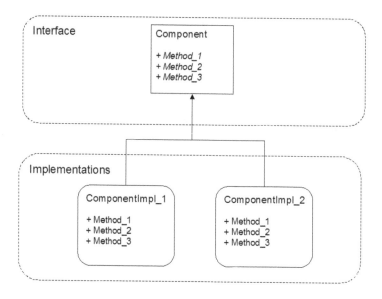

cation can interact with the component. Because an application is restricted to invoking only the methods that are defined in the component's interface, the component implements the details of satisfying the method invocation in any way that is appropriate so long as it agrees with what is specified in the interface (see Figure 5.3). Because the component's interface provides a layer of abstraction to the external application, the component's underlying implementation can be changed completely and, as long as it still conforms to the published interface, the application will not be affected. In a sense, the component's implementation is irrelevant from the point of view of the application. The application's only concern is that there exists some underlying implementation for the component that it can use.

The separation of interface from implementation is critical in providing distributed access to a component. Because an application is not inherently aware of the underlying implementation of a component, the implementation can be replaced with, for example, a thin stub that only knows how to communicate with the real component living on another machine. This allows the developer of the component to control the development and maintenance of the component without having to distribute new versions of it to every application every time something in the underlying implementation changes. We have seen that the external applications are shielded from these types of changes, so long as the changes do not affect the component's interface. This mechanism is an example of a very basic distributed component model. The stub component interacts with the real component using some RPC protocol such as Java RMI, but the details of that communication are hidden from the applications.

STRUCTURE OF A DISTRIBUTED COMPONENT SYSTEM

Before going too deeply into the issues involved in supporting distributed components, let us first take a quick tour of the general structure of a distributed component system. In general, we can divide a distributed component system into three major parts: the server, the client, and the component itself. In addition to these software entities, a distributed component system also requires several facilities to provide the distributed communication.

Server

The server refers to any software application that manages components and controls access to them. This can be a special purpose application like a CORBA Object Request Broker (ORB) that leaves the management of resources external to the object to some other entity. Alternatively, the server can follow the model of a Java Application Server, which not only manages the life cycle of its distributed objects, but also provides and manages resources such as pooled database connections and Web server functionality.

Along with any other responsibilities it may have, the server is responsible within the context of a distributed component system, for managing the life cycle of a component as well as controlling access to it. The problem of managing a component's life cycle is more complicated than it might appear. First, the server must have some mechanism for creating a component. Although this function is seemingly simple, a problem arises when two separate components require different resources and information during their creation process. Consider as an example a component that calculates shipping costs for an e-commerce application. Such a component needs access both to the different shipping carriers' costs and to the product database to determine dimensions and weight for a given order. When the component is created, it requires information about where to find the product database as well as the shipping costs for the different carriers. On the other hand, a component that authorizes credit cards simply needs access to the orders database to certify that a given order has been charged to a particular credit card. There is no implication that any one database holds both product and billing information; thus our example components, in the general case, would require some mechanism for finding the external resources it needs. This is clearly a problem for the server, as it has no prior knowledge of any components that may be deployed on it.

There are several solutions to this problem that we can borrow from traditional object-oriented programming. The basic idea is to standardize the process of creating a component. This can be accomplished by creating an additional entity known as a factory, which is responsible for handling the details of creating the component. Whether the component acts as its own factory, or an external entity is created to act as the factory for the component, we have addressed only the issue of the mechanics of creating a component. The other major issue that must be addressed is the context in which a component is created. As a component becomes more complex, its ability to remain a self-contained entity is compromised by the need to leverage externally available reusable functionality. A component may, for example, choose to implement its own thread pooling or database connection pooling mechanism, or it can leverage those same pooling mechanisms that may be available elsewhere in the server.

Client

Along with the server, a distributed component system requires a client. Although this seems intuitive, it is nevertheless important to understand what the role and expectations of the client are in a distributed component system. The most basic definition for a client is an application that will use a remote component. We say that such an application is a client of the component. It should be noted that this definition places no restriction on the complexity of the client application. Indeed, the client application may be a very thin presentation-only application that defers most of its functionality to the components it uses. Alternatively, the client application can be a complex application in its own right with its own set of components.

Although the abstract definition of a client places no restriction on the complexity of the client, some distributed component technologies may place implicit restrictions on the client, such as the use of a particular programming language. As we will see later, it may be possible to overcome such implicit restrictions by creating a more abstract software architecture that allows more flexibility in developing complex applications using distributed components.

Component

The fundamental entity in a distributed component system is, not surprisingly, the component. We can regard a component as a software entity with a well-known published interface that provides some set of functionalities. Admittedly, this is a rather vague description of a component. Nevertheless, it serves as an adequate starting point to discuss the fundamental nature of a component. In particular, this vague description illustrates a very important point, namely that there is no specific or required syntax that will identify a piece of software as a component. Although technologies such as Java EJBs require that an object implement a specific interface or throw a particular exception, these are artificial constructs that are imposed on the object by the underlying technology and that do not, in and of themselves, say anything about the "componentness" of the object. These constructs are necessary evils for interacting with components in the given technology, but prove to be significant barriers in allowing an application to interact with components using a different underlying technology.

DISTRIBUTED COMMUNICATION

The basis for a distributed component system is the ability of a software application to interact with remote resources. Although seemingly obvious, this simple fact has a significant impact in almost all areas of a distributed component system's design. It is therefore important to understand the function of the communication mechanism as it relates to the distributed component system as a whole. The communication mechanism can be very specific or very vague about its infrastructure requirements. For example, the communication mechanism can explicit specific networking and transport protocols. In systems where performance is critical, the communication mechanism may specify protocols to provide performance guarantees for the applications. This type of fine-grained functionality is noticeably absent from more general-purpose communication mechanisms since their focus is on broad compatibility and not on highly tuned performance.

In addition to the underlying networking protocols, the communication mechanism also specifies the message format and the sequence of messages that make up a valid transaction between a client and server. These are very low-level issues that are implemented by the server application and the client-side communication libraries, which are generally hidden from typical software developers creating or accessing a distributed component. Unfortunately, each distributed component mechanism uses different communication protocols, each with different semantics for communicating with a distributed component. As we have seen, the notion of an interface creates a layer of abstraction between the clients of a component and the underlying implementation of the component. We can adapt this paradigm to apply to the communication infrastructure. The basic idea is to separate a component's business logic interface from the underlying RPC technology implementation. A component's interface thus becomes RPC protocol–neutral. Such protocol neutrality allows for great flexibility for both component developers and client application developers. A component developer can simply focus on implementing the required functionality for the component without needing to worry about managing any of the remote communication details.

Data Marshaling and Object Serialization

Fundamental to a system's ability to support communication with objects remotely is the data marshaling mechanism. Data marshaling refers to the process of packaging the data that are passed as parameters to a method into the underlying communication mechanism's required data and message format. More specifically, the marshaling process involves converting the data from the types specified by the method's signature within the programming language into an appropriate representation of the data within the context of the communication protocol. Similarly, unmarshaling refers to the inverse process of unpacking the data from the remote message and constructing a valid object within the context of the current run-time environment.

The mechanics of such a conversion are relatively simple, though somewhat tedious. The essential problem lies in defining the mapping from programming language objects and data types to the data types supported by the RPC protocol. The problem is quite difficult, even before we consider the issue of complex objects. For example, consider the case of serializing a floating point number. Such a serialization requires that the RPC protocol support some mechanism of representing the number with the appropriate level of precision; otherwise, the resulting deserialized object might represent a slightly different number. The problem becomes even more complex when we consider complex objects. Even simple concepts such as arrays and linked lists require that the underlying RPC protocol support some mechanism of representing enumerations of objects. For that matter, the RPC protocol must provide a mechanism for representing composite objects such as a list of customer objects, each of which contains an address object.

Object serialization introduces several subtle problems for distributed component systems. First, what is the expectation of the state of the object when it is deserialized? Is the deserialized object a snapshot of the source object? Is it strictly a copy of the object? Or is it perhaps a reference to the original object? In particular, are the effects of changes to the deserialized object expected to be automatically reflected in the original object? And, of course, all these goals must be met while also maintaining good performance. An efficient mechanism for handling these task is Java RMI, for example, which allows for the use of Java in high-performance scientific applications (Maassen et al. 2001).

Name Binding and Lookup

A critical process in distributed component systems is assigning a name to a component that is to be made available, thus enabling the corresponding client-side process of finding a component. Unless a component is being developed for a customized system and will not be deployed elsewhere, a mechanism needs to exist that allows the server to publish the component to the world. The process of publishing involves binding a component instance to a name that uniquely identifies the instance. In its most basic form, this is simply a hash table that stores a mapping of component names and network locations for each component. Even this simple level of indirection offers advantages over statically defined locations for components, since all that is required to specify an alternate location for a component is to update the component's entry in the lookup table. The name binding and lookup facility can additionally be integrated into a larger resource location mechanism, as in the Java Naming and Directory Interface (JNDI). This model is very attractive because it provides a unified point of contact for an application to acquire any resource it needs as well as allow the lookup facility to cache communication stubs for components. No matter what level of complexity is chosen for the lookup facility, it is clear that some form of lookup facility is necessary in order to maintain and exploit the flexibility of the component architecture.

ISSUES IN DISTRIBUTED TECHNOLOGIES

Currently, a developer who wishes to create a distributed application must choose one of the available distributed component technologies and develop the application around that distributed component Application Programming Interface (API). This poses several problems. First, it forces the application to exist within only one RPC protocol domain. If the need arises to make all or part of the application available in a different RPC domain, the application must be modified to take into account the new communication requirements. This situation leads to another problem: it requires component developers to have specific knowledge of all the RPC protocols that might be used to access the component. Additionally, maintaining separate code for the different RPC mechanisms is prone to errors and bugs.

A desirable approach would allow component developers to eliminate the communication-specific code from their implementations. The component interface and implementation can then be considered clean. Additionally, a mechanism would create translators that convert a clean component to a protocol-specific object without needing to access the original component's source code. The translation is automated and occurs after compile-time. Either the translation occurs within the run-time system if the system supports introspection and reification or it could happen as a sort of just-in-time translation in which a translation layer is generated and compiled at deployment and run-time. This same mechanism could handle the creation of protocol-specific, data-type conversion and serialization.

API Syntactical Issues

Different APIs have varying syntactical requirements for objects that are to be used within the communication mechanism. For example, Java RMI requires that all remotely accessible methods throw java.rmi.RemoteException, and the Apache/IBM XML-RPC API requires methods to have signatures that contain only native primitives and certain supported object types. This situation is not always the case. It is only true if a component wants to be made available through the XML-RPC API from Apache/IBM using the default data serializers/deserializers. But a component is free to implement custom handlers for its methods that can handle the required data types.

Forcing a component to comply with many different rules that are imposed on it by all the protocols and APIs would quickly lead to syntax conflicts in the definition of the component. In addition, any client of the component would also have to be altered to take into account the changes in the API. These conflicts are even more undesirable as it forces clients to change in order to support something that they may not use. So requiring source code changes to the component is not only undesirable, but also counterproductive because the goal of being able to use multiple communication RMI protocols is to make a component available across many domains and not to force the component and all its clients to exist within all domains. This last point becomes important when clients are written in multiple languages or exist on platforms with no support for certain communication mechanisms. Modifying a component's source code to use a new protocol may not be feasible, or even possible. For example, if a component is distributed without source code, then it is, for practical considerations, impossible to change the original source code and recompile it because the run-time system does not have access to it.

Object Serialization

A big hurdle to overcome is the problem of object serialization, both in terms of both data types and binary format and the more abstract issues of serialization semantics. One fundamental requirement for remote method calls is serializing or (un)marshaling parameters and return values to and from method calls. Ideally, the run-time system would support pluggable serialization formatters. These would allow the run-time system to retain control of access to the internal structures of a serialized object, but provide a mechanism to specify the representation of the serialized data.

Serialization Semantics

Although the concept of serializing an object is conceptually simple, the semantics of the serialization process can be very different for different object serialization implementations. For example, is the entire internal state of an object serialized? If so, what entity has access to the private members of the object in order to serialize it? If only the externally accessible data is serialized, is the deserialized object guaranteed to be in an internally consistent state? The semantics of object serialization can be categorized into two broad classes: strong and weak serialization semantics. A taxonomy for these different classes of semantics is as follows:

> *Weak serialization semantics:* This refers to serializing only the publicly accessible fields of an object. Although conceptually simple, this can lead to problems when the critical internal state is omitted and the deserialized object is constructed and left in an unknown or inconsistent state. However, weak semantics allow for loose coupling between data and the mechanisms required to access them, such as when components are written in different programming languages.
> *Strong serialization semantics:* This refers to the serialization of the entire internal state of an object. This serialization is more difficult to implement as it requires access to the object's internal (read: private) members and fields, which, by definition, are not accessible to external entities. For this reason, strong serialization semantics benefit greatly from support by the run-time system producing a tight coupling between data and implementation of the data-type as the object expects that the internal state will be consistent when the data are unmarshaled. Strong semantics are, therefore, very difficult to apply when components are written in multiple languages. Strong serialization semantics also apply in applications where code mobility is required as it is expected that an object can transfer itself, including its state, to a remote host and execute there.

Unlike weak serialization semantics that allow for more abstraction due to a looser coupling between definition and implementation, strong serialization semantics are less abstract and more dependent on implementation. By their very nature, there exists a tight coupling between the implementation and the definition of the object. For cases in which strong serialization semantics apply, a mechanism is needed to extract the internal state of an object. The memento design pattern (Gamma et al. 1995) does not apply to this situation because it requires the serializable object to be designed with support for externalizing its state ahead of time. However, it is possible to create a version of the object that supports externalization of its state like that described in the memento pattern. The main semantic issue is this: What is the expectation of the serialization semantics for an object? More specifically, when is that determination made? Must the component author decide that when the component is created?

Data-Type Conversion

Not all APIs support the same set of data types. Object serialization, therefore, requires that a translation mechanism exist to convert from the component's data types to the protocol's data types and vice versa. Ideally, translators should be defined as separate entities from an object. This separation, which is analogous to the separation of communication logic from a component, allows us to plug different formatters for objects at run time as well as support multiple, simultaneous serialization formatters.

Protocol Compliance

Protocols should be considered clean and not be modified to support any desired or required functionality. Any functionality that is not provided by the protocols must be addressed at the application level and not at the protocol level, because protocol usage should be opaque. That is, a client, as long as it conforms to the protocol, should not make any assumptions about the server and vice versa. Opaqueness of protocol usage is more relevant to the server, which might receive requests from many different types of clients over the same protocol and thus should not make assumptions about how the client handles its communications.

Component Management

One issue that may be considered minor, but in fact causes a lot of problems is the issue of separating the management of a component from its implementation and the communication mechanisms. This separation is important because a component not only uses resources on the server, but also is itself a resource that the server must manage. Many of the communication APIs require an actual object instance in order for the protocol to manage remote access to it.

Asynchronous Paradigms

Methods are, by their very nature, synchronous and blocking operations. Asynchronous communication paradigms require very different usage semantics from synchronous method calls. It is possible to simulate synchronous communications within asynchronous systems and vice versa. In fact, some RPC mechanisms may use that type of mechanism "under the covers." Because of the inherent difference in programming style, asynchronous paradigms are, therefore, not appropriate topics for discussion within the context of distributed component systems.

Component Usage Semantics

The main problem here is that different protocols and mechanisms support different usage semantics for the remote components. Examples of these different usage semantics are stateful versus stateless method invocations and shared versus exclusive access to the component. The problem exists only if we force all protocols to support the usage semantics of all other protocols. A component is considered to be clean, so it does not need to support any specific usage semantics. The details of these usage semantics can be encapsulated at the protocol level. The protocol-specific translation layer or proxy can then support stateful, stateless, and shared requests from clients by employing pools, shared objects, and intelligent routing of requests. The issue of component semantics is, as a result, complicated. Consider the example of EJB. Java RMI was originally designed to facilitate building distributed applications that used remote objects. Later, EJB was created on top of RMI to provide a distributed component framework for Java. With its introduction, certain semantic rules were introduced that are not enforceable at compile-time. Take as an example a method in EJB that returns an object of type java.lang.Object. It is therefore possible to have the implementation return the reference *this* in Java (as long as the Bean was serializable, of course). That would be a perfectly legitimate procedure as far as the Java compiler is concerned. However, it would lead to an inconsistent state within the application at run time because of the way the EJB container manages EJB instances. The container creates proxies and pools many instances of a Bean so that, for example with Stateless Session Beans, a client may actually invoke methods on two separate instances on two consecutive method calls. Furthermore, a Session Bean can be either stateful or stateless, and the decision as to which type it is will not be made until the bean is deployed. This means that the Java compiler makes no distinction between the two types of Session Beans. More importantly, the Bean developer must make assumptions about the final deployment mode and the corresponding semantics. Such assumptions illustrates the point that current languages like Java are not expressive enough to allow for higher-level definition of functionality, such as usage semantics, and developers must, therefore, resort to external validation mechanisms for their components.

DESIGN STRATEGIES

Now that we have a clear picture of some of the major issues involved in designing distributed component systems, we can shift our attention to ways in which we can address these issues. Unfortunately, no magic formula exists that can solve all of these problems in an optimal way. Rather, as with all of software engineering, we will identify the relationships between the different issues for supporting distributed components and analyze the trade-offs involved in addressing each issue.

Protocol-Neutral Component Design

The first step in supporting multiple RPC protocols in a distributed component system is to separate the definition and implementation of a component from the logic required to make that component available to remote client applications. As we have seen previously, this separation is necessary because each RPC mechanism has different, and sometimes conflicting, syntax requirements in its API for distributed components. Separating the component from its communication has other advantages. By being specified in a protocol-neutral fashion, a distributed component can be made upwardly compatible with any new RPC protocol that is introduced simply by creating the appropriate adapters to make the component available via the new protocol. This is a very powerful capability as it requires no source code changes to the original component in order to make it available using a new RPC protocol. This allows a company, for example, to purchase a component and deploy it on a server with any desired RPC protocols without having to have access to the source code of the component.

The key, therefore, lies in being able to create a protocol-specific view of the component from a protocol-neutral definition. The simplest solution would obviously be to create the adapters by hand. However, such an approach offers very little over simply creating different versions of the component for each protocol. A more desirable approach is to generate the necessary adapters automatically, either at compile time or at run time. The role of the adapter is to present a view of the component that is compatible with the RPC protocol. It handles any necessary data conversions and thus performs a metamarshaling of the data being passed to and returned by a method invocation. The manner in which these adapters are created is quite varied. The most flexible solution involves analyzing the protocol-neutral component at run time and dynamically generating all required adapters and helper objects. Currently, limitations in languages like Java restrict the ability to support a fully dynamic solution. This restriction is due to the lack of reification mechanisms in most modern programming languages. However, languages like Java do provide fairly rich introspection mechanisms that, when coupled with dynamic class loading, allow us to simulate a fully dynamic solution. This type of solution presents further motivation for creating richer reflection mechanisms in middleware platforms.

In the absence of introspection mechanisms or dynamic class loading in the run-time system, a suitable process would involve simply extracting the translation layer logic from the RPC handler and creating stand alone tools that can create the appropriate adapters just before run time. Although this mechanism does not provide the flexibility of run-time modification to the system, it is, nevertheless, beneficial from the perspective of software engineering as it still generates the protocol-specific component adapters after compile time.

Because each RPC protocol has a different format as well as different serialization semantics, the issue of object serialization poses a significant hurdle in designing a system that supports multiple RPC protocols. Fortunately, the adapter model can be leveraged to encapsulate the details of serializing data for the RPC protocol.

Stateless Versus Stateful Semantics

The state semantics of a component influence almost all areas of the distributed component system's design. Stateful semantics imply that a component can maintain some state information between method invocations by a client. For example, a stateful component that calculates the price for an online order might have methods to apply gift certificates and calculate tax and shipping cost. A client of this stateful component would make several successive method invocations on this component in order to calculate the order price. Inherent to this interaction is that the component stores information about the order between each method invocation. In contrast, a stateless version of this component would require the client to pass the customer identifier as well as the intermediate values of the calculations to each method call. The stateless component does not maintain any information and thus requires that each method invocation provide all the information needed to perform the desired action.

Upon initial inspection, it appears that stateful semantics are more restrictive and that stateless semantics are a subset of stateful semantics whereby the client passes extra information to each method call. This view implies that a distributed component system need only support stateful semantics because it would be able to support stateless semantics "for free." This, however, is not the complete picture, and such an implementation would not gain certain advantages that stateless semantics provide.

Indeed, stateless semantics represent a very basic communication model. However, this simplicity can be exploited to great effect to support load-balancing and fault-tolerance mechanisms at the server level. For example, a server may create a pool of several instances of a stateless component that get allocated to each incoming remote request for the component. By distributing the load of requests for a component in this way, the server can achieve better performance. A similar model can be applied to allow successive requests for a stateless component to span multiple servers. Since the client-to-component interaction is stateless, successive method invocations are independent of any previous method invocation and, by implication, are not dependent on any particular instance of a component. If a server can exploit this property internally to achieve better throughput, an external entity can also exploit this property to route requests for a component to instances distributed across a cluster of servers. This capability not only provides load-balancing for the server, but also provides a fault-tolerance mechanism. If the entity responsible for routing detects a failure on any of the servers in the cluster, it can route requests for components to other servers in the cluster.

Although the routing mechanisms required to implement this load-balancing and fail-over are not trivial, they are significantly easier to implement for stateless semantics than the equivalent that would be required in a stateful communication model. To provide the same level of fault-tolerance and performance for a stateful distributed component system, the routing mechanism needs to be very sophisticated. The routing mechanism must account not only for routing around the failure, but also for tracking and recovering the state information in the failed component and replicating it to an alternate component instance. This is a very difficult problem to solve in a way that provides both high performance and maximum reliability.

The problem of state semantics in a distributed component system becomes quite difficult when dealing with multiple simultaneous RPC protocols. As an example, let us examine the problem from the point of view of the state semantics of the communication. To support stateful communications, an RPC protocol must contain the notion of a session. A session refers to a series of interactions between a particular client and a component. The notion of a session is necessary at the protocol level because, in order to route the request to the appropriate component instance, the server must determine the identity of the client from the message and guarantee that the request be serviced by the same instance of the component that the client had accessed on previous requests. An RPC protocol without session capabilities is limited to stateless communications.

A system that intends to support multiple RPC protocols must contend with this issue. A primitive solution is to force all communication to be stateless. Unfortunately, such measures are too restrictive and can often negate the benefit of the additional RPC protocols. To overcome this problem, a mechanism must be created that allows stateful communications to be simulated over a stateless RPC protocol. Fortunately, several mechanisms can be employed to achieve this effect. One possible solution is to leverage the component lookup facility to guarantee that the handle to the component instance that is returned to the client identifies a unique component instance. In this way, each communication between the client and server is a request for a specific component instance. This solution addresses the problem of providing stateful semantics over a stateless RPC mechanism. However, such a model limits the server's ability to pool instances of a component effectively because the decision about which component instance a client will access becomes the responsibility of the lookup facility and not the server. Similarly, this solution is vulnerable to failures of the server in which the component resides. These issues can be overcome by providing more sophisticated interaction between the server and lookup facility. Similarly, the issue of fault-tolerance can be addressed by creating intelligent client-side stubs for the component that can fail-over to a replicated instance of the component. However, these solutions require a much more complex communication infrastructure and server framework and, in turn, greater overhead in the system.

CASE STUDY: E-COMMERCE SOFTWARE ARCHITECTURE

As we have previously seen, Web applications—in particular, e-commerce applications—provide a good test bed for examining the issues involved in creating distributed component systems. These applications are typically composed of several smaller, discrete applications that interact with each other to provide the required functionality. Although the application appears to be a single, homogeneous entity from the point of view of a customer accessing the Web site, the truth is that such applications must integrate with various types of applications behind the scenes. These include not only legacy databases, but also remote applications located on the servers of a third-party company for such things as credit card validation and promotional campaigns. Providing seamless integration between such diverse applications demands a very flexible and robust distributed component technology. Currently, companies such as Sun and Microsoft have created distributed component systems that can address some of these issues. Early e-commerce applications, however, did not have the luxury of purchasing commercially available software to meet these needs because no such software existed at the time. The developers of those early Web applications therefore had to create custom solutions for all the distributed component problems. Not surprisingly, a great deal of the design of the current batch of distributed component technologies is a direct reflection of the techniques and solutions that were created by the developers of distributed applications. The following is a case study examining the software architecture and design decisions of an early e-commerce application that attempted to overcome some of the issues faced in distributed component system design.

Application Overview

The basic requirements of the application were flexibility, extensibility, and robustness. Specifically, the development team required the flexibility to use the most appropriate programming language or technology for each aspect of the application. To achieve this, the e-commerce application was split into several functional units following the basic three-tier architecture: presentation layer, business logic, and data sources (see Figure 5.1). In particular, the system architecture used multiple data sources as well as separate presentation logic and systems for each of the two main Web applications (StoreFront and ProductManager). Figure 5.4 shows a diagram of the major functional units and the communication connections between them for this system. The following is a brief description of these functional units and the role they played in the overall structure of the application as well as their relationship to the other components.

StoreFront

The StoreFront application is responsible for interacting with the user of the Web site. Its responsibility is to capture HTTP requests and determine the appropriate action to take based on the request. This involves not only inspecting the URL, but also parsing data from forms or other user input. On the response end, the StoreFront is responsible for formatting the data and generating HTML to be rendered on the client's browser.

When the Web site was created, very few tools existed for creating dynamic content on the Web. The StoreFront was implemented using the Apache Web server and the Mod_Perl module, which was, at the time, the best option both in terms of performance and flexibility for generating dynamic content.

Figure 5.4 **Web Application System Architecture**

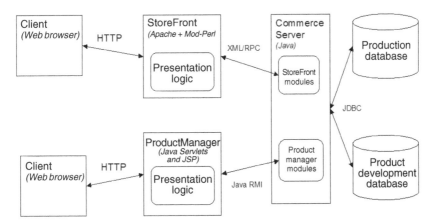

Databases

The application consisted of several databases. The main database contained all the product information as well as all information for all customers and all orders. This database, which was deployed on a cluster of servers with high-speed Redundant Arrays of Independent Disks (RAID) arrays running Oracle 8i, provided load balancing and fault tolerance. In addition to the main database, the system also contained a separate product development database.

ProductManager

The role of the ProductManager application is to manage the life cycle of a product beginning when the product is first identified by the merchandising department and ending when the product is added to the Web site. This process requires many revisions to the product description, many images and pictures of the product, dimensions, and statements of origin for the product. All information and revisions are kept in the product development database. When the product is ready to be sold through the Web site, the ProductManager transfers the information from the product development database to the main database, where it becomes a "live" product available for purchase through the Web site.

Since the editors, photographers, and merchandisers were not situated in a central location, the decision was made to develop the ProductManager as a Web-based application. The only requirement for any of the remote users is access to the Internet and a Web browser. This allowed the development team to add incremental enhancements to the user interface, functionality, and work flow of the ProductManager without needing to worry about distributing the new version of the application to each user.

The ProductManager was developed in response to the problem of an ad hoc, inconsistent, and increasingly time-intensive product development process. Due to the timing of the development of the ProductManager, the developers were able to create the presentation layer for the ProductManager using Java Servlets and Java Server Pages (JSP), technologies that were not available when the StoreFront was being created. Since the ProductManager was intended to be an internal application, the developers were able to experiment with this new technology. This application also served as a proof of concept for our software architecture since the ProductManager, written in Java, could coexist with the StoreFront application, written in Perl.

Modules

In the object model, the development team used the term *module* to describe the components that were available to remote applications (e.g., the StoreFront). A module exposes an interface that clients use to interact with it. This interface encapsulates the implementation of any business logic functionality performed by the module. For example, the AddressModule allowed an application to create and edit addresses for customers. Modules were intended to be discrete components of business logic for use by client applications like the StoreFront and ProductManager.

CommerceServer

The CommerceServer is the heart of the e-commerce application. In early 1999, when the CommerceServer was developed, there were no commercially available Java application servers that the development team considered stable enough for the production environment. This lack forced the development team to create a custom application server, dubbed the CommerceServer, in addition to the business logic required for the e-commerce application and the necessary software infrastructure to allow remote procedure calls using XML.

Software Architecture

The software architecture was a direct reflection of the requirements of the application. As with most other e-commerce sites, the software for the Web site had to be built from the ground up because no technologies were available that were stable and mature enough to rely upon for a production environment. The decision was made to leverage the best available technologies for each facet of the application, and the development team would create all the custom code necessary to make the design work. Oracle 8i was chosen for the back-end database as it provided the necessary functionality for performance and transaction processing. For similar reasons, the development team selected the Apache Web server with Mod_Perl as the front-end HTTP and HTML engine. Although Perl and Apache had proved themselves a formidable combination for building Web sites with dynamic content, it was decided the Perl alone did not provide an adequately structured platform (in terms of software engineering) to build such a complex application. In addition, at the time, the database connectivity available in Perl was very unstable. Java, on the other hand, had much better database connectivity and its native object-oriented model provided a much more structured platform for long-term software engineering, so it was decided that the business logic for the Web site would be implemented in Java. It should be evident that a significant development hurdle was introduced with the developers' decision to use Java for the business logic: how does a Perl application running on one machine interact with a Java application running on a separate machine? The solution was a custom RPC protocol based on XML.

XML-RPC MECHANISM

The decision to use XML was a very natural one, since XML provided a platform-neutral mechanism for exchanging data. The RPC protocol was therefore very simple. A client would construct a message in the form of an XML document and send it to the server. The server parsed the XML in the message, determined the component and which method within the component to invoke, and returned the result as another XML document in a response message. The structure of these XML messages was well defined by an XML Document Type Definition (DTD). The DTD for the protocol defined the allowable data types and structure for specifying component names, method names, and the parameters that were passed to each method invocation.

The use of an XML-based RPC protocol has some very clear advantages in terms of cross-platform integration and portability. All that is needed by a client is a mechanism for composing and parsing XML data. This allows client applications to be written in any language that is appropriate for that application. Additionally, unlike technologies like CORBA that require a complex infrastructure on each platform, XML requires, at its most basic level, a simple mechanism for parsing text. With such minimal requirements, an XML-RPC mechanism can be ported to platforms with limited resources, such as embedded or wireless devices, in addition to the wide array of other platforms that have XML parsers available.

In the case of this e-commerce application, the XML-RPC protocol was a very effective solution as it allowed a Perl application that handled HTTP requests to interact with Java components that handled business logic. In contrast, consider the use of a platform-specific protocol such as Java's Remote Method Invocation. The use of RMI would require that the client applications also be written in Java. Although Java is a language well-suited for certain types of software development tasks, it is not always the best choice for every type of application. The use of platform-specific protocols such as Java RMI renders the distributed component system unnecessarily restrictive and therefore out of place in a design philosophy that strives to maximize the choices available to developers.

The XML-RPC mechanism met the development team's requirements for portability and cross-platform integration very well. Not surprisingly, however, such success comes at the cost of speed, or, more precisely, efficiency. Because XML is a text-based mechanism, all data must be represented as a string. For example, consider the issue of passing an integer value of 12,345,678 as a parameter to a remote method invocation. In XML, that number must be passed as a string and thus occupies a minimum of eight bytes. In contrast, a traditional RPC mechanism with a byte-oriented message structure could represent that number in four bytes. Although this is a decidedly contrived example, it illustrates the inherent inefficiency of using a text-based mechanism instead of a traditional byte-based mechanism. The problem of efficiency becomes even more pronounced when we consider the structure and metadata required to send a message. With XML, not only are the values themselves being sent, but the structure of the message itself is encoded into the message in the form of the XML tags required to identify the different elements of the XML document. A traditional byte-based RPC protocol would have a clearly defined message structure that is known by both parties participating in the communication. All that is needed is that the data in the message be arranged according to the predefined format, and therefore each message contains only the raw data.

Each XML message must not only transmit its content, but also a description of its structure. It is worthwhile to note that this does not mean that each XML message must also include its DTD. Indeed, an intelligent system would probably cache the DTD for future reference, and thus there would be no need to send it on subsequent messages. More to the point, the DTD does not describe the contents of the message; it describes the syntax of a valid message. Each message must still describe its own contents within the syntax specified by the DTD.

Efficiency was not the only problem faced by the development team. The other major problem encountered was serializing objects as XML. On the surface, this does not appear to be a difficult problem. The system should take a snapshot of the state of the object and represent that snapshot as an XML document. The representation of the object as XML is not in and of itself difficult, since the XML-RPC protocol has a DTD defining the structure of such a representation. The problem with serializing an object becomes apparent when examining the expected semantics of serializing an object and the facilities available to create the serialized object.

Two separate and important factors led to the decision to use weak serialization semantics for the XML-RPC protocol. First, although Java natively provides a mechanism for serializing an object (including its internal nonvolatile or transient data), the resulting serialized object is formatted in Java's own format. Unfortunately, Java does not provide any means of specifying the desired serialization format. In order to use XML as the target serialization format, the implementation was limited to serializing only public member data of the object because it could not leverage the virtual machine's access to the internal state of the object for its serialization. The second, and perhaps more compelling, reason to use weak serialization semantics was the fact that the client applications would not necessarily be written in Java. In fact, the main client application was written in Perl. In such an environment, the internal state of a Java object is essentially meaningless within Perl. The use of weak serialization semantics degenerated the objects that could be passed via the RPC protocol to *structs* in the classic C/C++ sense. This can limit how a client application interacts with the component.

The XML-RPC protocol required that external serializers be created. Although this seems straightforward enough to understand, the initial design called for a custom serialization code to be created for each XML-serializable object and the XML serialization code was embedded into the objects themselves. Furthermore, these serializers had to be hand-coded and thus needed recompiling each time a change was required. Because the serialization code was incorporated into each object, supporting Java's RMI concurrently with the XML-RPC mechanism was very difficult since each RPC mechanism had different syntax requirements for its API and the objects that would be used with it.

The developers created a more robust approach for the second-generation architecture. The second approach separated the object from the serialization mechanism used. This allowed the object to remain clean and allowed developers to add support for new RPC mechanisms, in addition to the native XML-RPC mechanism, by adding new serializers for the objects. This split also gave the developers more freedom to implement the serializers in the most appropriate manner for their particular requirements. For example, the initial approach used hand-coded serializers within each object. However, because the XML-RPC protocol used weak serialization semantics, the serialization code could be generated automatically by inspecting the object and determining which fields would be serialized. In languages like Java that have rich introspection APIs, this can be done dynamically at run time. Alternatively, serializers could be generated at compile time in order to eliminate the overhead of introspection and reflection or on platforms with no such APIs. By separating the object from the mechanisms used to represent it in a serialized form, the second approach not only facilitated supporting multiple RPC protocols simultaneously, but also allowed for customization of the serialization process to meet the needs of the developers.

Overall, the main design goals of the application were reached by the second-generation of the software. Indeed, even the initial implementation provided more flexibility for the development team than was available at the time. By separating the business logic from the presentation logic, the development team was able to deploy two separate Web applications (StoreFront and ProductManager) backed by a common middle-tier application server (CommerceServer). Additionally, by representing the interface of the object in a platform- and language-independent manner using XML, the developers were able to create applications in multiple languages (Perl and

Java) that used the defined components. Similarly, separating the component from the RPC mechanism allowed for each application to use the most appropriate RPC mechanism: XML-RPC for Perl and RMI for Java. These techniques, although new and innovative at the time, were by no means unique to this project. In fact, because they were a natural evolution from previous technologies, these techniques were pioneered by many different developers and researchers, forming the basis for new standards like SOAP as well as Microsoft's .NET and Sun's Enterprise JavaBeans.

NOTES ON FUTURE RESEARCH OPPORTUNITIES

As we move forward, new technologies will emerge that will enable an unprecedented level of integration across a broad range of systems and networks and, in turn, allow developers to create increasingly sophisticated distributed applications. The challenge for researchers is to identify and explore new areas that show potential for the development of next-generation distributed component technologies. This section describes several potential research areas for new distributed component technology through either the evolution and integration of current technology or the application of principles from other research areas to the distributed component model.

Code Migration

Location transparency and independence are very powerful abstractions. They allow developers to create applications that make use of distributed components without specifying at compile time the actual locations of the remote components. This flexibility is beneficial not only to the application developer, but also to the developer of the server. The server, for example, can use replicas of a component on another host for fault tolerance. The details of the fail-over to the replica component are hidden from the client and also, in turn, from the developer of the client application by both the server and the underlying distributed communication mechanism.

A natural extension of this model is to support components that can migrate from one host to another. This implies that all the code necessary to execute the component must be transferred to the new host(s). The Java virtual machine model, for example, supports this natively with the use of remote class loaders. Although there are very good reasons to support code migration in distributed systems (performance, local caching of components, fault tolerance), the current mechanisms used for code migration are extremely limited in their effectiveness and performance.

Aspect-Oriented Programming

The proliferation of so many distributed object and component technologies brings with it a wide range of RPC protocols. Each of these protocols may be optimized for different functionality. For example, Java's RMI and EJB technologies are optimized for ease of integration within the Java programming language, but are neither efficient nor easily accessed by non-Java programming languages. Mechanisms like SOAP and other XML-RPC mechanisms are optimized to provide ease of integration among the widest range of programming languages and run-time environments; however, because these mechanisms rely on XML, a great deal of overhead is introduced for each message because the contents of the message must be text strings with extra markup. This makes these protocols attractive to applications that benefit from portability and accessibility, as long as they do not require maximum performance. Conversely, the RPC protocols used by Grid computing applications are optimized for performance, but a great deal of work must be done in order to port the communication APIs to new programming languages and run-time platforms.

It should not be a surprise, therefore, to realize that it is highly unlikely that any one particular distributed component or object mechanism or RPC protocol could be optimized for performance, ease of use, or portability without sacrificing one or more of the other attributes. This seems to indicate that developers are not likely to succeed in finding or creating a new mechanism that can optimally provide all three attributes. However, as systems become more complex, the need for them to interact with remote resources increases. Given that distributed component systems use such a wide variety of communication mechanisms, it seems reasonable to expect that more and more systems will need to interact with systems that use one or more different distributed technologies. It should be clear that an apparent conflict emerges between two opposing trends: the need to provide unified interfaces for distributed component communications and the inability to provide a particular RPC protocol that is simultaneously efficient, easy to use, portable, and available on many platforms and in many programming languages.

This conflict indicates that future research might not be very effective at finding a low-level communication protocol that can provide such a high level of unification. Nonetheless, because we do have different low-level RPC protocols that are optimized for the different needs, it appears that researching the problem from the software engineering and architecture perspective can make more progress. That is, it seems promising to focus research on creating higher-level distributed APIs that can abstract the details of the distributed protocols instead of researching new RPC mechanisms that attempt to be good at everything but turn out not to be optimal at any one thing. Such an approach would allow distributed component applications to support multiple RPC protocols simultaneously for each distributed component, even if the different RPC mechanisms have conflicting APIs.

An area that offers some promise is aspect-oriented programming (Constantinides et al. 2000; Duclos et al. 2002; Elrad et al. 2001). A simple way of understanding aspects is by examining an example. Consider the need to provide a unified logging mechanism in a large, complex application. The logging functionality can be thought of as cutting across all aspects of a complex application. All the internal subsystems and components benefit from access to a unified logging API. However, the logging functionality itself does not inherently belong to any one component. In a similar manner, communications and, specifically, RPC communication can be thought of as an aspect that cuts across many components in an application.

Single Address-Space Systems

A somewhat more exotic avenue for research is the exploration of distributed component technologies within single address-space systems (Chase et al. 1992). The premise behind this model is that a system that natively supports 128 bits or greater for memory addresses has a large enough memory space to allow every program and object to be allocated a globally unique address. The operating system still manages security and protection so that programs do not access unauthorized memory locations, but programs and objects would coexist within the same virtual memory space instead of the current model of each program existing within its own address space.

The implication of this model for operating system design of distributed systems is that, on a global scale, every system can share the same virtual memory space. This means that an object can be accessed directly via its globally unique address. More specifically, an object's address can uniquely identify it within the entire distributed system since every client and server share the same address space. This is a very powerful abstraction as it allows clients of distributed components to access the component as if it were a local object, in the traditional sense, since the client needs only the address of the object.

This abstraction, however, introduces new problems that must be overcome. For example, if each host in the distributed system shares the same view of the virtual memory space, a great deal of work must be done by the operating system to maintain accurate mappings that translate virtual memory locations to actual physical locations of the objects. Therefore, the management infrastructure for component location, name-binding, load-balancing, and fail-over must be tightly integrated with the operating system.

A more interesting issue arises when we consider that single address-space systems may not impose any requirements on the different hosts that make up the distributed system. More specifically, the system may imply that all hosts share the same virtual address-space, but force no requirements on the compatibility of the underlying hardware. This introduces some rather difficult problems when dealing with code migration for distributed components. It appears that such a model might benefit from either the virtual machine approach taken by Java or the byte code Just-In-Time compilation mechanisms used by Microsoft's .NET framework.

In addition to the inherent low-level mechanisms needed for communications, this model introduces certain issues and implications for the programming model that must be addressed. For example, distributed objects can themselves be used as arguments and return values for methods. Essentially, the use of a global address for each object allows distributed objects to behave within the context of a single address-space distributed system like traditional objects behave within traditional virtual memory systems. That is, by passing the address of the component, either explicitly (e.g., C++ pointers) or implicitly (Java), references to the object can be passed as arguments and return values of methods.

CONCLUSION

Components provide a powerful development paradigm for creating complex applications. The power of components is magnified when building applications that must integrate with many heterogeneous systems. Often such applications are required to communicate with remote components through some RPC mechanism. As these applications grow, they must communicate with an increasingly diverse set of components and resources through an equally diverse set of RPC mechanisms. The success of these applications is determined by how well they can adapt to the demands of communicating with many diverse resources. An application with a framework and software architecture designed from the outset to support multiple RPC mechanisms for distributed component communication will provide the needed flexibility and robustness. As we have seen, however, many issues must be considered when addressing the problem of distributed component communication. In the development of a system that supports multiple RPC mechanisms, the relationship between these issues must be carefully considered in order to create a truly flexible, robust, and functional distributed component system. Indeed, the critical issues for distributed component systems must be addressed at all levels of development. Software architects must make decisions about not only the overall system architecture, but also the distributed component technology that will be employed, the overall software architecture and object model, as well as the programming semantics used for distributed communications. Ultimately, applying current technologies to solve problems is what highlights the shortcomings of these technologies and, in turn, provides direction and motivation for new developments.

REFERENCES

Chase, J.S., M. Baker-Harvey, H.M. Levy, and E.D. Lazowska. 1992. Opal: A single address space system for 64-bit architectures. *Operating Systems Review* 26, no. 2: 9.

Constantinides, C.A., A. Bader, T.H. Elrad, P. Netinant, and M.E. Fayad. 2000. Designing an aspect-oriented framework in an object-oriented environment. *ACM Computing Surveys* 32, 1 (March) Electronic Symposium on Object-Oriented Frameworks.

Duclos, F., J. Estublier, and P. Morat. 2002. Describing and using non functional aspects in component-based applications. In *Proceedings of the 1st International Conference on Aspect-Oriented Software Development,* 65–75. New York: ACM Press.

Duncan, N.B. 1995. Capturing flexibility of information technology infrastructure: A study of resource characteristics and their measure. *Journal of Management Information Systems* 12, no. 2: 37–57.

Elrad, T., R.E. Filman, and A. Bader. 2001. Aspect-oriented programming: Introduction. *Communications of the ACM* 44, no. 10: 29–32.

Gamma, E., R. Helm, R. Johnson, and J. Vlissides. 1995. *Design Patterns: Elements of Reusable Object-Oriented Software.* Boston, MA: Addison-Wesley.

Maassen, J., R. Van Nieuwpoort, R. Veldema, H. Bal, T. Kielmann, C. Jacobs, and R. Hofman. 2001. Efficient Java RMI for parallel programming. *ACM Transactions on Programming Languages and Systems (TOPLAS)* 23, no. 6: 747–775.

CHAPTER 6

PATTERNS, PATTERN LANGUAGES, AND SOFTWARE ARCHITECTURE FOR CBDi

THE LESSONS OF THE ADAPTOR EXPERIMENT

ALAN O'CALLAGHAN

Abstract: *Component-based development and integration has become a practical proposition in the last few years with the emergence of industrial standards and component execution environments on the one hand, and the beginnings of a genuine marketplace for software components, considered as units of deployment and replacement, on the other. However, so far these advances appear to be quantitative rather than qualitative in their impact on the so-called software crisis— the gap between expectation and actuality in software-intensive systems. No new industrial revolution has as yet materialized. Software development remains a highly labor-intensive process, with quality and productivity depending on the skill and experience of development staff.*

We argue that the recent major advances in the technology of components, though undeniably gains, could never deliver an analogue to manufacturing's industrial revolution because software development is a creative, essentially intellectual and human process. What is required is the emergence of a set of software engineering disciplines based on a design culture specific to software development: this is what we regard as software architecture. Pattern languages for software development are presented as one potential way for delivering such cultures of design. The argument is presented by tracing the history of the development of the ADAPTOR pattern language: a language for the migration of large-scale systems to object technology and component-based development.

Keywords: *ADAPTOR, Patterns, Pattern Languages, Architecture, Component-Based Development and Integration*

INTRODUCTION

Component-based development and integration (CBDi) can be considered to have been the holy grail for software engineering for the last thirty-five years. Indeed, it was at the famous 1968 Garmisch conference (Naur and Randell 1968) (where the term *software engineering* was coined) that a solution to the software crisis was proposed that was an analogue to industrial manufacture: the making of products by assembling prebuilt parts, most productively in an automated, assembly-line production process.

CBDi has become a practical option only just recently. Component execution environments (CEEs) such as .NET, the Java 2 platform Enterprise Edition specification (J2EE), and Common Object Request Broker Architecture (CORBA) components make it possible today to construct systems that are, to some degree at least, composed of prebuilt independent units of deployment and replacement usually together with some hand-crafted code.

CBDi has both capitalized upon important gains in our collective understanding of how to structure large-scale and distributed systems and reinforced their significance. Although Szyperski (1997), for example, is careful, quite correctly, to distinguish between components and objects, there is no doubt that the best CBDi practice is based on object-oriented principles. Amongst the most important we would include:

- *encapsulation*: the explicit definition of access protocols
- *information hiding*: the hiding of design decisions that the client need not know
- *polymorphism*: the separation of abstract behavioral interfaces from their algorithmic implementations

These principles have been at the heart of object-oriented theory (if not always its practice) for three and a half decades, and they can be shown to have strongly influenced current thinking on component-based construction, particularly in the modeling of component systems (Cheesman and Daniels 2000). At the same time, the particular demands of CBDi have required practitioners to go beyond mere object-oriented practice and deal explicitly with notions of software architecture, for example, in order to deal with the very practical difficulties of putting together systems whose discrete parts have been made separately in time and space.

Advances in our ability to construct software components have not necessarily translated into the anticipated benefits at project level, however. The Standish Group's CHAOS report showed that between 1994 and 1998 only 26 percent of projects were delivered successfully on time and within budget (Standish Group 1998). These headline figures obscure the fact that most of these all too few successful projects were small ones. The success rate reported was 55 percent for projects with development teams of about six people, a time span of six months, and a budget of less than $750,000. Projects double that size had a success rate of only 33 percent. Projects above that size scored progressively less than average in the survey. Projects staffed by 250 or more people, with budgets between $6 million and $10 million and a target length of two years or more, were recorded as successful in only 8 percent of their efforts. The disturbing thing here is that it is precisely these kinds of enterprise-scale systems at which CBDi is targeted. The news is not all gloom; the average cost of projects to large companies has fallen by more than a half in the period covered, according to the same report. This suggests that there have been strong improvements in productivity, to which it is reasonable to believe that software components have contributed, but much weaker gains in quality. In the sections below, we examine the apparent contradiction between the rise of software reuse through CBDi and the apparent intractability of the software crisis.

The chapter is organized in the following way:

- The *Introduction* presents the contemporary background, including the state of software development today.
- *How Software Patterns Address the Process Issue* explains how the concept of pattern languages as presented by Christopher Alexander differs from the popular (mis)conception of software patterns and describes how pattern languages represent process as well as describe structures.
- *Patterns and Software Architecture: The Janus Project* explains how the initial experiences with ADAPTOR led to the Janus project and a reevaluation of the meaning of software architecture.
- *Janus and Pattern-Driven Architecture* describes future planned work in the Janus project.

- *Conclusion: Pattern Languages and CBDi* completes the circle by showing how, despite the evolution of the original ideas behind ADAPTOR, the promise of truly generative software pattern languages could act as a complement to, rather than any replacement of, the gains to date of CBDi.

HOW SOFTWARE PATTERNS ADDRESS THE PROCESS ISSUE

The progress that has been made in our ability to produce usable software components has not been matched by advances in our understanding of the *process* of building fit-for-purpose software-intensive solutions. While important steps forward have been made in the area of product-line processes (where generic components are targeted at a specific family of software products), there has been no generalized advance in understanding how complex software products are created, either with or without components.

Blum (1996) and Jackson (1994, 1995, 2001) among others have long argued that the collective computer science and software engineering disciplines have been too "solution-centred," resulting in an industry that has gained a reputation for finding "solutions" to the wrong problem. In this perspective, the technical gains of CBDi have accelerated our ability to create new such solutions, but they are still, by and large, imperfectly matched to the needs they are trying to serve. One promising advance in redressing the balance has been the emergence within the object-oriented community (and latterly the component-based development community also) of software patterns (e.g., Alur et al. 2003; Berry et al. 2002; J2EE Patterns Repository 2005; and Völter et. al. 2002).

Simply stated, a pattern describes a recurring, general design problem and an approach to solving the problem (a solution) in a particular context (O'Callaghan 1999). Note therefore that a pattern is a problem-solution-context triple. Patterns originated in the built environment with the works of the radical architect Christopher Alexander, and after a gestation period of about five years following their introduction to the object-oriented community (Cunningham and Beck 1997) were popularized by the book Design Patterns (Gamma et al. 1995). Since then, design patterns, in particular, have become an integral part of object-oriented practice, powerfully influencing, for example, the design of the Java 2 platform libraries. A key difference to date, however, has been that software patterns have been presented either as stand-alone entities or loosely grouped together in pattern catalogs. Alexander, on the other hand, did not conceive of individual patterns that existed outside of a pattern language (Alexander et al. 1977; Alexander 1979) in which each pattern was interdependent with the others in the language.

The ADAPTOR Pattern Language

An effort to construct a pattern language for software construction has been under way for some time at the Software Technology Research Laboratory at De Montfort University in Leicester, U.K. The acronym for this language is ADAPTOR (Architecture-Driven and Patterns-based Techniques for Object Reengineering). It is useful to examine the history of ADAPTOR in order to trace the clearly different stages of the evolution of our understanding of pattern languages. As the name suggests, ADAPTOR arose out of efforts to reengineer legacy systems for object-oriented and/or component-based development that have been reported elsewhere (O'Callaghan 2000, 2001, 2002). The first group of ADAPTOR patterns were mined from a series of five different migration projects in different domains within the telecommunication sector, beginning in 1993. Originally, the lessons of these projects were not captured as patterns, but this became a conscious aim from 1995 when, at first, individual design patterns were collected in a catalog. Very quickly it became clear that other kinds of patterns, notably organizational patterns (Coplien 1995), were needed to deal with some of the challenges that routinely emerge when efforts are being made to transform an existing, brittle structure into one that is more flexible to change. At the same time, interconnections between individual patterns suggested that there was a possibility of developing less a catalog of individual, stand-alone patterns and more of a pattern language whose patterns, when applied in context in an appropriate sequence, could generate solutions. The ADAPTOR project became a conscious one from 1995 onward though, as just stated, some of the patterns were mined as early as 1993. Subsequent experiences of projects in the defense industry, the oil exploration industry, and the retail buying industry permitted the mining of yet more patterns for the language (O'Callaghan 2002).

We should note here that in the early evolution of ADAPTOR, some key issues had to be confronted. Our first efforts were completely characterized by comments made by Alexander in his keynote speech to the 1996 Object-Oriented Programming, Systems, Languages, and Applications (OOPSLA) conference. He warned the software development community that although it was using patterns as a "nice and useful format" that allows the documentation of "good ideas about software design in a way that can be discussed, shared, modified, and so forth," it was in danger of missing the point (Alexander 1996).

Forms of Patterns

The particular form adopted to present the ADAPTOR patterns in the public domain (some of the patterns are held in different template form in-house by the companies that hosted the original project from which they were mined) was the Coplien form (Coplien 1995). The relevant sections of this template are:

- context
- forces
- solution
- resulting context
- rationale

The attractiveness of this form is that the context and resulting context sections hint at sequential links in the language, giving a vision of its systemic properties to its users even before they start applying them. The resulting context of applying one pattern to a system creates, potentially, the actual context for the next pattern in the sequence. Coplien developed his form to present his ideas for a generative-development process pattern language, of course, and ADAPTOR contains these kinds of patterns as well as design patterns and other kinds of patterns, such as analysis patterns. In recognition of this, another section, classification, was added to the template. In writing the patterns, the problem section (which is always posed in the form of a question) and the first sentence of the solution section are highlighted to provide thumbnails for short descriptions of the patterns for searchability. A number of key patterns from ADAPTOR have been published in this format.

On reflection, it was clear that at that stage of ADAPTOR's evolution we had discovered a useful form for describing design rules of thumb that were applicable in a number of different contexts to solving a small number of problems that typically recurred in our area of expertise: the reengineering of legacy systems for object-oriented and component-based development. It is also clear in retrospect that many of our patterns, in common with almost everything that was being produced by the patterns movement at the time, were abstract descriptions of potential components.

Patterns Are Not Components; They Are Pieces of Process

Our view at this point corresponded to a popular, but essentially incorrect view, often expressed in today's literature, that a pattern is a problem-solution pair. If this were true and context could be ignored, design patterns could be regarded as being generic—essentially as reusable but abstract (in the sense of being implementation-free) components. Since most design pattern descriptions use Unified Modeling Language (UML) class diagrams to describe the static relationships between roles being played in the solution, it is easy to see how the idea that a pattern is just a common layout of classes has taken root.

One vehicle for popularizing patterns has been the unified process (UP) for software development—an evolving process framework for object-oriented and component-based development which, like the UML, is strongly associated with Rational Inc. (Jacobson et al. 2000). Many practitioners have been introduced to design patterns via the UP, but unfortunately, therefore, to the "two-part rule" (problem, solution) version.

Patterns are included as part of the UP framework but are defined there as "template collaborations" (Jacobson et al. 2000). UP uses the UML as its design notation, and in the UML a template means any parameterized element. Thus, in fact, a pattern in the UP is essentially what Grady Booch called a "mechanism": a reusable structure usually comprising a number of tightly coupled object classes, which collaborate to provide a higher-level functionality to satisfy some higher requirement of a problem (Booch 1990). Clearly, the notion of a mechanism that is reusable and that can be parameterized to fit into a specific application is close to that of a software component. It is extremely valuable and useful to specify such common mechanisms or template collaborations, especially if what they describe are common business components, and to use them as blueprints for implemented software components.

Components—and therefore also template collaborations—are best designed to provide some essential, unchanging functionality with context dependencies factored out into its various "plugs" and "sockets" (or used and offered interfaces), provided these can be kept to a reasonable minimum (Szyperski 1997). But patterns are by, contrast, context-specific, and the context in question is not merely local plug-points and the technical platform but, as we will see below, the entire system under construction. The distinction is not merely an academic one—it is critical to this discussion. Although Gamma and colleagues have written that "point of view affects one's interpretation of what is and what isn't a pattern" and that "one person's pattern can be another person's building block" (Gamma et al. 1995) the "template collaboration" viewpoint is undeniably a reductionist one.

Once we realized that many of our "patterns" were merely using the form as a convenience to describe generic components, we removed them from the ADAPTOR catalog, often rewriting them as component specifications for the appropriate libraries and repositories. One exception to this was a pattern called Get the Model from the People, which prescribed the use of interviewing techniques and so on, with maintainers of legacy systems as the main way in which to reverse-engineer information about them (as opposed to relying on specialist documentation tools, etc.). Interestingly, it was this pattern, which describes a piece of process rather than a particular technical substructure (and therefore looked less like a design pattern than anything else we produced), above any other that contributed visibility to the ADAPTOR project through the attention it attracted. It has subsequently been incorporated into other pattern catalog (see, for example, Demeyer et al. 2003).

The significance of Get the Model from the People was that it opened our eyes to the real nature of patterns. They describe not only a structure (as the general solution to a recurring problem), but also the key elements of the process by which that structure can be constructed. Of course, context is still important, because the particular way in which the process-steps of a particular pattern are applied is always determined by the current state of the system under construction. In the context of a language of patterns, the application of one pattern followed by another in a sequence has the potential of describing a complete, integrated, and yet perfectly individual solution to the entire set of design problems faced in the design and implementation of an arbitrarily complex product.

From the beginning, ADAPTOR's approach to legacy system migration was radically different from "traditional" approaches based on the application of formal methods to source code. Legacy systems are, by definition, living systems, and we found it no more appropriate to use methods akin to archaeology than we would if they were suggested for the diagnosis of systems of ill-health in living organisms such as people. The traditional approaches are characterized by efforts to systematically replace and exclude the human dimension in favor of automation. In the context of legacy business systems, this means that traditional approaches ignore two crucial factors: first, both the explicit and tacit knowledge of the system under redevelopment that is held exclusively in the heads of those who have developed and maintained it, and, second, the actual needs of the various classes of user of the system-to-build (i.e., the migrated system).

Sequences in ADAPTOR

Something of the open and generative character of the process that ADAPTOR aspires to can be gained from looking at the typical application of patterns to the early phases of a legacy system migration project. Underpinning ADAPTOR is an object-oriented, model-driven approach. Problem space models—for example, business concept models (Cheesman and Daniels 2000)—are composed of object types and the relationships between them. These models capture the behavior of key abstractions of the context of the system as well as the system itself. The model of behavior makes use of the pattern Archetype, which, together with Get the Model from the People and Pay Attention to the Folklore, is typically among the first to be used. The use of such a pattern leads to the creation of a flyweight model that depicts a global vision of the system through application of the pattern Modello. At an early stage, strategic what-if scenarios are run against this model using Scenario-Buffered System. Shamrock is applied in order to decouple concept domain object types from the purely computational system resources needed to deliver them at run time. Evoking the three-leaf shape of Ireland's national emblem, the pattern requires that the development team conceptualize the system in three parts: packages that contain conceptual (problem domain) classes, interaction classes graphical-user interface (GUI, machine-machine protocols, etc.), and infrastructural classes (dealing with persistence, concurrency, etc.). The concept domain "leaf" can then be factored internally using Time-Ordered Coupling to keep types with similar change rates (discovered through the scenario-buffering) together. Coplien's Conway's Law (Coplien 1995) can now be utilized to design a development organization that it aligns with the evolving structure of the system. Another Coplien pattern, Code Ownership (Coplien 1995), makes sure that every package has someone assigned to it with responsibility for it. An ADAPTOR pattern called Trackable Component ensures that these "code owners" are responsible for publishing the interfaces of their packages that others need to develop so that they can evolve in a controlled

Figure 6.1   **A Typical Opening Sequence of ADAPTOR Patterns**

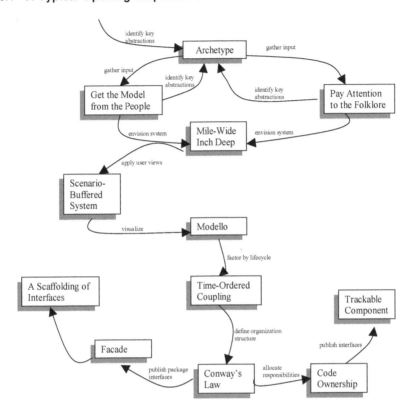

way. The Gamma pattern, Façade (Gamma et al. 1995), is deployed to enable *A Scaffolding of Interfaces* for the detailed structure of the system. It is at this point that decisions can be made as to which pieces of functionality require new code and which can make use of legacy code. The scaffolding ensures that these decisions, and their implementation consequences, can be dealt with at a rate completely under the control and at the discretion of the development team without fear of runaway effects.

This list of twelve patterns just described (depicted graphically in Figure 6.1) is a typical sequence of ADAPTOR patterns that might be used to start off a migration project. As a result of their application, a global vision of the system, its gross topology, the outline of the organization needed to develop and maintain it, and even a high-level work order is established. Other sequences exist to inform lower levels of the system architecture too. The ambition is for ADAPTOR—and similar generative languages—to have sufficient coverage and depth in its pattern vocabulary to completely generate whole systems by the use of such sequences. ADAPTOR is not yet at such a stage of development, however, and it is clear that many more patterns will need to be discovered and published before such a claim could be made for it.

PATTERNS AND SOFTWARE ARCHITECTURE: THE JANUS PROJECT

The realization that there existed a possibility to explore a pattern language for migration required more than just adding new patterns to the catalog and rearranging existing links. The original patterns themselves had to be recrafted. A general effect was that existing patterns became much smaller and apparently simpler (to the extent that some, when viewed in isolation, almost seemed *simplistic*) because some of the ground they covered was now addressed by newer patterns that were linked to them. The language, even in its current, immature form, is sophisticated, even complex, but that complexity is distributed through the language as a whole and is no longer apparent by viewing the individual patterns in isolation.

ADAPTOR was announced in 1998 as a "candidate, open, generative pattern language" (O'Callaghan 2000). It remains, even now, a candidate language for two reasons. First, despite the overwhelming success of the projects from which it is drawn, ADAPTOR is not comprehensive enough in its coverage or recursed to a sufficient level of detail to be, as yet, truly generative. Second, we have different levels of confidence in its individual patterns, with only those that have gone through various patterns workshops as being regarded as anything like fully mature. Patterns yet to prove themselves in this way are regarded as candidate patterns.

ADAPTOR is open in a number of other senses too. First, like any true language, both the language itself and the elements which compose it are evolvable. Many of the most mature patterns, such as Get the Model from the People, which was first presented in 1996 at the Patterns in Telecommunications (TelePLoP) workshop of OOPSLA, have gone through numbers of iterations of change. Second, since it aims to be inclusive, it unashamedly adds valuable patterns from other languages and even catalogs to itself. Third, following Alexander himself (Alexander 1979), its patterns are open abstractions themselves. Since no true pattern delivers a complete solution on its own, and every time it is applied it delivers different results (because of the different specific contexts to which it is applied), it resists the kind of formalization that closed abstractions such as rules can be subject to.

On reflection, it became clear over time that there was a deeper connection between ADAPTOR considered as a narrow reengineering approach and systems building more generally (i.e., including "Greenfield" development). Many of the individual patterns are not specific to legacy system migrations. Perhaps it is the case that the more constrained environment imposed by the special context of legacy systems highlighted some fundamental aspects of software development that are true for most, if not all, development projects, not just those of the legacy systems themselves. As we have seen from the sequence above, ADAPTOR relies on a model-driven approach. Typically, three kinds of models are built: problem space models (to understand the business need that the proposed software solution is designed to meet), solution space models (models of the software solution itself), and specification models designed to map between the two. These ideas, originated in the Syntropy method (Cook and Daniels 1994), have recently been validated to a degree in the OMG's Model Driven Architecture (MDA) (OMG 2003) and can also be found in the Cheesman-Daniels approach to CBDi (Cheesman and Daniels 2000). The approach is clearly, then, not specific to legacy systems.

These, and other similar, insights are what gave rise to the Janus project: the current vehicle for ADAPTOR research. Janus is an attempt to describe a generalized praxis that applies to both greenfield development and legacy system migration. The project was named after Janus, the Roman god who had two faces, one looking forward and one looking backward. The metaphor, besides reflecting the essential unity between reengineering (backward-looking) patterns and forward-engineering (forward-looking) patterns, also strongly reflects our intuition that software architecture itself looks simultaneously to the problem space and the solution space, thus providing the conceptual integrity that is needed to guide a software development project.

In fact, the entire ADAPTOR experience has enabled us to rethink not only our initial understanding of patterns, but also of the notion of software architecture. The current consensus, if there is one at all in this emerging discipline, is that software architecture is focused on structure: the static and dynamic relationship between software components and their interconnections (e.g., Bass et al. 1997). For most practitioners, even this focus on structure is narrowed further to the gross topology or top-level structure of a system. Our experience brings us toward a notion of software architecture that emphasizes two other characteristics: software architecture is also about process, and it is recursive down to its finest details. Incidentally, we believe that this understanding brings us closer to the Institute of Electrical and Electronics Engineers' (IEEE) definition of architecture than most will admit, as well as being consistent with the Royal Institute of British Architects (RIBA) use of the word *architecture.*

RIBA describes architecture as "design imagination" that requires the application of a knowledge base that includes technical and cultural ideas to a situation of need. It is also problem-centered in that the architect is chiefly the client's agent, not the builder's, and, finally, it requires knowledge of the building process and procurement (Duffy and Hutton 1998). From this perspective, an "architecture" is not a deliverable separate from the construction of the product itself and certainly not a mere blueprint as many would have it, but rather is a body of knowledge that is both systemic (it addresses the whole as more than the sum of its parts and never addresses parts separately from the context of the whole) and configurational (it deals with the complex interrelationships and cross-cutting features of the elements that make up the sequence). Software architecture, for us, is this kind of how-to-design knowledge.

Pattern languages, as understood through the lessons of ADAPTOR, are vehicles for the transmission of this kind of design knowledge. They capture and disseminate architectural knowledge by describing the kinds of structure established by previous practice as "good" solutions to the particular design problem under focus while leaving plenty of room for variation. But, because they also describe the general process-steps by which the structure is created, the designer, by applying them in sequences, can "grow" an overall, integrated solution piecemeal, addressing each design problem as it reveals itself in context.

Once the proposition that pattern languages are a vehicle for the transmission of (design) cultural norms is accepted, other arguments flow logically. For example, Alexander argues that an effective design culture must be slow-moving to enable it to gracefully digest elements of change that would otherwise undermine it (Alexander 1964). This suggests that many of the patterns within a pattern language must themselves be robust to many kinds of change. One of the most remarkable ADAPTOR patterns is Time-Ordered Coupling. This pattern is based on the principles of "shearing layers" that can be found in the writings of Brand (1994) and Duffy (1990) in the built environment, but it is also evident in biological systems. It turns out to be fully applicable to software. In essence, it suggests that elements with similar life cycles and change rates should be designed together in a logically layered structure, designing the slow-changing layers first and allowing them to constrain the progressively faster-moving layers. Applied to software, it could be argued that both the traditional separation of data and process in structured design (on the grounds that process is more volatile than data), and the principles in object-oriented construction, follow this deep-rooted pattern (e.g., Martin 1996a, 1996b). This would suggest that Time-Ordered Coupling is likely to be a fundamental pattern that will not change much through the evolution of the pattern language and is fairly generally applicable in software development. We expect that it will prove to be one of the stable centers of our future pattern language.

On the other hand, there are patterns that are more domain-specific and others that are more volatile. A truly generative pattern language requires a comprehensive coverage of its domain. Intuitively, we believe that the shape of such a language for software will necessarily include stable, slow-changing patterns at its core and more volatile, changeable patterns at its periphery. It seems likely that Time-Ordered Coupling will apply to the structure of any future pattern languages as well as to the systems it helps construct.

JANUS AND PATTERN-DRIVEN ARCHITECTURE

As mentioned above, ADAPTOR is a work in progress that may take many years to complete. In the meantime, its evolution has thrown up a number of important research questions that urgently need to be addressed. The Janus project is currently poised to address two of these questions:

(1) Is a truly generative, comprehensive pattern language possible for software?
(2) How should patterns and pattern languages be categorized in order to be accessible within a particular domain?

We address each of these questions in turn below.

Bits and Pieces

The problem, from a scientific point of view, is that design is almost always open-ended. For any given specification, let alone any particular set of needs that generate the specification in the first place, there are always many (and in many cases—theoretically, at least—an infinite number of) solutions. It is impossible to estimate the number of patterns that a language of the domain-scope of ADAPTOR (i.e., legacy system migration) would need to contain before it has sufficient coverage to be able to be truly generative. A truly generative pattern language would be one from which many complete systems could be developed simply by using sequences of its patterns. The explosion of variables involved makes any laboratory-based scientific judgment of its generativity extremely difficult, if not impossible.

However, if a highly constrained domain can be identified and a pattern language constructed for it, then the chances of forming valid conclusions about the generativity of pattern languages becomes more reasonable. In conjunction with the Patterns Movement and colleagues in universities in Europe, we have just started an experiment, which will run for at least a year, around what we currently call the Bits and Pieces pattern language.

The domain that Bits and Pieces addresses is that of Lego Mindstorms™ Robots. These robots contain a "programmable brick" with only three sensor (input) ports and three output ports plus an LCD display, an infrared transmitter, and four control buttons. In addition, the robots have three internal sensors, a timer, a message holder, and an ability to hold user-defined variables. The RCX bricks are connected to motors to drive the robots. As well as their native code for the message holder, there exist environments for programming the robots in C, Visual Basic, and Java as well as other languages (Bagnall 2002). In addition, each kit contains more than 760 Lego parts that can be assembled in different configurations to provide the physical aspects of the robot.

For some years, the eXtreme Programming (XP) community has been using these robots to demonstrate key features of XP (which is regarded as a lightweight, or agile, design and construction process) at various software conferences. In the Mindstorms Challenge, teams of five people, using XP practices, work to create and race a robot around an oval track. The robot that completes the course in the fastest time wins the race for its team.

We have borrowed the Mindstorms Challenge and are in the process of mining and collecting both hardware (the Lego brick configurations) and software patterns that have been used. Workshops based on the Challenge have already been run at EuroPLoP 2003 (European PLoP, held in Irsee, Germany) and VikingPLoP 2003 (held in Norway) for this purpose. To date, some forty candidate patterns already exist. The intention is to amass the patterns, opening up the process to the not inconsiderable Mindstorms community via a dedicated Web site, and to subject them to critical review at pattern writers' workshops—the standard procedure of the Patterns Movement (Rising 1998). The Challenge will then be repeated, under laboratory conditions, but with one or more teams armed with the mature Bits and Pieces language so that their effectiveness can be quantified. While the experiment is highly constrained and the domain of application of the patterns is artificial in that sense, nevertheless we believe that this experiment can be extremely valuable in providing insights as to the feasibility of generative systems' and software pattern languages.

Problem Frames and Pattern Languages

It seems clear that if the gains in productivity seen in the last few years are to be matched by advances in design quality, then domain-based knowledge bases, cultures of design, need to evolve. We have already argued that the lessons of ADAPTOR demonstrate a role that patterns and pattern languages can play in creating such cultures, but that argument raises the critical question of scope. While ADAPTOR contains some important general-purpose patterns such as Modello and Time-Ordered Coupling, it is clear that software architecture will be served not by a single pattern language, but by families of such languages. What, then, might the lines of demarcation be between them?

Michael Jackson proposes an approach he calls Problem Frames as a starting point for turning software development into a (set of) genuine engineering discipline(s) by identifying the key features of the different kinds of virtual machine that software developers typically build (Jackson 2001). Problem Frames are classifications of problems. Jackson presents an initial list of five such problem categories.

- *Required behavior:* The problem is to build a machine that will impose control on some part of the physical world to satisfy specified conditions.
- *Commanded behavior:* The problem is to build a machine that will accept commands from an operator, which will lead it to impose control over some part of the physical world in accordance with those commands.
- *Information display:* The problem is to build a machine that will continually obtain information about the behavior and states of some part of the physical world and present it in some required form.
- *Simple workpieces:* The problem is to build a machine that can be a tool for a user to create, edit, and otherwise manipulate graphics, text, or other computer-processable entities.
- *Transformation:* The problem is to build a machine that will produce output files in some form from computer-readable input files.

Jackson argues that very many, if not most, software development projects reflect a combination of these categories. More important he suggests that there are sufficiently different knowledge requirements and skill sets between these categories for them to form the basis of a new separation of concerns in software development that would allow the growth of real, but separate, engineering disciplines based upon them and, of course, any new Problem Frames that might be added to the list later. While this approach needs further research, it has the merit of stressing the importance of recognizing and taking full account of *context* in producing successful, quality-assured software.

In explaining his idea of Problem Frames as a basis for a new division of labor in software engineering, Jackson explains that they stand rather close in conception to the original idea of patterns as expounded by the radical architect of the built environment, Christopher Alexander. These ideas differ from design patterns as presented in the seminal work of Gamma, Helm, Johnson, and Vlissides (1995), he explains, in that those are rather solution-oriented while Problem Frames focus, as we have seen, on commonalities in the *problem* to be solved. We have already seen, in the second and third sections of this chapter, how the lessons of ADAPTOR have led to an evolution of the ideas contained in Gamma et al. (1995) to one much closer to Alexander's. But Jackson's work adds something new again: the suggestion of classifying patterns by the kinds of virtual machine they solve, in effect by the Problem Frames they serve. From this perspective, ADAPTOR could be refined to focus on Transformation, Simple Workpiece, and Information Display frames, while Bits and Pieces clearly addresses the Required Behavior frame. It may be that, taken together, Problem Frames and pattern languages offer one approach to the building of the domain-focused knowledge base for software engineering that is being advocated. This is another area that the Janus project hopes to address in the immediate future.

CONCLUSION: PATTERN LANGUAGES AND CBDi

If patterns are not abstract generic components, and pattern languages not merely catalogs of the same, where does this leave patterns in relation to CBDi? After all, the ADAPTOR experiment started as an approach to solving issues exactly in the field of legacy system migration to object-oriented and component-based development. Our argument has been that, to date, CBDi has probably contributed to the lowering of the costs of large, distributed systems through the gains in productivity it has generated but has not solved the underlying issues of the software crisis. In particular, the anticipated gains in design quality have not been achieved. Does this mean CBDi should be discarded? Our answer to this question is no, not at all. In speeding up the development process, CBDi has, perhaps more sharply than ever, revealed some gaps in our understanding of software architecture. The task is to fill those gaps and to complement the gains of CBDi with advances that strike more directly at the quality issue.

Garlan et al. (1995), identify architectural mismatch as the single biggest obstacle historically to the development of a component-based paradigm. It occurs when hidden assumptions about a component's expected execution environment conflict with different assumptions made by other units of deployment in the system in which it has been incorporated. Ironically, this phenomenon is actually exacerbated by the use of the hard-won modeling and programming principles of object orientation listed in the first section of this chapter, since to reveal, programmatically at least, such information would violate the principles of encapsulation and information-hiding described above.

Practices such as the special design-by-contract rules articulated by Cheesman and Daniels (2000) have ameliorated the impact of architectural mismatch. Even more important has been the emergence of the CEEs mentioned in the opening section. Major infrastructural concerns are abstracted away into the CEE standards, while many services come bundled with the middleware products that support them. Szyperski has shown in his seminal work *Component Software* (1997) that the attempt to make any given component maximally generic requires isolating its essential, common behavior and allocating its context dependencies into separate, configurable elements.

This is also one conceivable approach to dealing with architectural mismatch, incidentally, by providing as many interfaces for the component to as many different potential architectures (contexts) known to exist for it. However, as Szyperski shows, maximizing genericity (or potential reusability) along these lines actually results in a lowering of actual use since the number of potential configurations that an application developer or component assembler has to learn to use quickly becomes too unwieldy.

The emergence of a *small* number of standard environments, such as J2EE, the CORBA Component Model, and Microsoft technologies such as the Distributed Component Object Model (DCOM) and its successor, .NET, effectively reduces the number of context dependencies the component developer has to worry about. However, the problem has not been completely solved. What is required is making explicit the "why?" decisions of software design (i.e., "*Why* was this particular design solution chosen rather than alternatives?"), including at component and infrastructure level. This requires exactly the kind of holistic knowledge base, the culture of design, that pattern languages can promote. From this perspective, software components are the analogue to the materials that builders construct with and that architects of the built environment conceptualize when they design. Armed with pattern languages, together with the existing and future gains of CBDi, it may be possible to train software architects worthy of the name, able to design large, distributed, enterprise-wide systems that meet their full expectations and genuinely solve the business problems that spawned them in the first place.

REFERENCES

Alexander C. 1964. *Notes on the Synthesis of Form.* London: Harvard University Press.
———. 1979. *The Timeless Way of Building.* New York: Oxford University Press.
———. 1996. Keynote address. In *Proceedings of the Object Oriented Programming, Systems, Languages and Applications Conference.* New York: ACM Press.
Alexander, C., S. Ishikawa, M. Silverstein, M. Jacobson, M., I. Fiksdahl-King, and S. Angel. 1977. *A Pattern Language.* New York: Oxford University Press.
Alur, D., J. Crupi, and D. Malks. 2003. *Core J2EE Patterns: Best Practices and Design Strategies.* Upper Saddle River, NJ: Sun Microsystems Press.
Atkinson, C., J. Bayer, C. Bunse, E. Kamsties, O. Laitenberger, R. Laqua, D. Muthig, B. Peach, J. Wust, and J. Zettel. 2001. *Component-Based Product Line Engineering with UML.* Reading, MA: Addison-Wesley.
Bagnall, B. 2002. *Core Lego Mindstorms Programming: Unleash the Power of the Java Platform.* Upper Saddle River, NJ: Sun Microsystems Press.
Bass, L., P. Clements, and R. Kazman. 1997. *Software Architecture in Practice.* Reading, MA: Addison-Wesley.
Berry, C.A., J. Carnell, M.B. Juric, M.M. Kunnumpurath, N. Nashi, and S. Romanosky. 2002. *J2EE Design Patterns Applied: Real World Development with Pattern Frameworks.* Birmingham, UK: Wrox Press.
Blum, B.I. 1996. *Beyond Programming: To a New Era of Design.* New York: Oxford University Press.
Booch, G. 1990. *Object-Oriented Analysis and Design.* 2nd ed. Redwood, CA: Benjamin-Cummings.
Bosch, J. 2000. *Design and Use of Software Architectures: Adopting and Evolving a Product-Line Approach.* Reading, MA: Addison-Wesley.
Brand, S. 1994. *How Buildings Learn: What Happens to Them After They're Built.* London: Viking.
Cheesman, J., and J. Daniels. 2000. *UML Components: A Simple Process for Specifying Component-Based Software.* Reading, MA: Addison-Wesley.
Cook, S., and J. Daniels. 1994. *Designing Object Systems.* Englewood Cliffs, NJ: Prentice Hall.
Coplien, J.O. 1995. A generative development-process pattern language. In *Pattern Languages of Program Design,* ed. J.O. Coplien and D.C. Schmidt. Reading, MA: Addison-Wesley.
Cunningham, W., and K. Beck. 1997. Constructing abstractions for object-oriented applications. *Technical Report CR-87–25.* CRS. Techtronix.
Demeyer, S., S. Ducasse, and O. Nierstrasz. 2003. *Object-Oriented Reengineering Patterns.* San Francisco: Morgan Kaufman.

Duffy, F. 1990. Measuring building performance. *Facilities* 8, no. 5 (May).

Duffy, F., and L. Hutton. 1998. *Architectural Knowledge: The Ideas of a Profession.* London: E and F.N. Spon.

Gamma, E., R. Helm, R. Johnson, and J. Vlissides. 1995. *Design Patterns: Elements of Reusable Object-Oriented Software.* Reading, MA: Addison-Wesley.

Garlan, D., R. Allen, and J. Ockerbloom. 1995. Architectural mismatch: Why reuse is so hard. *IEEE Software* 12, no. 6 (July): 17–26.

Jackson, M. 1994. Problems, methods and specialization. *IEEE Software* 11, no. 6 (June): 757–762

———. 1995. *Software Requirements and Specifications: A Lexicon of Practice, Principles and Prejudices.* Wokingham, UK: Addison-Wesley.

———. 2001. *Problem Frames.* Wokingham, UK: Addison-Wesley.

Jacobson I., G. Booch, and J. Rumbaugh. 2000. *The Unified Software Development Process.* Reading, MA: Addison-Wesley.

J2EE Patterns Repository. 2005. TheServerSide.com, www2.TheServerSide.com/patterns/.

Martin R.C. 1996a. The Liskov substitution principle. *C++ Report* 8, no. 3 (March): 14–23.

———. 1996b. The dependency inversion principle. *C++ Report* 8, no. 6: 61–66.

Naur, P., and B. Randell, eds. 1968. *Proceedings, NATO Conference on Software Engineering. Garmisch, Germany.* Brussels: NATO Science Committee.

O'Callaghan, A. 1999. So you think you know about patterns? *Application Developer Advisor* 2, no. 6 (July/August): 28–31.

———. 2000. Patterns for change: Sample patterns from the ADAPTOR pattern language. In *Proceedings of the 4th European Conference on Pattern Languages of Programs* (EuroPLoP 1999). Konstanz: UVK.

———. 2001. Patterns for an architectural praxis. In *Proceedings of the 5th European Conference on Pattern Languages of Programs* (EuroPLoP 2000). Irsee, Germany.

———. 2002. Three patterns from the ADAPTOR pattern language. *Proceedings of the 6th European Conference on Pattern Languages of Programs* (EuroPLoP 2001) Konstanz: UVK.

OMG. 2003. MDA Guide Version 1.0.1. June 1, www.omg.org/mda/.

Rising, L. 1998. Design patterns: Elements of reusable architectures. In *The Patterns Handbook,* ed. L. Rising. Cambridge, UK: Cambridge University Press.

Szyperski, C. 1997. *Component Software: Beyond Object-Oriented Programming.* New York: ACM Press.

Standish Group. 1998. CHAOS—a recipe for success. *CHAOS Report.*

Völter, M., A. Schmid, and E. Wolff. 2002. *Server Component Patterns: Component Infrastructures Illustrated with EJB.* Chichester, UK: Wiley.

CHAPTER 7

TECHNIQUES AND STRATEGIES FOR TESTING COMPONENT-BASED SOFTWARE AND PRODUCT LINES

RONNY KOLB AND DIRK MUTHIG

Abstract: *Component-based software development and software product lines are recent approaches to software development that are based on the systematic reuse of software components and other development artifacts. They promise to improve the productivity of the software development process and so to reduce both cost and time of developing and maintaining software systems. However, the move toward component-based software development and product lines also highlights the need for more effective methods and techniques for ensuring the quality of software components that are intended for reuse. In fact, a high level of quality is required in order to achieve the promised benefits, since poor quality parts not only lead to an end product with low quality but also propagate this low quality into all the products that use them. Therefore, quality assurance in general and testing as still the most prevalent approach for ensuring quality in practice become crucial in every reuse effort. To date, however, very few papers address the problems and challenges that arise in testing software components intended for the purpose of reuse as well as product lines and applications engineered under the heavy reuse of existing software artifacts.*

This chapter will provide—based on our experience in technology transfer projects with our industrial customers and on our work on PuLSE and KobrA—an overview of the difficulties and challenges that come up when testing in a reuse context. In particular, it investigates the implications of component-based software, generic components, and software product lines from the perspective of testing. The chapter will identify how the process of testing in a reuse context needs to be different from traditional software testing. Furthermore, it will present a number of potential techniques and strategies for efficiently and thoroughly testing component-based systems and product lines.

Keywords: *Testing, Test Planning, Testing Techniques, Testing Strategies, Component-Based Software, Product Lines*

INTRODUCTION

During the last decade, component-based software and software product lines have emerged as promising paradigms to conceptually improve the productivity of the software development process and thus to reduce both the cost and the time of developing and maintaining software systems. The potential benefits of these paradigms are primarily based on the assumption that a significant portion of a new software product can be built through the systematic reuse of existing artifacts or components. Although the move toward component-based software development and software product lines offers many promises for improved productivity, it also highlights the need for more effective methods and techniques for ensuring the quality of software artifacts that are intended for reuse. In fact, reusable artifacts must be of good quality, since poor quality parts not only lead to an end product with low quality but also propagate this low quality into all the products that use them.

As a high level of component quality is required, testing as still the most prevalent approach in industry today for detecting software defects and ensuring software quality becomes a crucial part of every reuse effort. Rather than focusing on optimized test approaches, however, most research has been focusing on the definition and realization of reusable artifacts, as well as on their instantiation and integration while constructing concrete applications to date. That is, only some work investigates and addresses the unique issues of testing components developed for reuse, product line infrastructures, and applications assembled from existing artifacts. Although some specific techniques have been proposed recently, there is neither an overall test process nor specific strategies for efficiently testing component-based software and product lines.

Consequently, in practice, the same test techniques and strategies proved in traditional (single-system) development projects are applied also in the context of component-based software and product lines. Traditional test techniques and strategies, however, do not sufficiently match the requirements on a test approach in the context of these paradigms. This is mainly due to the characteristic of these development paradigms of splitting the software life cycle into the two conceptual phases "development for reuse" and "development with reuse." That is, they do not systematically exploit the fact that the subject under test was tested, at least partially, in similar contexts before. Therefore, testing component-based software and product lines is done in an inefficient way in most cases.

This chapter addresses this problem by presenting test techniques and test strategies for the two development paradigms, component-based software and product lines. In addition, it describes a test planning framework that guides the systematic definition of an efficient test plan, which among others prescribes the usage of test techniques and the scope of testing, for a given reuse context. The chapter is structured as follows. The remainder of this first section gives a brief introduction to software testing and then discussed the position of testing in the software life cycle and the relations between the development and test processes. Furthermore, a general framework for test planning is presented. The issues and challenges to be faced in testing component-based software and product lines are discussed in the second and third section, respectively. Both sections point out why testing issues are more critical and complex in a reuse context than for single software systems. Also, these sections present potential test techniques and strategies for each of these two development paradigms. Implications for research and practice of the test planning framework and the proposed test strategies are discussed using an example that is derived from a real-world situation in the fourth section. The fifth section then draws some conclusions.

SOFTWARE TESTING FUNDAMENTALS

Although there are many published definitions of software testing, all of these definitions actually stress the same points and boil down to essentially the same thing: software testing is the process of executing a piece of software or system in a controlled manner and evaluating the results with the intent of uncovering defects and revealing problems. The Institute of Electrical and Electronics Engineers (IEEE) *Standard Glossary of Software Engineering Terminology* (IEEE Computer Society 1990) defines testing as "the process of operating a system or component under specified conditions, observing or recording the results, and making an evaluation of some aspect of the system or component."

Software testing determines whether a software component or system behaves as specified and basically compares what is with what should be. Although testing can be used to measure various different quality attributes such as security or performance, it is most widely used during construction for the detection of failures, that is, undesired effects and deviations from the expected results.

Today, organizations must deliver high-quality software systems on time and within budget to remain competitive in their marketplace. The motivation for testing software is to provide confidence in the quality of software. Although extensive testing helps to ensure software quality, testing is still a very labor-intensive and thus expensive activity within the software development process. In fact, many studies show that up to 50 percent of the cost of software development is spent on detecting and correcting defects rather than on developing software. Because exhaustive software testing is usually just not possible from practical and economical perspectives, testing always involves a trade-off between limited resources and schedules, and inherently unlimited test requirements. Thus, a common problem is to decide how much testing is sufficient and when to stop testing. In general, what is considered adequate testing will vary from one organization to another.

Traditionally, testing has been carried out after the implementation phase in virtually every software development process, since it requires executable code to be performed. Actually, however, testing activities are applied at various points during the software development process, not just at the point where executable code is finally available. Thus, the testing process is separate from, but intimately related to, the development process. The development process feeds the testing process with specifications and realizations. The testing process, on the other hand, feeds identified failures to the development process, so the developers can identify the defect causing the observed failure and modify the software under test to eliminate the suspected faults. Then, the revised development products are fed back to the test process.

Because testing is a very labor-intensive and thus expensive activity of the software development process (Beizer 1990), savings in the testing process have a significant impact on the overall performance of a development project. The ultimate goals are to reduce the time to test a software product, to reduce the number of test case executions needed to test the software thoroughly, and to increase the productivity of the testers. As a consequence, it is critical to carefully plan and execute tests and to clearly assign responsibilities for the various stages of testing in the project to personnel. Moreover, test planning should begin as early as possible, and test plans and procedures must be systematically and continuously refined as development proceeds. Both the cost of testing and the elapsed time necessary for its completion can be reduced through careful planning and systematic execution. Finally, experience shows that software testing is generally more effective when conducted by an independent party rather than the original developers.

Test Planning Framework

In this section, we present a general framework for test planning that consists of development paradigms, test techniques, and test strategies.

Test planning is the initial activity in the general software test process as shown in Figure 7.1. In addition to test planning, the test process covers activities that are performed according to the test plan, namely the design of test cases; their execution, including the collection of the produced test results; and the analysis and interpretation of the test results to create a test report.

The test planning activity produces a test plan, which is an evolving document that focuses on the managerial aspects of testing and that describes the objectives, scope, approach, and focus of

Figure 7.1 **General Software Test Process**

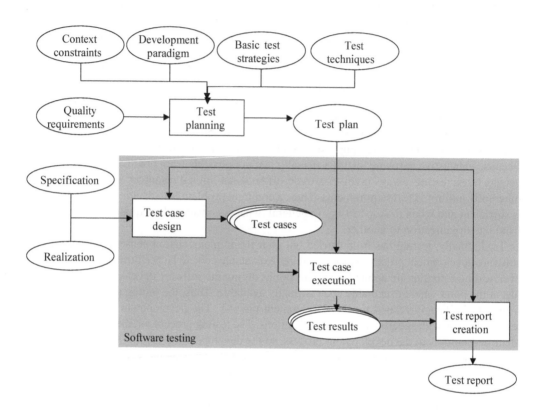

a software testing effort. The test plan states what the items to be tested are, at what level they will be tested, what sequence they are to be tested in, how each item will be tested, and what the test environment is. It also provides a summary of criteria for test case selection and completion of the test effort. The basic information that should be covered in a test plan is defined, for example, by the IEEE Standard for Software Test Documentation.

From a software engineer's point of view, the test plan defines a set of activities as the means to ensure a certain software quality, which is acceptable with respect to both quality requirements and context constraints (e.g., available resources or given time schedules). Most of the activities defined in the test plan must be coordinated with development activities. Therefore, the test plan is tailored to a particular development process or, at a more abstract level, to the underlying development paradigm. The role of the development paradigms for testing is discussed below. Typically, quality requirements, context constraints, and development paradigm are defined before and independent of the test planning activity. The planner then selects from a broad range of existing test techniques those best suited for the already defined context. Our classification of test techniques is introduced below. In general, there are many potentially valid test plans for a given context; the selection of the eventually implemented plan depends on the overall test strategy. We then present two basic strategies that may serve as starting points for the test planning activity, which then adapts the selected strategy.

Figure 7.2 **Relationship Between Development and Test Process**

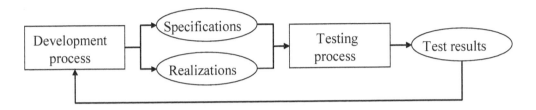

Development Paradigms

Software testing activities, as shown in Figure 7.2, are separate from but intimately related to the development process. The development process continuously triggers test activities by delivering development artifacts from various life-cycle stages. Testing consumes these artifacts and eventually returns identified failures in the form of test results. Based on the test results, developers identify the defects causing the observed failures, modify the software under test to eliminate the suspected faults, and trigger further test activities.

The detailed interaction between the two processes is determined by the development process and is in all details unique for any implemented development process. At a less detailed level, the interaction between the development process and test activities can be described with respect to the underlying development paradigm. Development paradigms, such as component-based software or product lines, define the software life cycle and development artifacts at a general, conceptual level. Hence, in order to define a good test plan, the development paradigm must be considered.

Reuse-oriented paradigms, for example, conceptually split the overall development process into two phases: development for reuse and development with reuse. Thus, test plans must address the development of not only a single system but a series of such development projects in order to be effective. The second and third sections discuss the impact of two reuse paradigms, component-based software and software product lines, on the definition of a test plan.

Test Techniques

To test software, a number of different techniques can be applied and numerous test techniques have been proposed (Beizer 1990). Fundamentally, there are two distinct types of test techniques that are differentiated according to the information they use for creating test cases. Techniques that make use only of the information provided by a specification of an artifact are called specification-based techniques. Techniques that rely on the realization, and thus primarily on the code, of a software artifact for creating test cases and performing tests are called realization-based techniques.

The concrete meaning of specification and realization can be discussed only in relation to the underlying development paradigm. For example, a component-based realization deals with collaborating components rather than with program paths as the realization of a monolithic piece of software.

Depending on the actual development paradigm and context, different techniques are required to test software artifacts thoroughly and efficiently. Further, as different types of faults tend to occur at different development stages, different techniques are needed to find them.

Test Strategies

In practice, specification-based and realization-based techniques are typically applied in combination rather than independently as there is no single ideal technique for testing a software artifact. We refer to the combination of different test techniques as a test strategy.

Generally, there are two extremes: optimistic and pessimistic strategies. On the one hand, optimistic strategies anticipate development artifacts of good quality and successful, effective test techniques. Pessimistic test strategies, on the other hand, tend to expect low-quality artifacts and are skeptical with respect to the effectiveness of techniques.

Typical factors in a test strategy are how much is tested, what is tested, when it is tested, and who tests it. Pessimistic and optimistic strategies for our two development paradigms, component-based software and software product lines, are discussed in the following sections.

Purely optimistic or pessimistic strategies represent extremes that are typically not implemented in practice. Moreover, depending on the development organization, one of the extreme strategies is selected as a starting point and then adapted to particular needs. Thus, realistic test strategies usually combine optimistic and pessimistic elements and are determined by considerations of cost, schedule, maturity levels of the involved organizations, and criticality of the application.

TESTING OF COMPONENT-BASED SOFTWARE

This section discusses testing for component-based software systems, whether built using in-house components or commercially available components from third-party vendors. In particular, it provides an overview of the major difficulties and challenges to be faced in testing reusable software components and component-based software systems and presents potential techniques and strategies for addressing these issues.

As systems are primarily built by assembling reusable components, the benefits of component-based software engineering are largely dependent on the quality of the components: the expected reductions in development time and effort will arise only if separately developed software components are of high quality and can be made to work effectively together with minimal effort in the given context. Therefore, testing, as the most prevalent approach in industry today for detecting software defects, becomes a crucial part of component-based software engineering. However, the nature of component-based development introduces a number of unique problems and challenges for testing, and reusable components exhibit certain characteristics that not only make them difficult to test but also render many traditional test techniques inadequate or inappropriate (Weyuker 1998; Ghosh and Mathur 1999). According to Szyperski (1998), probably the single most demanding aspect of component-based development is the testing of reusable components because all future usage of a software component cannot be known and thereby cannot be tested. As a result, component-based software engineering calls for new test techniques, strategies, processes, and tools in order to realize the promised benefits fully.

According to Harrold et al. (1999), the issues arising in the test of component-based software systems can be viewed from two different perspectives: the perspective of the provider of a component and the perspective of the user of a component. The component provider designs, builds, and tests the components that are adopted by the component users to construct systems according to the specific requirements of a particular customer or market segment. To be truly reusable, components must be designed to support a broad range of systems. The problem, however, is that the component provider cannot predict all future usages of the component, so it is thus impossible to test the component in all possible contexts and environments. Further, a reusable software component might provide a significant amount of functionality that will never be used in a particular software system, but may lead to interoperability and performance problems and unpredictable side effects in the system. As reusable components are typically tested in a few contexts only, it is not obvious that they function optimally in combination with others in a system, and so components often have to be tested again by the component users. From an economic point of view, therefore, another major problem in testing reusable components and component-based systems is that generally a lot of time and resources are wasted in repeated testing. Typically, components are tested separately by the component producer and then together in some particular manner by the component user, leading to frequent retesting of the component. In order to test individual components, test stubs (i.e., partial implementations to simulate the behavior of software components on which the tested component depends) and test drivers (that execute the component under test and pass data), have to be constructed. The construction of test drivers and stubs in an ad hoc fashion, however, becomes very costly and ineffective, especially for rapidly evolving components.

In component-based software development, systems are built by assembling a number of existing components, potentially from many different providers, according to the given requirements at hand. Therefore, component users have to focus their test effort on ensuring that the individual components work together properly. Testing at the system level is then very much the same as for traditional systems, and there should be little impact due to component-based development.

Each time a component changes or a new component is going to be used in an already tested system, regression testing on the constructed system has to be performed. Since regression testing is a very costly process, selective regression testing strategies, by which only a subset of test cases are selected and rerun, are often preferred to the strategy of rerunning all test cases. For component-based systems, however, the most critical decision due to the lack of relevant information in software components is to determine which test cases to rerun in order to minimize the test effort. Finding out the features and parts to be tested again can be costly and time-consuming.

Finally, complications of component-based software from the perspective of testing are generally represented by components, such as commercially acquired components from third-party vendors, whose source code is unavailable. For testing such components, component users can only apply techniques that do not require the source code and instead rely merely on the specification of a software component. Often, however, the specification of a component lacks relevant information, making it difficult to test the component for the required use effectively and thoroughly.

Test Techniques

In this section, we discuss specification-based and realization-based techniques for testing reusable software components and component-based software and describe coverage measures and the notion of built-in tests.

To test reusable components and component-based software systems, several techniques are commonly used in practice. In most cases, however, these techniques have originally been developed for procedural or object-oriented software and hence do not take the special issues of reusable components and component-based software into account. While some traditional test techniques are to some extent still applicable to component-based software, many others are no longer appropriate or adequate. This is because traditional test techniques assume that a component is tested in, and for, exactly the software system in which it is used. In the component-based development paradigm, however, the same component might be used in building several different software systems and therefore has to be tested independently of the concrete system and configuration. Unfortunately, only a very limited number of specific test techniques for system-atically testing individual software components intended for reuse (component testing) and sys-tems built using reusable software components (integration and system testing) currently exist. Some techniques and approaches addressing the issues in testing a component-based system are described in Atkinson and Gross (2002), Beydeda and Gruhn (2001), Bhor (2001), Harrold et al. (1999 and 2001), Hörnstein and Edler (2002), Wang et al. (1999), and Wu et al. (2001).

Testing in the context of component-based software primarily includes the two distinct activi-ties of testing the reusable software components that are used to build specific systems and testing the systems built using these components. For testing reusable software components and compo-nent-based systems, there is no single ideal technique, since different testing techniques are ap-propriate at different times. Further, depending on the expected quality of a component or component-based system and the availability of the code of components, different testing tech-niques need to be used. At the level of system tests, for example, at which the system is deemed as one entity and where primarily the required functionality of the system is validated, the avail-ability of code is not absolutely necessary and thus specification-based techniques can be applied. It is important to choose the right combination of testing techniques at the right time in order to test reusable components and component-based systems thoroughly and efficiently.

For testing reusable components, either specification-based or realization-based techniques can be applied. Whereas the former make use only of information provided by the specification of a component and thus do not require knowledge of design and implementation details or the applied programming language, the latter rely on the realization of a component. Although source code is primarily deemed as the realization of a software component, we also consider architec-ture descriptions, design documents, or component interaction diagrams as part of the realization of reusable software components. Specification-based techniques are language-independent and can be used if the source code of a component is not available (e.g., when components have been acquired from third-party vendors), but require the specification of a component to be complete and correct for effective and thorough testing. As no source code is required, test cases can be developed as soon as the specification of a software component has been finished and before implementation actually starts. Due to the independence from the actual implementation, test cases are still valid even if the implementation changes but may leave parts of a component untested. Realization-based techniques, on the other hand, can take advantage of knowledge of the source code and implementation details for defining effective test cases, but it might be diffi-cult, and too complex, to examine the code of large components. Further, test case design cannot start until code or design documents are available, and test cases might become redundant every time implementation changes.

To measure how completely a software component has been exercised by the tests that have been applied to it, coverage measures can be used. For specification-based techniques, coverage measures might be the percentage of requirements or use cases exercised or the ratio between the number of methods executed in a component and the number of methods provided by the soft-ware component. Examples of coverage measures for realization-based techniques might be method coverage, interface coverage, and interaction coverage.

Aiming at simplifying testing and to reduce test costs, particularly at the user side, built-in tests are a relatively new and promising approach to testing components (Wang et al. 1999; Gao et al. 2002). The basic idea is to build tests into software components. Built-in tests, which are gener-ally activated in test mode only, can range from simple assertions to complete test cases and are used to verify the behavior of a component in its environment, as well as the interactions between a software component and other components. The problem, however, is that the tests embedded

Table 7.1

Component-Based Test Strategies

Optimistic strategy	Pessimistic strategy
Component provider	
• Tests components in one configuration only	• Tests components in a large number of configurations
• Uses a single test technique	• Uses at least two different test techniques
• Developers perform testing	• Independent team performs testing
• Very limited set of test cases for built-in components	• Exhaustive set of tests for built-in components
Component user	
• No acceptance test for reused components	• Acceptance test for every reused component
• Integrates all components at once	• Integrates and tests components incrementally
• Selective regression testing	• Thorough regression testing
• Only very limited system test	• Extensive system test as for traditional software systems
• Developers perform testing	• Independent team performs testing
• Built-in tests are run only once, when components are integrated	• Built-in tests are executed once a component has been acquired, when it is integrated with others, whenever a new or changed component is added, and when the resulting system is deployed

within a component add a lot of overhead to the component and so affect component size and execution speed negatively. Therefore, it is generally not feasible to build complete test cases into a component. Instead, the goal is to find a good balance between test requirements and overhead. A recent approach to avoid these performance and size problems is to place the test cases outside the actual component (Atkinson and Gross 2002; Hörnstein and Edler 2002). The testable software component itself only provides the information that is needed to execute the tests that are implemented in an external component. The essential question regarding this test approach is how to generate the testable software components and the external tester components in a systematic and cost-effective way.

Test Strategies

As mentioned above, two extreme strategies exist for testing software. In the following, we describe the optimistic and pessimistic strategies for testing in the context of component-based software from the perspective of both the provider and the user of a software component. The two strategies are summarized in Table 7.1. Further, we briefly discuss the consequences of both strategies on quality and test effort.

Anticipating development artifacts of good quality as well as effective test techniques, the optimistic strategy for testing reusable components and component-based systems is entirely different from the pessimistic strategy. Whereas in the optimistic strategy, a reusable software component is tested only in one configuration using a single technique by the developers of that component, an independent test team is responsible for testing the software component in a large number of configurations using at least two different techniques in the pessimistic strategy. In order to obtain the best results, at least one specification-based technique and one realization-based technique has to be applied to the component under test.

Due to the execution of tests in multiple configurations, the usage of several techniques, and an independent test team, the pessimistic strategy is considered to yield higher component and product quality compared to the optimistic strategy, but at the cost of a much larger test effort for the component provider. From the perspective of a component user, however, test effort can be reduced because the software component has been extensively tested in numerous configurations and a large extent of the results of the previous tests can be assumed. Nevertheless, in the pessimistic strategy, a component user always anticipates the components used to build a system to be of low quality and is not sure if they are appropriate for the given requirements. Therefore, before assembling the system, the component user subjects every reused component to some acceptance test, resulting in an increase in both test effort and quality. Every time a component has been changed, this testing has to be performed again. In fact, in the pessimistic strategy, the component user subjects a changed component and the system making use of it to a thorough regression test each time the component has been changed. For the regression test, the original component test suite and additional test cases are used to achieve high coverage. Contrary to that, component users following the optimistic strategy do not perform a thorough regression test each time a software component has been changed. Instead, they run only a very limited subset of the test cases on the changed component. The limited set of test cases contains only test cases considered most critical for the component under test.

Testing on the component user side is done by the developers of the systems in the optimistic strategy and by an independent test team in the pessimistic strategy. Since the developers generally bring a bias concerning their own work, testing done by an independent team is considered to be more effective but is also more expensive.

When it comes to building the specific software system by assembling the individual components, the focus of testing shifts to the interactions that occur between already tested software components. Whereas in the optimistic strategy the component user integrates all components at once, components are integrated and tested incrementally in the pessimistic strategy. Although this incremental integration testing allows to figure out the cause of a failure more easily, it requires more effort than the approach suggested by the optimistic strategy.

Once the assembly of the system is finished, the complete system is subjected to a system test. Whereas in the optimistic strategy only a very limited system test is performed since the individual components, and so the resulting system, are anticipated to be of good quality due to prior testing, a thorough system test as in traditional development is performed in the pessimistic strategy. Although this might detect failures not detected by the component provider and component user before and thus might increase quality, it greatly increases the test effort.

To simplify testing, built-in tests can be used. In the optimistic strategy, only a very limited set of test cases is embedded in a component and these tests are only run once the component is integrated with others. Contrarily, the component providers in the pessimistic strategy build an exhaustive set of tests in every reusable component. The component users execute these tests once the component has been acquired, when it is integrated with others, whenever a new or changed component is added, and when the resulting system is deployed.

SOFTWARE PRODUCT LINES

In this section, testing of software product lines will be discussed. It is concerned with testing the generic software components included in the product line infrastructure as well as the products built using these reusable components. The section provides an overview of the most significant differences between testing product lines and testing single software systems and examines the effect of generic software components on testing. Assuming that testing contributes to a large extent to the success or failure of a product line effort and that there are some similarities to testing component-based software systems, we will also discuss how testing in a software product line can take advantage of reuse. Finally, the section discusses techniques and strategies for testing software product lines.

Software product lines are a rather new, highly promising approach to software system development. By facilitating reuse of previous development efforts, the product line approach enables organizations not only to reduce both development and maintenance costs but also to achieve impressive productivity and time-to-market gains. According to Clements and Northrop (2001, 1), a software product line is "a set of software-intensive systems sharing a common, managed set of features that satisfy the specific needs of a particular market segment or mission and that are developed from a common set of core assets in a prescribed way." Core assets are reusable artifacts, such as components, architectures, requirements specifications, or documents, which are generic enough to support the development of the different products in a product line.

While software product lines can significantly reduce both the development and maintenance effort of software systems, no significant reduction of the overall testing effort has been seen to date. Moreover, testing issues have become even more critical and complex for product lines since quality problems in an artifact can have a particularly high impact on the numerous products in the software product line depending on it. As fixing a fault revealed in a core asset component by the product developers would typically entail a much higher cost than fixing a similar fault detected earlier on by the core asset developers, the need to detect errors early in the development is even higher than for single systems, and therefore it pays to test the core asset components thoroughly. To conclude, the testing process contributes to a large extent to the success or failure of a product line approach, and the potential benefits of software product lines can be lost if the testing process does not take into account the issues specific to software product lines.

In general, testing of product lines encompasses testing the generic core asset components that are used across various product line members, as well as testing the product-specific components and the members of the product line that have been derived from the product line infrastructure. Although there are some similarities to testing single software systems and component-based software, testing product lines has significant differences, and product line organizations face unique challenges in testing. Nevertheless, not much has been written so far about the miscellaneous problems and challenges in testing product lines (Clements and Northrop 2001; McGregor 2001), and testing is still a process to be improved and adapted to support the product line approach.

In addition to the challenges posed by reusable components and component-based software development, software product lines present a number of significant test challenges. First, the genericity of the core asset software components makes testing all their functionality problematic as it is often impossible in practice to test all possible combinations that result from the large number of variation points and possible variants at each variation point. Consider, for example, a component with just ten variation points and three possible variants at each variation point. There are yet 59,049 variants that need to be tested. Second, due to the large number of products making use of the core asset software components and because of the interdependencies between product line components and product-specific components, regression testing becomes complex. The challenge is to test all products making use of a component every time the component efficiently and effectively has been changed.

Although testing product lines is very similar to testing component-based software, software

Table 7.2

Product Line Test Strategies

Optimistic strategy	Pessimistic strategy
Product line developer	
• Does not test the variants of a core asset component, but only the common aspects	• Tests every possible combination of variants of a core asset component
• Use a single test technique	• Uses at least two different test techniques
• Developers perform testing	• Independent test team performs testing
• No built-in tests	• Built-in tests and external tester component for every variation point
Product developer	
• No acceptance test for core asset components	• Acceptance test for every core asset component
• Tests only the required functionality of a core asset component	• Tests the complete functionality provided by a core asset component
• Integrates all components at once	• Integrates and tests components incrementally
• Selective regression testing	• Thorough regression testing
• Only very limited system test	• Extensive system test as for traditional software systems
• Developers perform testing	• Independent test team

product lines have some unique characteristics, such as an explicit product line architecture or the large amount of domain documentation, that ease testing. Further, it is generally possible for the product developers to access the source code of a core asset component when needed and to have access to the personnel and expertise used in the creation of the component. In summary, the issues in testing software product lines compared to single systems and component-based software are mainly caused by the fact that components are typically generic.

Test Techniques

In essence, the same techniques used for testing component-based software can be applied for testing product lines. Due to the genericity of software components, however, these test techniques alone are not sufficient to test product lines efficiently and adequately. Thus, test techniques that take into account the generic aspect of components and that can handle variability are required. A promising direction is the idea of generic test cases. Just as a generic software component can be instantiated for a particular product, so can the generic test cases for that component be instantiated and then used to efficiently test the instantiated component. Another approach for testing generic components is the notion of built-in tests. For the diverse variants of a generic software component, different external tester components are developed and then used together with the generic component for a concrete test.

Test Strategies

This section presents the optimistic and pessimistic strategies for testing product lines and thus for testing the generic core asset components as well as the products in a product line. Table 7.2 gives a summary of the optimistic and pessimistic strategies for testing product lines.

Just as the same techniques used for testing reusable components and component-based software are to a large extent applicable for software product lines, so can the test strategies for component-based software be applied to product lines. Rather than discriminating between component provider and component user, Table 7.2 makes a distinction between product line developers and product developers. The major difference compared to the strategies for component-based software is due to the genericity of the product line components.

IMPLICATIONS FOR RESEARCH AND PRACTICE

The test-planning framework introduced in this chapter clearly separates quality issues related to the different development paradigms, component-based software and product lines, respectively. Although the purpose of this framework is to enable organizations to understand the different aspects and sources of their quality problems, there are still several open issues in research and in practice to be solved.

In this section, these issues and their implications for research and practice are discussed. To illustrate the intended role of the framework in the future, a small visionary example is introduced first to set the context of the discussion.

Worked Example

This subsection introduces an example application of the described test-planning framework. The example is based on a real situation taken from a technology transfer project with an industrial customer and from our work on Product Line Software Engineering (PuLSE) (Bayer et al. 1999) and Komponentenbasierte Anwendungsentwicklung (German for component-based application development (KobrA) (Atkinson et al. 2001).

The context of the example is characterized, as discussed above, by organizational characteristics, the organization's underlying development paradigm, and the particular quality requirements for the software to be developed.

- *Organizational characteristics.* The organization has one "standard" application that it markets and that represents the typical software solution for customers operating in their application domain. Therefore, it is sold and initially installed at every customer's site. In most cases, however, the standard application does not fully satisfy the customer and thus it must be extended and customized.
- *Development paradigm.* The standard application is component-based whereby customer-specific variants are integrated into the components that resolve the variation dynamically at run time. The resolution evaluates various database flags and entries that are configured manually for every customer. Because of the very small size of the development team, there is no separation between the development of the components for the standard application and their customization for particular customers. Consequently, there is no separation between development for and development with reuse, and developers are responsible for all test activities.
- *Quality requirements.* The software interacts with the overall enterprise-resource-planning (ERP) system and thus quality requirements with respect to correctness are high, whereas nonfunctional requirements such as performance are much less dominant. The current problem of the organization is to ensure functional correctness for all its variants. This is mainly because testing becomes increasingly complex because of the extensive usage of run-time variability mechanisms.

The initial step during test planning is the decision on the basic test strategy: an optimistic or a pessimistic strategy. In the example, the optimistic strategy was chosen for the following reasons:

- Project-independent testing of reusable components is not useful because the same developer is responsible for the development of a component for reuse and for using and customizing this software component in an application-engineering project.
- Separation of development and test staff is not possible because of the small size of the organization.
- Beta testing at the customer site is easily possible since the personnel of the customer is first educated in using the system within a test environment before failures may affect the customer's ERP system.

After the basic test strategy has been selected, it is tailored to the particular context. In this case, a pessimistic regression test was chosen in order to continuously ensure that the evolving standard application still allowed previously delivered systems to be updated in the future without massive manual adaptations. Thus, the organization decided to test, not after every change of a component but before every externally visible release of the standard application, all software components of the standard application for all configurations delivered.

The test techniques used stayed the same, that is, only the overall system is fed with test data from the customers and the output data are validated against the expected results as delivered by the customer. Therefore, the system as a whole is tested based on its specification. The test of single software components, as well as collaborations among components, is done only in cases of reported failures.

Implications for Research

The process of the example assumes the use of several tools, or information which do not exist today. Hence, research effort is required to make these tools available in the future. The three missing elements are as follows:

- Reliable information on the characteristics of testing techniques and strategies
- A method for systematically gathering information on an organization's characteristics, applied development paradigms, role and priority of quality requirements
- Guidelines for defining a quality strategy that perfectly combines available techniques into a homogeneous quality strategy, as well as guidelines for systematically implementing the ideal strategy starting from the organization's individual applied test activities

The first item implies that the efficiency and effectiveness of existing techniques are analyzed in a way that allows the performance of these techniques to be objectively compared for diverse contexts. In addition to the analysis results for each single technique, the mechanisms by which the quality attributes of single techniques can be combined must be explored in order to enable an evaluation of the performance of a quality strategy that combines several techniques.

The second item emphasizes the need for understanding the attributes of a software organization that vary from one organization to another, as well as the impact of the particular values of these attributes on the performance of test techniques and strategies. If these attributes are known, on the one hand, a method for assessing the concrete value for a given organization can be defined, and on the other hand, the variation in these attributes can be handled by defining appropriate customization factors for test techniques and strategies.

The third item explicitly recognizes that a theoretically optimal strategy may not be the best for a real-world organization in practice. This is because a new strategy with potentially new techniques means changing an organization. Hence, a process is required that considers the current status of an organization.

Implications for Practice

If an ideal framework including all the knowledge described in the previous subsection, were available, it would not automatically enhance software organizations' practices. Instead, organizations must accept software quality as a result of an engineering discipline rather than an art.

The application of the test-planning framework requires the systematic assessment of the current status of an organization. That is, information on organizational characteristics, development paradigms, and quality requirements are systematically elicited. As a result, the organization understands its software product line, the role of components in their development and maintenance processes, and the role and priorities of diverse quality requirements on their software. This information is required to apply the guidelines for defining a combined quality strategy in a useful way.

Before the identified strategy is implemented in an organization, the currently implemented strategy must be known to systematically plan the organization-specific series of migration steps that eventually leads to the intended strategy.

In addition to the required attitude to be able to make use of the test-planning framework, there is another kind of implication for practice. That is, the organizations must collect experience and data for existing techniques in practice and this data must be fed back into research in order to improve the framework and make it more reliable.

CONCLUSION

In this chapter, a framework and basic strategies have been presented that help in systematically defining an efficient test plan for a given reuse context. In particular, the issues that arise when testing component-based software and software product lines as well as potential test strategies for these two development paradigms have been discussed.

The heavy reuse of components implied in both component-based software engineering and the product line approach offers the promise of shorter development cycles with accompanying reduction in development costs. However, component-based software and product lines require a high level of component quality in order to be successful. Thus, more than for traditional, single-system software development, testing becomes a crucial part of the development process for these two novel software development paradigms.

There are a number of unique issues to be faced when testing software product lines. The problems and challenges, however, are, in principle, the same as in testing component-based software systems. That is because both approaches imply the large-scale reuse of previously developed components. To summarize, the most significant differences of testing in a reuse context compared to single software systems stem from the genericity and variable usage of components, as well as their changeable environment and dependencies.

In order to enable organizations to test component-based software and product lines effectively and efficiently, a number of open issues still have to be addressed. For example, more comprehensive and efficient techniques for testing generic components and for identifying inter-action defects among software product line variants are required. Also, general guidelines for selecting or defining the test strategy most appropriate in a particular context or for a specific organization have to be developed. The ultimate goal will be a practical, consistent, and cost-effective approach for adequately testing component-based software and product lines. The ap-proach should minimize the number of tests and hence the overall effort and amount of resources required for testing in a reuse context while still testing all functionality and thus ensuring ad-equate testing. As it is widely recognized today that the earlier a problem or defect can be identi-fied, the easier and cheaper it is to fix, it is also important to integrate techniques that can identify defects early in the development process, such as inspections and reviews, into a quality assur-ance approach for reuse-based development paradigms.

REFERENCES

Atkinson, C., J. Bayer, C. Bunse, E. Kamsties, O. Laitenberger, R. Laqua, D. Muthig, B. Paech, J. Wust, and J. Zettel. 2001. *Component-Based Product Line Engineering with UML.* London: Addison-Wesley.
Atkinson, C., and H.G. Gross. 2002. Built-in contract testing in model-driven component-based develop-ment. Paper presented in Workshop on Component-Based Development Processes at the Seventh Inter-national Conference on Software Reuse, Austin, Texas, April.
Bayer, J., O. Flege, P. Knauber, R. Laqua, D. Muthig, K. Schmid, T. Widen, and J. DeBaud.1999. PuLSE: A methodology to develop software product lines. In *Proceedings of the Fifth ACM SIGSOFT Symposium on Software Reusability,* 122–131. New York: Acm Press.
Beizer, B. 1990. *Software Testing Techniques.* 2nd ed. New York: Van Nostrand Reinhold.
Beydeda S., and V. Gruhn. 2001. An integrated testing technique for component-based software. In *Proceed-ings of the ACS/IEEE International Conference on Computer Systems and Applications,* 328–334. Los Alamitos, CA: IEEE Computer Society Press.
Bhor, A. 2001. *Component Testing Strategies.* Technical Report UCI-ICS-02–06. University of California, Irvine.
Clements, P., and L.M. Northrop. 2001. *Software Product Lines: Practices and Patterns.* Boston, MA: Addison-Wesley.
Gao, J., K. Gupta, S. Gupta, and S. Shim. 2002. On building testable software components. In *Proceedings of the First International Conference on COTS-Based Software Systems,* 108–121. Berlin: Springer.
Ghosh S., and A.P. Mathur. 1999. Issues in testing distributed component-based systems. Paper presented at the International ICSE Workshop on Testing Distributed Component-Based Systems, International Con-ference on Software Engineering. Los Angeles, California.
Harrold, M.J., D. Liang, and S. Sinha. 1999. An approach to analyzing and testing component-based sys-tems. Paper presented at the First International ICSE Workshop on Testing Distributed Component-Based Systems, International Conference on Software Engineering. Los Angeles, California.
Harrold, M.J., A. Orso, D. Rosenblum, G. Rothermel, M.L. Soffa, and H. Do. 2001. Using component metadata to support regression testing of component-based software. In *Proceedings of the International Conference on Software Maintenance.* Los Alamitos, CA: IEEE Press.
Hörnstein, J., and H. Edler. 2002. Test reuse in CBSE using built-in tests. Paper presented at Workshop on Component-Based Software Engineering, Composing Systems from Components, Lund, Sweden.
IEEE Computer Society. 1990. *IEEE Standard Glossary of Software Engineering Terminology, IEEE Std 610.12–1990.* Los Alamitos, CA: IEEE Computer Society Press.
McGregor, J.D. 2001. *Testing a Software Product Line.* Technical Report CMU/SEI-2001-TR-022. Soft-ware Engineering Institute, Carnegie Mellon University, December.
Szyperski, C. 1998. *Component Software: Beyond Object-Oriented Programming.* Harlow, UK: Addison-Wesley.
Wang, Y., G. King, and H. Wickburg. 1999. A method for built-in tests in component-based software main-tenance. In *Proceedings of the Third European Conference on Software Maintenance and Reengineering,* 186–189. Los Alamitos, CA: IEEE Computer Society Press.
Weyuker, E.J. 1998. Testing component-based software: A cautionary tale. *IEEE Software* 15, no. 5 (Sep-tember/October): 54–59.

Wu, Y., D. Pan, and M.H. Chen. 2001. Techniques for testing component-based software. In *Proceedings of the Seventh IEEE International Conference on Engineering of Complex Computer Systems.* Los Alamitos, CA: IEEE Computer Society Press.

PART II

MANAGING COMPONENT-BASED DEVELOPMENT

PART II

MANAGING CONFLICT THROUGH
DEVELOPMENT

CHAPTER 8

ORGANIZING FOR SOFTWARE PRODUCT FAMILIES

JAN BOSCH

Abstract: *The notion of a software product family forms one of the most successful approaches to component-based development, as can be judged by its increasingly wide adoption in the software industry. The organizational aspects of product family development require analysis. Most authors focus on the technical and process aspects, while assuming an organizational model consisting of a domain engineering unit and several application engineering units. In our cooperation with several software development organizations applying software product family principles, we have identified several other organizational models that are successfully employed as well. We present a number of organizational alternatives, organized around four main models: development department, business units, domain engineering unit, and hierarchical domain engineering units. For each model, its characteristics, applicability, advantages, and disadvantages and the mapping of core product family processes to organizational units are discussed and exemplified. Based on an analysis of these models, we present three factors in the choice of the organizational model. These factors are product family assets, the responsibility levels, and the type of organizational units.*

Keywords: *Software Product Families, Organizational Models, Project Management, Organizational Culture, Responsibility*

INTRODUCTION

Achieving reuse of software has been a long-standing ambition of the software engineering industry. Ever since the paper by McIlroy (1969), the notion of constructing software systems by composing software components has been pursued in various ways. Most proposals to achieve component-based software development assume a market divided into component developers, component users, and a marketplace. However, these proposals proved to be overly ambitious for most types of software. In response, there has been, in addition to worldwide reuse of components, a strong development of organization-wide reuse of components, thus intraorganizational rather than interorganizational. Parallel to this development, the importance of an explicit design and representation of the architecture of a software system has become increasingly recognized. The combination of these two insights leads to the definition of software product families.

A software product family consists of an architecture, a set of reusable components, and a set of products derived from the shared assets.

Existing literature on software product families (Bayer et al. 1999; Dikel et al. 1997; Jacobsen et al. 1997; Macala et al. 1996) tends to focus on the technology and the processes that surround product family–based software development. The processes associated with a software product family depend on the phase in which the product family currently finds itself. We identify four phases: initial development, evolution, reengineering, and retirement. Of these phases, we identify the evolution phase as the normal case. Evolution is typically organized as an iterative process consisting of the following four activities: scoping, impact analysis, development, and validation. These activities, however, need to be mapped to organizational units. In the existing literature, the organizational structure of software development organizations that is needed for the successful evolution of a software product family is not discussed. It is, nevertheless, necessary to impose an organization on the individuals that are involved in the product family and to assign the core product family processes to organizational units.

We shall discuss four primary organizational models that can be applied when adopting a product family–based approach to software development. For each model, we describe in what situations the model is most applicable, the advantages and disadvantages of the model, the mapping of processes to the organizational units, and an example of a company that employs the model. In addition, we discuss some factors that influence the choice of the most appropriate organizational model. Based on an analysis of the presented models, we have identified three dimensions that are organizationally relevant. These dimensions are the assets that are considered product family–wide, the levels of responsibility employed in the organization, and the nature of the organizational units. These dimensions are used to present a space of organizational alternatives.

The contribution of this chapter is that it identifies and categorizes the organizational alternatives for companies employing software product families and discusses the different ways of mapping the primary software processes to each of these organizational alternatives. It extends considerably over existing proposals for software product family organization that assume a division in domain and application engineering units.

The remainder of this chapter is organized as follows. In the next section, we present the four main life cycle phases of a software product family and, for each phase, the main processes. In the third through sixth sections, four organizational models are discussed in more detail and the mapping of software processes to these organizational models is discussed. The seventh section discusses four influencing factors and their effects on selecting the optimal organizational model. In the eighth section, we discuss the dimensions that can be used to describe a space of organizational alternatives. Finally, related work is discussed in the ninth section and the chapter is concluded in the tenth section.

SOFTWARE PRODUCT FAMILY PROCESSES

Software product family–based software development consists of several software processes. The exact processes depend on the phase in which the software product family currently exists. We identify four phases: initial development, evolution, reengineering, and retirement. Below, each phase is briefly presented.

Initial Development

The initial development of a software product family is concerned with converting the current way of working, which typically is organized around individual products, into a product family–centric way of working. This requires changes to the technology, processes, organization, and business models. First, initial versions of the shared artifacts, that is, the product family architecture and components, need to be constructed. Second, new development processes are required because new products now need to be created based on the product family artifacts and existing products need to be recreated. Third, the organization of the software development department needs to be adapted to the new situation. A number of organizational alternatives are discussed in

Figure 8.1   **Three Main Types of Product Family Artifacts and Associated Processes**

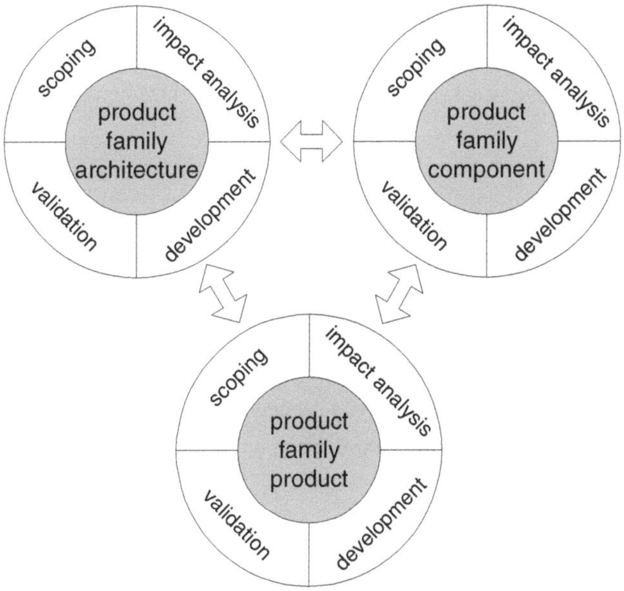

this chapter. Finally, several business issues are affected by the presence of a software product family. However, these issues are outside the boundaries of the chapter.

Evolution

The second phase, evolution, is also the normal case. Now, the shared artifacts and the products have been developed. Based on new requirements, due to innovating customers and technological opportunities, these artifacts evolve by incorporating new features in existing products and through the introduction of new products in the family. The organization typically employs some kind of technological road map in which it plans the evolution of all artifacts in their next release. Several processes occur during this phase, including the four primary ones discussed below. First, in the scoping process, the supported requirements and features are determined as well as the division between the shared and product-specific artifacts. Typically, only a subset of the suggested new requirements and features can be implemented, so some selection process is required. Second, in the architecture evolution process, the architecture evolves in response to new requirements and features. Third, for each component or related set of components, there is a component evolution process again in response to the evolution of the requirements on the system as well as the evolution of the architecture. Finally, individual products evolve in response to new product-specific requirements, new component versions, and new product family architecture versions that affect the product architecture. These processes are similar to the processes discussed in Jacobsen et al. (1997). In Svahnberg and Bosch (1999), we present the results of a case study addressing evolution in software product families and identify a number of typical evolution categories.

Figure 8.1 presents the three main types of artifacts in a software product family, which are the product family architecture, the components, and the products. Each of these artifacts has four core processes associated with itself: scoping, impact analysis, development, and validation. All artifacts are depending on each other, indicated by the arrows. For instance, extending the scope of the product may require additional functionality to be implemented by the architecture and some of the components. Similarly, any change to the software architecture will typically affect one or more components and most of the products in the product family.

Reengineering

The third phase, not necessarily reached by all product families, is reengineering. The goal of a reengineering project is typically not to add or change the functionality of a software product family, but rather to improve one or more quality attributes of the system. Typically, due to software erosion and lack of documentation, the modifiability of the software artifacts has been affected negatively. The intention of a reengineering effort is then to improve this. A second example occurs when a new quality requirement is imposed on the product family or the required level for an existing quality requirement is changed drastically. Since unplanned changes in quality requirements typically have architectural impact, a reengineering effort may be required.

Retirement

The fourth phase is the retirement of the software product family. Since this phase typically takes place concurrently with the initial development of the next software product family, this phase is primarily concerned with the reuse of the ideas and (part of) the software artifacts of the old product family in the new product family.

The latter two phases, reengineering and retirement, are the atypical situation and have little effect on the organization of software development units. Therefore, we do not discuss the associated processes in detail. The evolution phase, on the other hand, is the normal activity in a software company and the identified processes need to be mapped to organizational units. Depending on a number of factors, including the size of the organization, we identify four primary organizational alternatives that can be employed. These are discussed in the subsequent sections.

DEVELOPMENT DEPARTMENT

The development department model imposes no permanent organizational structure on the architects and engineers that are involved in the software product family. All staff members can, in principle, be assigned to work with any type of asset within the family. Typically, work is organized in projects that dynamically organize staff members in temporary networks. These projects can be categorized into domain engineering projects and application (or system) engineering projects. In the former, the goal of the project is the development of a new reusable artifact or a new version of it, for example, a software component. The goal is explicitly not a system or product that can be delivered to internal or external customers of the development department. The system engineering projects are concerned with developing a system, either a new one or a new version, that can be delivered to a customer. Occasionally, extensions to the reusable assets are required to fulfill the system requirements that are more generally applicable than just the system under development. In that case, the result of the system engineering project may be a new version of one or more of the reusable assets, in addition to the deliverable system.

In Figure 8.2, the development department model is presented graphically. Both the reusable

Figure 8.2 **Development Department Model**

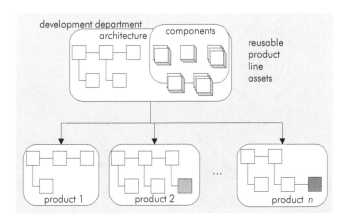

product family assets and the concrete systems built based on these assets are developed and maintained by a single organizational unit.

Applicability

The development department model is primarily applicable for relatively small organizations and for consultancy organizations, that is, organizations that sell projects rather than products to their customers. Based on our experience, our impression is that this model works for up to thirty software-related staff members in product-based organizations. If the number of staff members exceeds thirty, generally some kind of organizational structure needs to be imposed anyhow, independent of the use of a product family.

Advantages and Disadvantages

The development department model has, like most things in life, a number of advantages and disadvantages. The primary advantage is simplicity and ease of communication. Since all staff members are working within the same organizational context, come in contact with all parts of the system family, and have contact with the customers, the product family can be developed and evolved in a very efficient manner with little organizational and administrative overhead. A second advantage is that, assuming that a positive attitude toward reuse-based software development exists within the department, it is possible to adopt a software product family approach without changing the existing organization, which may simplify the adoption process.

The primary disadvantage of this approach is that it is not scalable. When the organization expands and reaches, for example, more than thirty staff members, it is necessary to reorganize and to create specialized units. A second disadvantage is that staff members within organizations are, depending on the local culture, typically more interested in either domain engineering or system engineering, that is, working with a particular type of engineering has higher status in the informal organization. The danger is that the lower-status type of engineering is not performed appropriately. This may lead to highly general and flexible reusable components, but systems that do not fulfill the required quality levels, or vice versa.

Figure 8.3 **Process Mapping in the Development Department Model**

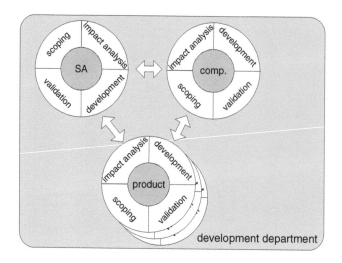

Process Mapping

Since the organizational model is rather simple in the case of a development department, there is no specialization with respect to the processes that take place during the normal evolution of the software product family. Each of the processes, or a combination of these, is performed as a project. Very often, the organization decides to introduce a new product or some new features in an existing product (product scoping). This typically has consequences on the product family architecture and shared components as well. Consequently, typically several artifacts evolve as part of a product development project.

Example

A company that employed this organizational model is Securitas Larm, Sweden. All its product development, including hardware and software, is concentrated in a single development department. This department maintains a product family in the domain of fire-alarm systems, as we describe in Bosch (2000). The department has an engineering staff of about twenty-five persons, so it fits our applicability requirement. In fact, until about a decade ago, development was organized in product business units. Each product unit was responsible for sales, marketing, installation, and development of the product. However, development especially did not function well in this organizational form. Generally only up to five engineers worked with the product development, which was too few to create an effective development organization. Consequently, Securitas Larm decided to reorganize development into a single development department (Figure 8.3).

BUSINESS UNITS

The second organizational model that we discuss is organized around business units. Each business unit is responsible for the development and evolution of one or a few products in the software product family. The reusable assets in the product family are shared by the business units. The evolution of shared assets is generally performed in a distributed manner, so that each business unit can extend the functionality in the shared assets, test it, and make the newer version available to the other business units. The initial development of shared assets is generally performed through domain engineering projects. The project team consists of members from all or most business units. Generally, the business units most interested in the creation of, for example, a new software component put the largest amount of effort into the domain engineering project, but all business units share, in principle, the responsibility for all common artifacts.

Depending on the number and size of the business units and the ratio of shared versus system-specific functionality in each system, we have identified three levels of maturity, especially with respect to the evolution of the shared artifacts.

Unconstrained Model

In the unconstrained model, any business unit can extend the functionality of any shared component and make it available as a new version in the shared asset base. The business unit that performed the extension is also responsible for verifying that, where relevant, all existing functionality is untouched and that the new functionality performs according to specification.

A typical problem that companies using this model suffer from is that, typically, software components are extended with too system-specific functionality. Either the functionality has not been generalized sufficiently or the functionality should have been implemented as system-specific code, but for internal reasons, for example, implementation efficiency or system performance, the business unit decided to implement the functionality as part of the shared component.

These problems normally lead to the erosion or degradation of the component, that is, it becomes, over time, harder and less cost-effective to use the shared component, rather than developing a system-specific version of the functionality. As we discussed in Bosch (2000), some companies have performed component reengineering projects in which a team consisting of members from the business units using the component reengineers the component and improves its quality attributes to acceptable levels. Failure to reengineer when necessary may lead to a situation in which the product family exists on paper, but the business units develop and maintain system-specific versions of all or most components in the product family, thus invalidating all advantages of a software product family approach, while maintaining some of the disadvantages.

Asset Managers

Especially when the problems discussed above manifest themselves with increasing frequency and severity, the first step in addressing these problems is to introduce asset managers. An asset manager has the obligation to verify that the evolution of the asset is performed according to the best interest of the organization as a whole, rather than optimal from the perspective of a single business unit. The asset manager is explicitly not responsible for the implementation of new requirements. This task is still performed by the business unit that requires the additional functionality. However, all evolution should occur with the asset manager's consent, and before the new version of the asset is made generally accessible, the asset manager will verify through regression testing and other means that the other business units are at least not negatively affected by the evolution. Preferably, new requirements are implemented in such a fashion that even other business units can benefit from them. The asset manager is often selected from the business unit that makes most extensive and advanced use of the component.

Although the asset manager model, in theory at least, should avoid the problems associated with the unconstrained model, in practice it often remains hard for the asset manager to control the evolution. One reason is that time-to-market requirements for business units often are prioritized by higher management, which may force the asset manager to accept extensions and changes that do not fulfill the goals, for example, they are too system-specific. A second reason is that, since the asset manager does not perform the evolution directly, it is not always easy to verify that the new requirements were implemented as agreed upon with the business unit. The result is that components still erode over time, although generally at a slower pace than in the unconstrained model.

Mixed Responsibility

Often, with the increasing size of the system family and an increasing number of staff and business units, the organization reaches a point where it is still unwilling to adopt the next model (domain engineering units), but wants to assign the responsibility for performing the evolution of shared artifacts to a particular unit. In that case, the mixed responsibility model may be applied. In this model, each business unit is assigned the responsibility for one or more shared artifacts, in addition to the product(s) the unit is responsible for. The responsibility for a particular asset is generally assigned to the business unit that makes the most extensive and advanced use of the component. Consequently, most requests for changes and extensions will originate from within the business unit, which simplifies the management of asset evolution. In this model, the other business units no longer have the authority to implement changes in the shared component. Instead, they need to issue requests to the business unit responsible for the component whenever an extension or change is required.

The main advantage of this approach is the increased control over the evolution process. However, two potential disadvantages exist. First, since the responsibility for implementing changes in the shared artifact is not always located at the business unit that needs those changes, there are bound to be delays in the development of systems that could have been avoided in the approaches described earlier. Second, each business unit has to divide its efforts between developing the next version of its product(s) and the evolution of the component(s) it is responsible for. Especially when other business units have change requests, these may conflict with the ongoing activities within the business unit, which may prioritize its own goals over the goals of other business units. In addition, the business unit may extend the components it is responsible for in ways that are optimized for its own purposes, rather than for the organization as a whole. These developments may lead to conflicts between the business units and, in the worst case, the abolishment of the product family approach.

Conflicts

The way the software product family came into existence is, in our experience, an important factor in the success or failure of a family. If the business units already exist and develop their systems independently and, at some point, management decides to adopt the software product family approach, conflict between the business units is likely because giving up the freedom that they had up to that point will be difficult. If the business units exist, but the product family gradually evolves because of bottom-up, informal cooperation between staff in different business units, this is an excellent ground to build a product family upon. However, when cooperation is changed from optional to obligatory, tensions and conflicts may appear anyhow. Finally, in some companies, business units develop through an organic growth of the company. When a company ex-

Figure 8.4 **Business Unit Model**

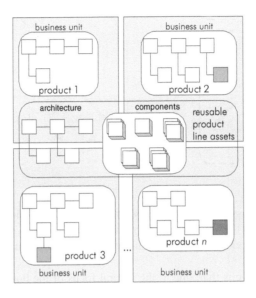

pands the set of systems that it develops and maintains, at some point, a reorganization into business units becomes necessary. However, since the staff in those units earlier worked together and used the same assets, both the product family and cooperation between business units develop naturally, and this culture often remains long after the reorganization, especially when it is nurtured by management. In all these cases, conflicts and tensions between business units must be resolved by management early and proactively since they imply considerable risk for the success of the product family.

In Figure 8.4, the business unit model is presented graphically. The reusable system-family artifacts are shared by the business units, with respect to both use and evolution.

Applicability

As discussed above, when the number of staff members is too low, for example, below thirty, organization into business units is rarely optimal since too few people are working together and the communication overhead over unit boundaries is too large. On the other hand, our hypothesis, based on a number of cases that we have studied, is that when the number of staff members exceeds one hundred, domain engineering units may become necessary to reduce the n-to-n communication between all business units to a one-to-n communication between the domain engineering unit and the system engineering units. Thus, with respect to staff size, we believe that the optimal range for the business unit model is between thirty and one hundred, although this figure, to a large extent, depends on the specific context as well.

Advantages and Disadvantages

The advantage of this model is that it allows for effective sharing of assets, that is, software architectures and components, between a number of organizational units. The sharing is effective

Figure 8.5   **Process Mappings in the Business Unit Model**

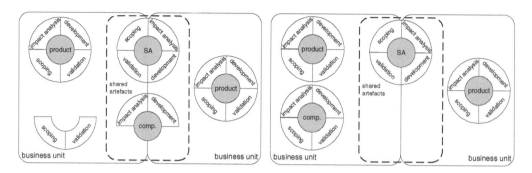

in terms of access to the assets and particularly effective in the evolution of assets (especially true for the unconstrained and the asset manager approaches). In addition, the approach scales considerably better than the development department model, for example, up to one hundred engineers in the general case.

The main disadvantage is that, due to the natural focus of the business units on systems (or products), there is no entity or explicit incentive to focus on the shared assets. This is the underlying cause for the erosion of the architecture and components in the system family. The timely and reliable evolution of the shared assets relies on the organizational culture and the commitment and responsibility felt by the individuals working with the assets.

Process Mapping

The business unit model has three alternative implementations: the unconstrained, asset manager, and mixed responsibility model. In the first model, all processes for all shared artifacts can be initiated and performed by any business unit. Each business unit is responsible for its own products, but when new product requirements have effects on shared artifacts, the business unit can take a shared component, extend its functionality, run it through validation, and make it available for all units. In the asset manager model, the scoping and validation processes are assigned to an individual in one of the business units. Whenever one of the business units intends to extend an existing component, the asset manager has to give permission. Once the change has been implemented, the asset manager will evaluate the result and validate the functionality. Only if this process is performed successfully is the new version of the component made generally available. In the mixed responsibility model, all processes associated with shared components are assigned to one business unit. If other units desire changes, these have to be requested at the unit managing the component. This unit will perform the change and subsequently release the new version of the component. The software architecture is, in all alternatives, subject to a shared evolution process. Because of the impact of architectural changes, the units have to reach consensus before changes take place. The asset manager and mixed responsibility models are presented graphically in Figure 8.5.

Example

Axis Communications, Sweden, employs the business unit model. Its storage-server, scanner-server, and camera-server products are developed by three business units. These business units share a common product family architecture and a set of more than ten object-oriented frameworks that may be extended with system-specific code where needed. Initially, Axis used the unconstrained model with relatively informal asset managers, but recently the role of asset managers has been formalized and they now have the right to refuse new versions of assets that do not fulfill generality, quality, and compatibility requirements. The asset managers are taken from the business units that make the most extensive and advanced use of the associated assets. Within the organization, discussions were ongoing whether an independent domain engineering unit, or, alternatively, a mixed responsibility approach would be needed to guarantee the proper evolution of assets. Whenever new assets or a major redesign of some existing asset is needed, Axis has used domain engineering projects, but disguised these projects as system engineering projects by developing prototype systems. The advantage of the latter is that the integration of the new artifact with the existing artifacts is automatically verified as part of the domain engineering project.

DOMAIN ENGINEERING UNIT

The third organizational model for software product families is concerned with separating the development and evolution of shared assets from the development of concrete systems. The former is performed by a so-called domain engineering unit, whereas the latter is performed by product engineering units. Product engineering units are sometimes referred to as application or system engineering units.

The domain engineering unit model is typically applicable for larger organizations It requires considerable amounts of communication between the product engineering units, which are in frequent contact with the users of their products, and the domain engineering unit, which has no direct contact with customers, but needs a good understanding of the requirements of the product engineering units. Thus, one can identify flows in two directions: the requirements flow from the product engineering units toward the domain engineering unit, and the new versions of assets, including the software architecture and the components of the product family, are distributed by the domain engineering unit to the product engineering units.

The domain engineering unit model exists in two alternatives—first, an approach in which only a single domain engineering unit exists and, second, an approach in which multiple domain engineering units exist. In the first case, the responsibility for the development and evolution of all shared artifacts, that is, the software architecture and the components, is assigned to a single organizational unit. This unit is the sole contact point for the product engineering units, which construct their products based on the shared assets.

The second alternative employs multiple domain engineering units. One unit is responsible for the design and evolution of the software architecture for the product family and, for each architectural component (or set of related components), a component engineering unit manages the design and evolution of the components. Finally, the product engineering units are, also in this alternative, concerned with the development of products based on the artifacts. The main difference between the first and second alternatives is that, in the latter, the level of specialization is even higher and the product engineering units need to interact with multiple domain engineering units.

Figure 8.6 presents the organizational model for the domain engineering unit. The domain engineering unit is responsible for the software architecture and components of the product family, whereas the product engineering units are responsible for developing the products based on the shared assets.

Figure 8.6   **The Domain Engineering Unit Model**

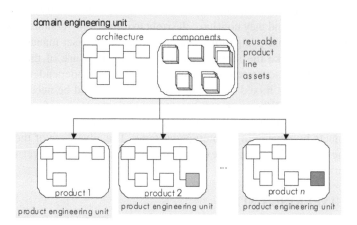

Applicability

Small companies, especially, are very skeptical of domain engineering units. One of the reasons is that, just because domain engineering units are concerned with reusable assets rather than products that are relevant for users, these units may not be focused on generating added value, but rather may lose themselves in aesthetic, generic, but useless abstractions. However, based on our experience, our impression is that when the number of staff members working within a product family exceeds a hundred software engineers, the amount of overhead in the communication between the business units causes a need for an organizational unit or units specialized on domain engineering.

Multiple units rather than a single domain engineering unit become necessary when the size of the domain engineering unit becomes too large, for example, thirty software engineers. In that case, it becomes necessary to create multiple groups that focus on different component sets within a product family software architecture. In some cases, although component engineering units exist, no explicit product family architecture unit is present. Rather, a small team of software architects from the component engineering units assumes the responsibility for the overall architecture.

Finally, at which point the complexities of software development even exceed the domain engineering unit approach is not obvious, but when the number of software engineers is in the hundreds, the hierarchical domain engineering units model, discussed below, may become necessary.

Advantages and Disadvantages

Despite the scepticism in small organizations, the domain engineering unit model has a number of important advantages. First, as mentioned, it removes the need for *n*-to-*n* communication between the business units, reducing it to one-to-*n* communication. Second, whereas business units may extend components with too product-specific extensions, the domain engineering unit is responsible for evolving the components such that the requirements of all products in the product family are satisfied. In addition, conflicts can be resolved in a more objective and compromise-oriented fashion. Finally, the domain engineering unit approach scales up to much larger numbers of software engineering staff than the aforementioned approaches.

Figure 8.7 **Process Mapping for the Domain Engineering Unit Models**

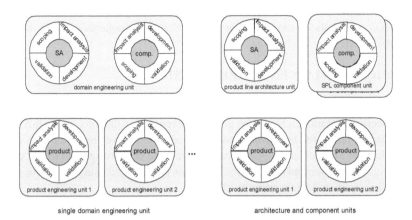

Obviously, the model has some associated disadvantages as well. The foremost is the difficulty of managing the requirements flow toward the domain engineering unit, the balancing of conflicting requirements from different product engineering units, and the subsequent implementation of the selected requirements in the next version of the assets. This causes delays in the implementation of new features in the shared assets, which, in turn, delays the time-to-market of products. This may be a major disadvantage of the domain engineering unit model since time-to-market is the primary goal of many software development organizations. To address this problem, the organization may allow product engineering units to create, at least temporarily, their own versions of shared artifacts by extending the existing version with product-specific features. This allows the product engineering unit to improve its time-to-market while it does not expose the other product engineering units to immature and instable components. The intention is generally to incorporate the product-specific extensions, in a generalized form, into the next shared version of the component.

Process Mappings

The domain engineering unit model clearly separates the responsibility for the evolution of shared artifacts from the responsibility of specific products by assigning these processes to different organizational units. As we discussed earlier, two alternative models exist, that is, a single domain engineering unit and multiple domain engineering units, organized as a product family architecture and one or more component units. All evolution processes for an artifact are assigned to one organizational unit, which provides a clear separation of responsibility. However, substantial amounts of interaction are necessary between the various processes, and these are typically complicated by the assignment of processes to different units. The alternative models are presented graphically in Figure 8.7.

Example

The domain engineering unit model is used by Symbian. The EPOC operating system consists of a set of components, and the responsibility of a number of subsets is assigned to specialized organizational units. For each device family requirement definition (DFRD), a unit exists that composes and integrates versions of these components into a release of the complete EPOC operating system to the partners of Symbian. The release contains specific versions and instantiations of the various components for the particular DFRD. Some components are only included in one or a few of the DFRDs.

HIERARCHICAL DOMAIN ENGINEERING UNITS

As we discussed in the previous section, there is an upper boundary on the size of an effective domain engineering unit model. However, generally even before the maximum staff member size is reached, often already for technical reasons, an additional level has been introduced in the software product family. This additional layer contains one or more specialized product families that, depending on their size and complexity, either can be managed using the business unit model or may actually require a domain engineering unit.

In the case that a specialized product family requires a domain engineering unit, we have, in fact, instantiated the hierarchical domain engineering units model that is the topic of this section. This model is only suitable for a large or very large organization that has an extensive family of products. If, during the design or evolution of the product family, it becomes necessary to organize the product family in a hierarchical manner and a considerable number of staff members is involved in the product family, then it may be necessary to create specialized domain engineering units that develop and evolve the reusable assets for a subset of the products in the family.

The reusable product family assets at the top level are frequently referred to as a platform and not necessarily identified as part of the product family. We believe, however, that it is relevant to explicitly identify and benefit from the hierarchical nature of these assets. Traditionally, platforms are considered as means to provide shared functionality, but without imposing any architectural constraints. In practice, however, a platform does impose constraints, and when considering the platform as the top-level product family artifact set, this is made more explicit and the designers of specialized product families and family members will derive from the software architecture rather than design it.

In Figure 8.8, the hierarchical domain engineering units model is presented graphically. For a subset of the systems in the product family, a domain engineering unit is present that develops and maintains the specialized product family software architecture and the associated components. Only the components specific for the subset in the product family are the responsibility of the specialized domain engineering unit. All other components are inherited from the overall product family asset base. The specialized domain engineering unit is also responsible for integrating the specialized with the general reusable assets.

Applicability

As mentioned in the introduction, the hierarchical domain units model becomes the preferred model when the number and variability of systems in the family is large or very large and hundreds of staff members are involved. Consequently, the model is primarily suitable in large organizations and long-lived systems in the family, since the effort and expenses of building up this organizational model are substantial.

The complexities involved in the implementation and use of this organizational model are beyond the scope of this chapter, but a considerable maturity with respect to software development projects is required for this approach to succeed. This model is the fourth and most complex

Figure 8.8 **Hierarchical Domain Engineering Unit Model**

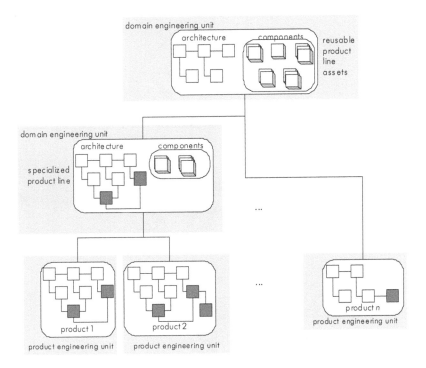

model that we discuss, and if the product family cannot be captured within this model, it is reasonable to assume that the scope of the family has been set too wide.

Advantages and Disadvantages

The advantages of this model include its ability to encompass large, complex product families and organize large numbers of engineers. None of the organizational models discussed earlier scales up to the hundreds of software engineers that can be organized using this model.

The disadvantages include the considerable overhead that the approach implies and the difficulty of achieving agile reactions to changed market requirements. Typically, a delicate balance needs to be found between allowing product engineering units to act independently, including the temporary creation of product-specific versions of product family components, versus capitalizing on the commonalities between products and requiring product engineering units to use shared versions of components.

Process Mapping

The fourth approach to assigning processes to organizational units is provided by the hierarchical domain engineering unit model. In this case, the shared artifacts are decomposed into basic and more specialized parts. The evolution of the basic shared artifacts is the responsibility of the top-level domain engineering unit model, whereas specialized domain engineering units evolve more specific versions of the artifacts. Figure 8.9 presents this model graphically.

Figure 8.9 **Process Mapping for Hierarchical Domain Engineering Units**

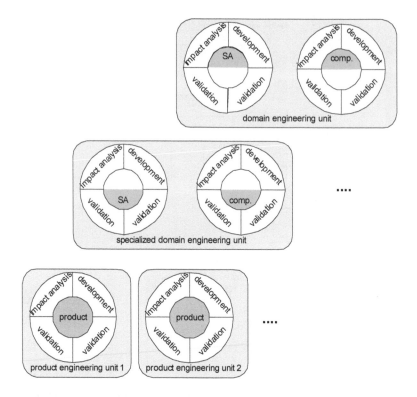

Example

An example of an organization that has successfully adopted the hierarchical domain engineering units model is Nokia Mobile Phones. This company develops and maintains a wide variety of products in the wireless information devices domain, in particular mobile phones. The company has applied a product family approach to its mobile phone development for several years. The software product family consists of two levels. The top level, a platform, is developed and maintained by a top-level infrastructure group, and consists of a product family architecture and a set of components, which are shared by all mobile phone products and ported to different hardware platforms. For subsets of products in the product family, specialized groups exist that develop, especially, components specific for the family members in the subset. These domain engineering units have frequent contact and exchange considerable amounts of information, but are organized as independent units.

INFLUENCING FACTORS

Up to this point, we have presented the size of the product family and the engineering staff involved in the development and evolution of the product family as the primary factors in selecting the appropriate organizational model. Although, in our experience, the above factors indeed are the most prominent, several other factors should be allowed to influence the selection decision as well. Below, we present some factors that we have identified in industry as relevant in this context.

Geographical Distribution

Despite the emergence of a variety of technological solutions aiming at reducing the effects of geographical location, for example, telephone, e-mail, video conferencing, and distributed document management, the physical location of the staff involved in the software product family still plays a role. It simply is more difficult to maintain effective, efficient communication channels between teams that are in disparate locations and, perhaps, even time zones than between teams that are located in the same building. Therefore, units that need to exchange much information should preferably be located closer to each other than units that can cooperate with less information.

For instance, geographical distribution of the teams developing the systems in the family may cause a company to select the domain engineering unit model because it focuses the communication between the domain engineering unit and each product engineering unit, rather than requiring the n-to-n communication of the business unit model.

Project Management Maturity

The complexity of managing projects grows exponentially with the size of the project (in virtually any measure). Therefore, the introduction of a software product family approach requires, independent of the organizational model, a relatively high level of maturity with respect to project management. Projects need to be synchronized over organizational boundaries and activities in different projects may become dependent on each other, which requires experience and proactiveness in project management.

To give an example, incorporating new functionality in a product family component at Axis Communications, as previously mentioned, requires communication with the other business units at the start, the actual execution, and at the end of the project: at the start, to verify that no other business unit is currently including the same or related functionality; during the project, to verify that the included functionality and the way in which it is implemented are sufficiently general and provide as much benefit as possible to the other business units; and after the end of the project, to verify that the new version of the component provides backward compatibility to systems developed by the other business units.

Organizational Culture

The culture of an organization is often considered a hard-to-use concept, which is obviously the case. However, the attitude that each engineer has toward the tasks that he or she is assigned to do and the value patterns exhibited by the informal organizational groups have a major influence on the final outcome of any project. Thus, a kind of "cowboy" or "hero" culture, in which individual achievements are valued higher than group achievements, can seriously inhibit a successful software product family approach, which is highly dependent on a team culture that supports interdependency, trust, and compromise.

For instance, at one company, which will remain unnamed, we discussed the introduction of a software product family approach. The company had extensive experience in the use of object-oriented frameworks and within each business unit reuse was widespread and accepted. However, when top management tried to implement product family–based reuse, business unit managers revolted and the initiative was canceled. The reason, it turned out, was that each business unit would have had to sacrifice its lead architect(s) for a considerable amount of time during the development of the reusable product family assets. In addition, the conversion would have delayed several ongoing and planned projects. These two effects of adopting a product family approach, among others, would have led to highly negative effects on the bonuses received by, especially, business unit management. One explanation could be that these managers were selfish people who did not consider what was best for the company as a whole. However, our explanation is that top management had, over many years, created a culture in which business units were highly independent profit centers. This culture conflicted directly with the product family approach that top management tried to introduce.

Type of Systems

Finally, an important factor influencing the optimal organizational model, but also the scope and nature of the system family, is the type of systems that make up the family. Systems whose requirements change frequently and drastically, for example, due to new technological possibilities, are substantially less suitable for the large, up-front investments that a wide-scoped, hierarchical software product family approach may require than systems with relatively stable requirement sets and long lifetimes. Medical and telecommunication (server-side) systems are typical systems that have reasonably well understood functionality and that need to be maintained for at least a decade and often considerably longer.

For instance, consultancy companies that typically are project-based are able to adopt a software product family approach. Since subsequent projects often are in the same domain, the availability of a product family architecture and a set of reusable components may substantially reduce lead time and development cost. However, the investment made by such a company to develop these artifacts can never be of the same order of magnitude as that for a product-based company with clear market predictions for new products. The consultancy company has a significantly higher risk that future projects are not in exactly the same domain, but in an adjacent one, invalidating or at least reducing the usefulness of the developed assets. Consequently, investment and risk always need to be balanced appropriately.

ORGANIZATIONAL DIMENSIONS

Once we had identified the four organizational models and their variants, we performed an analysis of their characteristics. Based on this analysis, we have identified three dimensions that play a role in the selection of the most appropriate organization for software product family–based development. These dimensions are the assets that are considered product family–wide, the levels of responsibility employed in the organization, and the nature of the organizational units. When combined, these dimensions form a space of organizational alternatives. Below, each dimension is discussed in more detail. The section ends with a discussion of the relation between the dimensions and the discussed organizational models.

Product Family Assets

A software product family consists of a number of artifacts, which are the product family architecture, the product family components, and the product-specific software. In the traditional organizational model, the product family architecture and shared components are the responsibility of the domain engineering units, whereas the product-specific software is the responsibility of the application engineering units.

In our experience, the way artifacts are treated depends on the type of products and the type of organization employing a product family approach. Therefore, the assets considered by the organization as a whole may vary from just the product family architecture to all assets, including the product-specific code. Below, we describe four levels:

- *Architecture:* In organizations with little integration between the various units, a first step toward achieving a software product family may be to synchronize around a common architecture for the products where possible. In this case, only the architecture is the shared asset.
- *Platform:* Once a shared architecture is in place, it becomes possible to define some basic functionality as shared components. Typically, this functionality is shared by all products. In this way, the increased integration between different units provides obvious benefits and no or few disadvantages. Often, this type of sharing between product units is referred to as using a platform.
- *Components:* As in traditional software product families, the next level is to share both the product family architecture and most of the software components that are shared among two or more products. At this point, some products typically experience disadvantages of using the product family. This requires the organization to explicitly stress the overall advantages, which, obviously, should outweigh the local disadvantages.
- *Product specifics:* The highest level of integration is achieved when product-specific code is explicitly considered at the product family level. The reason for focusing on product-specific code is typically that much of this code, at some point in the future, is used in other products as well. Thus, by designing and developing product-specific code carefully, the organization will make future integration in the shared product family assets considerably easier.

Responsibility Levels

A second dimension is the way responsibility for product family assets is handled. Again, traditionally a clear division between domain engineering and application engineering units exists. However, in many cases, the actual assignment of responsibility is more fine-grained. We have identified three levels of responsibility within organizations applying software product families.

- *Shared responsibility:* Especially in organizations where a product family appeared in a bottom-up manner, the responsibility for the shared product family assets may, at least initially, be shared among the organizational units.
- *Managed responsibility:* At some point, typically an individual or a small team is assigned to be responsible for the particular asset. However, this does not mean that the evolution of the asset is performed by those responsible for it. The responsibility of the person or team is limited to ensuring that changes do not violate the requirements of other users or decrease future modifiability.
- *Engineered responsibility:* The highest level of responsibility is achieved when a team is responsible for the development and evolution of a particular asset. This requires users of the asset to request changes from the team. The team has the responsibility to respond to change requests in a fair and timely manner.

Organizational Units

The third dimension that we have identified as relevant for the organization of software product family–based development is the way staff is organized into units. Our cooperation with the software industry has identified four perspectives:

Figure 8.10   **Dimensions Organizing Software Product Families**

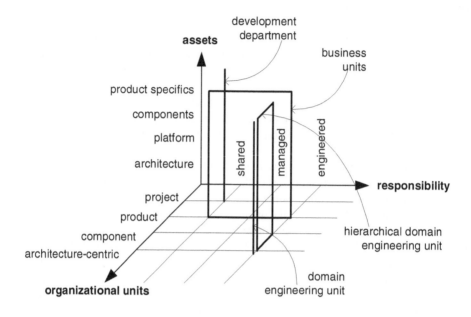

- *Project:* The first model does not employ a permanent assignment of staff to units. In such a project-based type of organization, staff is assigned to teams for the duration of projects.
- *Product:* The second model is to organize staff around products. Because staff members are permanently assigned to a particular product, their experience leads to increased levels of efficiency. However, this experience is not shared between different products.
- *Shared components:* When considerable overlap between different products is identified, the company may decide to exploit this by identifying and defining a number of components that are assigned to units that act as service providers to the product units.
- *Architecture-centric:* The final model for organizing staff centers on a software architecture that is shared among the products. This architecture defines the shared components and the product-specific code and, consequently, the organizational units. Unlike in the previous model where the product units are in control, in this model the software architecture and associated staff typically control development.

Organizational Alternatives

The three dimensions discussed above define a three-dimensional space that can be used to categorize organizational approaches to product family development. In earlier sections, we discussed four organizational models of software product family–based development. Figure 8.10 illustrates the relation between the dimensions and the organizational models. Development department and domain engineering units are presented by a single family, whereas business units and hierarchical domain engineering form planes, since alternatives exist for these models.

What is clear from this three-dimensional space is that several alternatives exist that we have not discussed in the earlier sections. However, this does not mean that these are not viable alternatives. We are convinced that organizations exist that employ these alternative models. When adopting a software product family, it is advisable to understand what alternatives are available and to evaluate these, rather than blindly adopting a standard model.

RELATED WORK

As we discussed in the introduction, most publications in the domain of software product families address issues different from the organizational ones. Macala et al. (1996) and Dikel et al. (1997) were among the first researchers to describe experiences of using software product families in an industrial context. Although the authors do address organizational, management, and staffing issues, both articles assume the domain engineering unit model and present it as the de facto organizational model. Jacobsen et al. (1997) also discuss organizational issues, but focus on a number of roles that should be present and do not address the overall organization of software product family–based development. Clements and Northrop (2002), addressing organizational issues of software product families, identify four functional groups: the architecture group, the component engineering group, the product family support group, and the product development group. The authors note that these functional groups may be mapped to organizational units in various ways. Finally, Bayer et al. (1999) provide a methodology for developing software product families and discuss organizational guidelines, but no organizational models.

CONCLUSION

Component-based software development can be divided into two categories: interorganizational and intraorganizational reuse of components. Interorganizational components are typically rather generic and provide little application domain- or product-specific functionality. Intraorganizational components are highly application domain-specific and provide considerable benefit to the organization. Software product families provide the most successful approach to intraorganizational, architecture-driven reuse of software artifacts. This approach has been adopted by a variety of industrial software and system development organizations. A software product family typically moves through a number of phases: initial adoption, evolution, reengineering, and retirement. Of these phases, the evolution phase is the normal case and the core processes associated with this phase need to be mapped to an organizational model. During this phase, for each artifact, one can identify a scoping, impact analysis, development, and validation process.

Traditional literature assumes the domain engineering unit model, whereas we have experienced that several organizational models are employed in the software industry. In this chapter, we have discussed four organizational models for software product families and discussed, based on our experiences, the applicability of each model, its advantages and disadvantages, the mapping of the core processes to organizational units, and an example of an organization that employs the particular model. The approaches are summarized below and in Table 8.1.

Development Department

In this model, software development is concentrated in a single development department; no organizational specialization exists with either the software product family assets or the systems in the family. The model is especially suitable for small organizations. The primary advantages are that it is simple and communication between staff members is easy, whereas the disadvantage is that the model does not scale to larger organizations. Because of the lack of specialization in

Table 8.1

Summary of Software Product Family Models

Type	Applicability	Advantages	Disadvantages
Development department	Staff less than 30	Simple; ease of communication	Limited scalability
Business units	Staff between 30 and 100	Effective sharing of software artifacts	High design erosion of shared artifacts; complex communication
Domain engineering unit	Staff between 100 and several hundred	Scalable; higher-quality shared artifacts	Managing requirements and evolution difficult
Hierarchical domain engineering units	Staff greater than several hundred	Effective organization of very large research and development teams	Risk for high administrative overhead and lack of agility

this organizational model, there is no specific mapping of processes to units. Instead, all processes are performed in the development department.

Business Units

The second type of organizational model employs a specialization of system types in the form of business units. Three alternatives exist: the unconstrained model, the asset manager model, and the mixed responsibility model. Some of our industrial partners have successfully applied this model for up to one hundred software engineers. An advantage of the model is that it allows for effective sharing of assets between a set of organizational units. A disadvantage is that business units easily focus on the concrete systems rather than on the reusable assets. With respect to the core processes, the product-specific processes are assigned to business units and the architecture-specific processes are performed jointly by all business units. The mapping of component-specific processes depends on the selected alternative. In the unconstrained model, all processes can be initiated and performed by any business unit. In the asset manager model, the scoping and validation processes are performed by the asset manager, whereas the other processes can be performed by any business unit. Finally, in the mixed responsibility model, all processes for a component are assigned to a particular business unit.

Domain Engineering Unit

In this model, the domain engineering unit is responsible for the design, development, and evolution of the reusable assets. Product engineering units are responsible for developing and evolving the products built based on the product family assets. The model is widely scalable, from the boundaries where the business unit model reduces effectiveness up to hundreds of software engineers. Another advantage of this model is that it reduces communication from n-to-n in the business unit model to one-to-n between the domain engineering unit and the system engineering units. Finally, the domain engineering unit focuses on developing general, reusable assets, thus addressing one of the problems with the aforementioned model, that is, too little focus on the reusable assets. One disadvantage is the difficulty of managing the requirements flow and the evolution of reusable assets in response to these new requirements. Since the domain engineering unit needs to balance the requirements of all system engineering units, this may negatively affect time-to-market for individual system engineering units. In the single domain engineering unit model, all architecture- and component-specific processes are assigned to the domain engineering unit, whereas the product-specific processes are assigned to the product engineering units.

Hierarchical Domain Engineering Units

In cases where a hierarchical product family has been necessary, a hierarchy of domain units may also be required. The domain engineering units that work with specialized product families use the top-level assets as a basis to found their own product family upon. This model is applicable especially in large or very large organizations with a sizable variety of long-lived systems. The advantage of this model is that it organizes large numbers of software engineers effectively. One disadvantage is the administrative overhead that easily builds up, reducing the agility of the organization as a whole, which may affect competitiveness negatively. In this model, architecture- and component-specific processes are also assigned to domain engineering units, but the architecture and component artifacts are decomposed into basic and specialized artifacts.

We have discussed a number of factors that influence the organizational model that is optimal in a particular situation. These factors include geographical distribution, project management maturity, organizational culture, and the type of systems.

Based on an analysis of the four organizational models, we have identified three dimensions that are organizationally relevant: the assets that are considered product family-wide, the levels of responsibility employed in the organization, and the nature of the organizational units.

REFERENCES

Bayer, J., O. Flege, P. Knauber, R. Laqua, D. Muthig, K. Schmid, T. Widen, and J.M. DeBaud. 1999. PuLSE: A methodology to develop software product lines. In *Symposium on Software Reuse,* 122–131. New York: ACM Press.

Bosch, J. 1999. Product-line architectures in industry: A case study. In *Proceedings of the 21st International Conference on Software Engineering,* 544–554. New York: ACM Press.

———. 2000. *Design and Use of Software Architectures: Adopting and Evolving a Product-Line Approach.* Harlow, UK:Addison-Wesley.

Clements, P., and L. Northrop. 2002. *Software Product Lines : Practices and Patterns.* Harlow, UK: Addison-Wesley.

Dikel, D., D. Kane, S. Ornburn, W. Loftus, and J. Wilson. 1997. Applying software product-line architecture. *IEEE Computer* (August): 49–55.

Jacobsen, I., M. Griss, and P. Jönsson. 1997. *Software Reuse: Architecture, Process and Organization for Business Success.* Harlow, UK:Addison-Wesley.

Macala, R.R., L.D. Stuckey, and D.C. Gross. 1996. Managing domain-specific product-line development. *IEEE Software* 13, no. 3 (May): 57–67.

McIlroy, M.D. 1969. Mass produced software components. In *Software Engineering, NATO Science Committee,* ed. P. Naur and B. Randell, 138–150. Garmisch, Germany: NATO Science Committee.

Svahnberg, M., and J. Bosch. 1999. Evolution in software product lines: Two cases. *Journal of Software Maintenance* 11, no. 6: 391–422.

Chapter 9

BUSINESS ENGINEERING OF COMPONENT-BASED SYSTEMS

Marijn Janssen and René W. Wagenaar

Abstract: Component-based information systems focus on building information systems by combining and matching predeveloped components and leveraging the investments in legacy systems. Although component-based systems have many advantages, most organizations are reluctant to adopt them. Many companies do not understand the opportunities and advantages of component-based systems and lack sufficient insight into how to identify components and align them with business processes.

Business engineering approaches are crucial for aligning information systems within their organizations' context, assessing the value of information systems, and communicating implications to stakeholders. The business engineering approach aims at defining business processes, mapping processes to components, evaluating the pros and cons of component-based systems, and helping stakeholders to create a shared understanding. This chapter presents a business engineering approach aimed at formulating, specifying, and evaluating organizational and technological aspects of component-based systems within a particular organizational context.

The approach is described, applied, and tested in a case study. A simulation is used to demonstrate visually how a component-based architecture could allow for more flexible, customer-driven service provisioning as opposed to the current situation. The case study highlights (1) the need for identifying components based on existing and future business processes and interdependencies between tasks in business processes, and (2) the need for modeling and visualizing technical infrastructure, applications, components, and business processes along with their interdependencies.

Keywords: Business Engineering, Component-Based Development, Organizational and Technological Aspects, Architecture

INTRODUCTION

Modern organizations operate within a continually changing environment and are subject to constant adaptation of their business processes and technologies in order to reduce their operational costs. However, organizations and their supporting information systems are seldom structured. On the contrary, most of today's business structures and processes have not been designed at all, but have emerged over time. This has led to the existence within organizations of unrelated and fragmented computer applications with overlapping functionality and content. In response, the concept of component-based information systems appeared, aimed at enabling reuse of functionality, reduced development times, and cost reductions. With the advent of Web services technology, it is possible to create components deployed as services that are modular, easy to access, well described, implementation-independent, and interoperable (Fremantle 2002). Once developed to support one business process, the same component can be reused in various other business processes; moreover, new business processes can be constructed within a shorter time by combining and matching predeveloped components.

The component concept is a very generic and most diversely defined term, referring to many different types and levels of software. Components can be either coarse- or fine-grained and used at different levels of information systems development. Fine-grained components are small-sized, capturing source code; coarse-grained components are large, encapsulating complete business functions or complex systems. Current methods address components usually in a fine-grained connotation and provide little or no support for mapping business architectures to component-based software architectures (Arsanjani 2002). In this chapter we look at coarse-grained components supporting businesses to create a flexible and adaptive architecture.

Although various companies already use component-based systems, most organizations are relatively slow in adopting such approaches. This is mainly due to the difficulties related to the identification of components and the assessment of the organizational implications of the adoption of component-based approaches. Experiences show that the component paradigm hinges to a large extent on the enterprise business context (Arsanjani 2002), where the linking of business processes and information systems is essential (Lee et al. 2003). Business engineering can be viewed as the integral design of both organizational structures and information systems and aims at aligning information systems and the organizational context (Fan et al. 2000; Janssen et al. 2002; Meel 1994). As such, a business engineering approach should help decision makers gain insight into the possibilities and implications of a component-based system. Business engineering of component-based systems has, however, received little or no theoretical and methodological support. Therefore, in this chapter, we will develop and discuss a business engineering approach for developing component-based systems. The business engineering method should align business processes and software components and provide insight into the implications for stakeholders.

The following section discusses two issues: deriving coarse-grained components and providing insight into the implications, targeted by our business engineering approach. In the third section, we describe the foundations of this approach by discussing the way of working and the way to identify components, along with modeling and visualization support. The modeling described in this chapter is based on simulation and is used to understand and visualize the behavior of existing information systems and organizations. Thus, simulation is used as a means to study the impact of component-based information systems on organizations. In the fourth section, we apply and test the business engineering approach in a case study. In the case study opportunities for components in the information and communication technology (ICT) architecture of municipalities are derived. The existing and "to be" situations (with components) are simulated and visualized. Our approach shows that a component-based architecture could allow for a more flexible, customer-driven service provisioning in contrast to the use of monolithic applications supporting business processes. Components can be used for building information systems supporting all kinds of processes and services and can be reused by other municipalities. In the fifth section, we draw conclusions and finally, in the last section, discuss implications for future research and business practice.

ISSUES IN BUSINESS ENGINEERING OF COMPONENT-BASED SYSTEMS

There are two important characteristics of components (Budgen 2003). The first is that they are commonly based upon well-defined functionality, making it easy to identify and search for suit-

Figure 9.1   **Design Phases and Stakeholder Involvement**

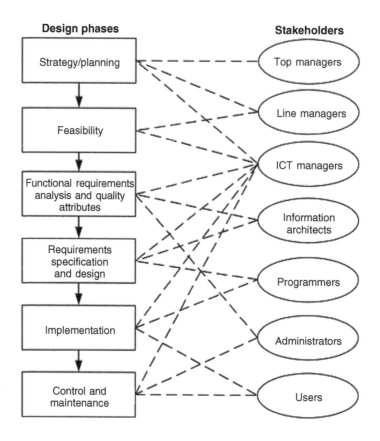

able components. The second characteristic is that components have well-defined interfaces, which enable the substitution of one component for another one. Component-based systems are largely driven by the concepts of reusability and openness (Crnkovic and Larsson 2001). The reuse concept can appear in two distinct ways. On the one hand, components can be developed to support a particular business process and can be reused to support many other business processes. On the other hand, within a component-based architecture a legacy system can be integrated and therefore the functionality and data in such a system can be reused. When existing systems are considered as components providing certain functionality, component-based systems can leverage investments in legacy systems (Arsanjani 2002). Enterprises do not want to get rid of their mission-critical legacy systems, as these are often reliable systems that required large investments and amounts of resources.

In many cases, component-based systems are intended to be a replacement or extension of existing systems. Such a design project starts by formulating a strategy and ultimately leads to the implementation and maintenance of an information system. The main design phases as identified by Kontonya and Sommerville (1998) are shown on the left side of Figure 9.1. Strategy planning is the decision to replace or enhance information systems. The results of the strategy process are often vague and require further detailing; moreover, the feasibility of such a system, the resources necessary, and the impact on existing systems should be determined. Thus a business case capturing the use of current systems, the new functionality offered by components, and the pros and cons should be made. This requires a thorough analysis of the existing situation. The next steps are the analysis of requirements and the specification and design of the ideal situation and the steps to be taken to realize this ideal situation. The requirements and design should lead to a successful implementation of the future system. Control and maintenance services are necessary to keep the system running. A business engineering approach is only one, however crucial, phase of the total life cycle of a component-based development project and is focused on bridging the gap between high-level strategy planning and feasibility, on the one hand, and functional requirements analysis on the other hand.

Rather than using the classic waterfall approach to system development, component-based systems are designed by analyzing the existing systems and by examining available components to see how they meet the requirements for identifying opportunities for improvements (Brown 2000). This is a highly iterative and interactive process of refining the requirements to match existing components of vendors and deciding which of the components can be best integrated to provide the necessary functionality. Currently, there is little or no support for defining business processes and then mapping them to component-based systems (Arsanjani 2002; Levi and Arsanjani 2002). Consequently, our business engineering approach has to address this issue.

As with any information systems development process, the design of component-based systems requires interactions and discussions between all kinds of heterogeneous stakeholders. Not only are designers and programmers involved, but also system integrators, information architects, investors, marketing investigators, and managers (Janssen et al. 2002). An example of stakeholders and their relationship with the design phases is shown in Figure 9.1. These stakeholders have varying backgrounds and their ICT knowledge can range from limited or no ICT knowledge to highly specific knowledge. Some stakeholders might have a natural resistance to or distrust of new initiatives, while others might not have enough technical knowledge to be able to discuss opportunities and implications. Stakeholders might be interested in different aspects, like advantages for the operational processes or customer value or ICT control and maintenance. All these actors are interested in different aspects of the system; however, they have the same goal to design a system and need to cooperate with each other.

Successful implementation requires strong communication, coordination, and cooperation between ICT and business personnel (Lee et al. 2003). Currently, most organizations lack sufficient insight into the possible opportunities and implications of component-based systems (Fan et al. 2000), and no support is available to communicate implications to stakeholders (Janssen et al. 2002). Existing business engineering approaches already provide support for visualization and communication of the implications of business processes of ICT (Janssen 2001; Meel 1994; Sol 1982). As such they provide a good starting point for a business engineering approach, as it is often argued that a business engineering approach should allow decision makers to focus on the relevant issues for designing component-based information systems (Sol 1982). Our business engineering approach supports the creation of a common understanding to enable discussions among heterogeneous types of stakeholders and to visualize the implications of component-based systems on their business.

A BUSINESS ENGINEERING APPROACH

There is no widespread definition of business engineering, although most people have an intuitive notion of the concept. The basic idea of business engineering is the integral design of both orga-

Figure 9.2   **Problem-Solving Cycle**

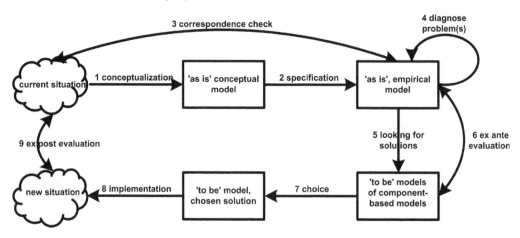

nizational structures and information systems (Meel 1994). In this respect, business engineering can be seen as consciously designing solutions to real-life organizational problems in a structured way. In the preceding section, we discussed main issues that need to be addressed by business engineering of component-based systems. In this section, we discuss how our business engineering approach deals with the identified issues.

Way of Working

The way of working concerns the steps taken in a business engineering approach to identify functionality of components, create a shared understanding, and show the implications of a component-based system. Business engineering involves in the first place understanding the current way organizations operate. This understanding should lead to the identification of problems or opportunities for improvement. The way of working is based on a problem-solving cycle (Mitroff et al. 1974; Sol 1982). A problem-solving approach can result in a clear understanding of the problem situation and the set of potential solutions to the problem under study. The problem-solving cycle consists of nine interactive activities divided into an understanding phase (activities 1–3) and a design phase (activities 4–9), as depicted in Figure 9.2. In an actual design effort, work will be carried out simultaneously at different levels of detail. Several activities can be conducted in parallel and possibly during several iterations and cycles.

The understanding phase starts with the first activity, the conceptualization of the problem situation (1), including the existing information systems, human activities, and organizational processes. The next activity is the specification of the problem situation (2) in order to construct a descriptive empirical model of the problem situation that can be experimented with to obtain quantitative results of the analysis and a diagnosis of the problem situation. The third activity is a correspondence check (3), which is aimed at validation of the descriptive empirical model.

The fourth activity initiates the design phase and is concerned with diagnosing the problem (4). Based on the diagnosis, alternative solutions can be formulated (5). These alternatives are worked out in "to be" models of possible solutions. In the ex ante evaluation (6), these "to be" models of possible solutions are experimented with to evaluate their quantitative and/or qualitative performance in comparison with the "as is" model of the current situation. The "to be" models of possible solutions can also be compared with each other. The final activities are the actual choice (7), implementation of the preferred solution (8), and the expost evaluation to validate the modeling effort (9).

During the problem-solving cycle, the original problem situation is reformulated a number of times and looked at from different points of view. In this way an interdisciplinary approach is created. An important aspect is the generation of one or more alternatives and the selection of that alternative that is better or best according to some kind of criterion. A problem-solving perspective can be used to tackle the problem situation, as there are many opportunities for components having different functionalities and granularity, and which alternative arrangements have the most advantages, and the possible need for reengineering of organizational processes, are not known. Decision making can be supported by comparing the benefits and disadvantages of "to be" models using a component-based information system with the "as is" model of the existing situation and by comparing various "to be" models of possible solutions with each other.

Component Identification

One of the main issues in designing component-based systems is that component identification and boundary definition are often a highly intuitive process, which can have ambiguous outcomes. Rather than relying only on experience and intuition, organizations should take a more structured, reliable approach that recognizes organizational characteristics and addresses the need for the commitment and contribution of stakeholders.

Often, use cases are proposed for identifying components; however, use cases are essentially a functional concept (Levi and Arsanjani 2002). As such they do not take into account the business processes consisting of tasks and dependencies between activities. Parnas (1972) proposes criteria for decomposing systems into modules and recommends that systems should be decomposed along lines encapsulating design decisions. Parnas looks primarily at identifying fine-grained modules at a software level. Levi and Arsanjani (2002) propose a systematic method where a goal-oriented model of a business is first created and then mapped to a component-based software architecture. They use business use cases to guide the decompositions of the business domain. Parnas (1972) and Levi and Arsanjani (2002) partition systems into the functional areas of the business. Major limitations of their approaches are as follows:

- They assume that there is a stable business environment, whereas business goals are agreed on by heterogeneous types of stakeholders.
- They assume that a component boundary is independent of the interdependencies between tasks that make up business processes.
- They do not look at existing components within an organization or components readily available from software vendors.
- They do not capitalize on stakeholders' knowledge and experience.

To ensure that coarse-grained components, supporting the business, are constructed in a traceable and demonstrable fashion during the information system's life cycle, organizations need to have explicit relationships between (1) components and existing legacy systems, (2) components and existing business processes, and (3) components and future business processes. Enterprises have typically invested vast amounts of resources to develop and maintain legacy systems, and it is critical to incorporate these resources into future systems. An approach should leverage the investments in legacy systems by analyzing the existing applications as components.

Components should be sufficiently general to cover the different aspects of their use; at the same time they must be concrete and simple enough to serve a particular task in an efficient way. Component boundaries should be defined in terms of tasks within business processes, which provide a natural, large-grained boundary that maps well to functional areas. We propose to identify components by making an explicit mapping between tasks in business processes and components, independent of the organizational structures containing functional departments. It is necessary to analyze how components can support individual tasks and which component functionality is required. This is similar to the approach proposed by Levi and Arsanjani (2002); however, they do not take into account the interdependencies between the tasks ("business use cases" in their terms). For example, they do not take into account that a number of highly interdependent tasks should be supported using one component to ensure simple relationships between components and that tasks having low interdependencies with other tasks can easily be supported using a single component. Considering interrelationships between tasks is crucial; therefore, business processes should be analyzed by modeling such interdependencies.

To support the identification of components per task, we derived five intuitive, appealing design guidelines: (1) information should be captured only once at the source and reused by other components, (2) communication between components should be kept to a minimum, (3) there should be a central process control component integrating business process steps with functionality provided by components, (4) the component should, whenever possible, be offered as reliable and proven commercial off-the-shelf (COTS) software products supplied by a vendor, and (5) a component should capture a business function.

Traditional software development often takes a top-down approach (Sametinger 1997), and the proposed approach described above is also top-down. Although we identified a structured method and design guidelines, the identification of components and boundary definition is still an intuitive process that requires the contribution of human experience and knowledge. To include these aspects, the structured top-down approach is combined with a bottom-up approach. In this way a middle-out approach is created. This type of approach is structured, but also takes into account the variety of stakeholders' knowledge and experiences. This knowledge is capitalized and contributes to the development process. Stakeholders can provide valuable information about the changing demands of the business environment, components readily available on the market, vendor characteristics, preferred suppliers, and commonly made mistakes in component-based development.

Modeling and Visualization Support

Modeling support is crucial for effective business engineering (Law and Kelton 1991; Sol 1982). The key issue in modeling is the choice of phenomena to include and to omit. Modeling should capture the essential requirements, but avoid presenting so much detail that decision makers and other participants require too much effort and time to understand the models. The visualization of a model plays an essential part in the communication process and can provide a reference for discussing opportunities and implications.

Existing information systems, components, and existing and hypothetical business processes and their dependencies should be modeled for supporting the identification of components. The dependencies between elements at different architectural levels—for example, organizational, process, application, and technical infrastructure—should also be included and modeled to create a complete architectural picture incorporating all constraints. Figure 9.3 shows the various layers, along with dependencies between and within layers. The process and application levels need to be modeled in detail; the other layers can be modeled at a lower level of abstraction.

Figure 9.3 **Architectural Levels**

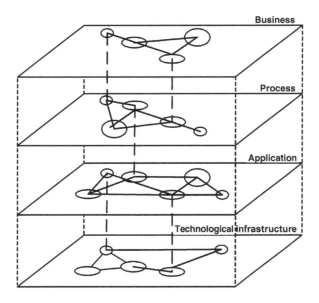

Different stakeholders have different objectives, concerns, perceptions, knowledge, skills, and means of expression. Design completeness and adequacy require that all relevant viewpoints be captured and eventually integrated. Visualization can help translate the outcomes of the model into explanations, conclusions, recommendations, and requirements (Vreede and Verbraeck 1996). Visualization can therefore be used for critical debate about the fit between information systems and organizational processes and as a means to involve and commit stakeholders to contribute to the process with their experience.

Simulation of business processes constitutes one of the most widely used applications of operations research, as it allows us to understand the essence of business systems, to identify opportunities for change, and to evaluate the effect of proposed changes on key performance indicators (Law and Kelton 1991; Shannon 1975). Discrete-event simulation means that the time aspects are modeled (Pegden et al. 1994). The philosophy behind simulation is to develop a dynamic model of the problem situation, experiment with this model, and experiment with alternatives for the problem situation (Sol 1982). Animation is often a standard feature of a simulation language (Swain 1999). As such, simulation is a suitable instrument for our purposes as it provides support for modeling and visualizing the interdependencies between and within the architecture layers. An animation model is a graphical model of both a problem situation and of a simulation of that situation (Vreede and Verbraeck 1996). An animation model's static part consists of representations of the relevant aspect of the problem situation and the simulation model with a static background. Its dynamic part depicts status-changes over time.

CASE STUDY

Dutch municipalities are free to design their information architecture and to choose appropriate software vendors. Within municipalities, departments can buy their own applications for each process. As a result, municipalities have a highly fragmented ICT architecture, consisting of legacy systems for each of the 290 products they offer. Examples of the 290 products are driver's license renewal, garbage collection, building licenses, rent subsidies, and social security services. To ensure a uniform structure between municipalities, the products are standardized and divided into eleven categories: (1) building and living, (2) life environment and safety, (3) life, traveling, and documents, (4) complaints, reporting and procedures, (5) environment and garbage, (6) entrepreneur, (7) education, (8) sports and culture, (9) traffic and transportation, (10) labor and income, and (11) health and welfare. The legacy systems supporting these products and services are often monolithic packages that are extremely difficult to reconfigure and to integrate with applications developed by other vendors. Each of these systems offers the same basic functionality. A similar problem arises between municipalities. The roughly 500 municipalities in the Netherlands have developed and implemented their own information systems independently. Information systems within one municipality offer similar functionalities as the systems in other municipalities. As yet, there is no coordination aimed at reusing systems or functionality.

The existence of isolated, highly fragmented, and unrelated computerized applications, overlapping in functionality and content, within the same public organization has resulted in a major reuse problem and has led to isolated islands of technology while information systems were viewed as being internal to the public organizations. As technology continues to evolve at an accelerating rate, nontrivial hardware and software will remain diverse and heterogeneous. The various legacy applications for the 290 products offered by the municipalities have grown over time, meaning that hardware and applications purchased years ago *must* interoperate with those purchased today and tomorrow. Driving factors such as multichannel support, the need for communication between back and front office and with external systems, and the call for a more customer-oriented organization create a need for a more interoperable and flexible system that can meet these future requirements efficiently and effectively.

Component-based systems seem to provide a solution to this problem and as such need to be investigated. For this purpose, the information managers of the Dutch cities have joined forces in a cross-municipality information-management council. This council initiated the "AnalysePilot" aimed at designing a functional architecture to provide guidance for the development of a component-based architecture and to determine the feasibility of component-based development (CBD). This should be accomplished by creating a shared, accepted vision of a component-based architecture and by making a business case aimed at supporting management in its decision making about the potential use of a component-based architecture. Management needs to be convinced of the system's flexibility in supporting existing and hypothetical future processes, the reuse of functionality for various products in different municipalities, and the incorporation of and gradual replacement of functionality offered by legacy systems. Animation will be used to familiarize management with the complex situation with and without the use of components.

Model Conceptualization and Specification

In our business engineering approach, we concluded that there is a need for having an explicit relationship between (1) components and existing legacy systems, (2) components and existing business processes, and (3) components and future business processes. We started our process analysis by modeling the tasks for one particular process found to be simple, understandable, and representative of other processes: the renewal of driver's licenses. The existing process is shown on the left side of Figure 9.4 and a hypothetical future process for online renewal is shown on the right side.

In the current process, a citizen goes to the counter of the town hall and requests a new driver's

Figure 9.4   **Mapping Components Onto Business Processes**

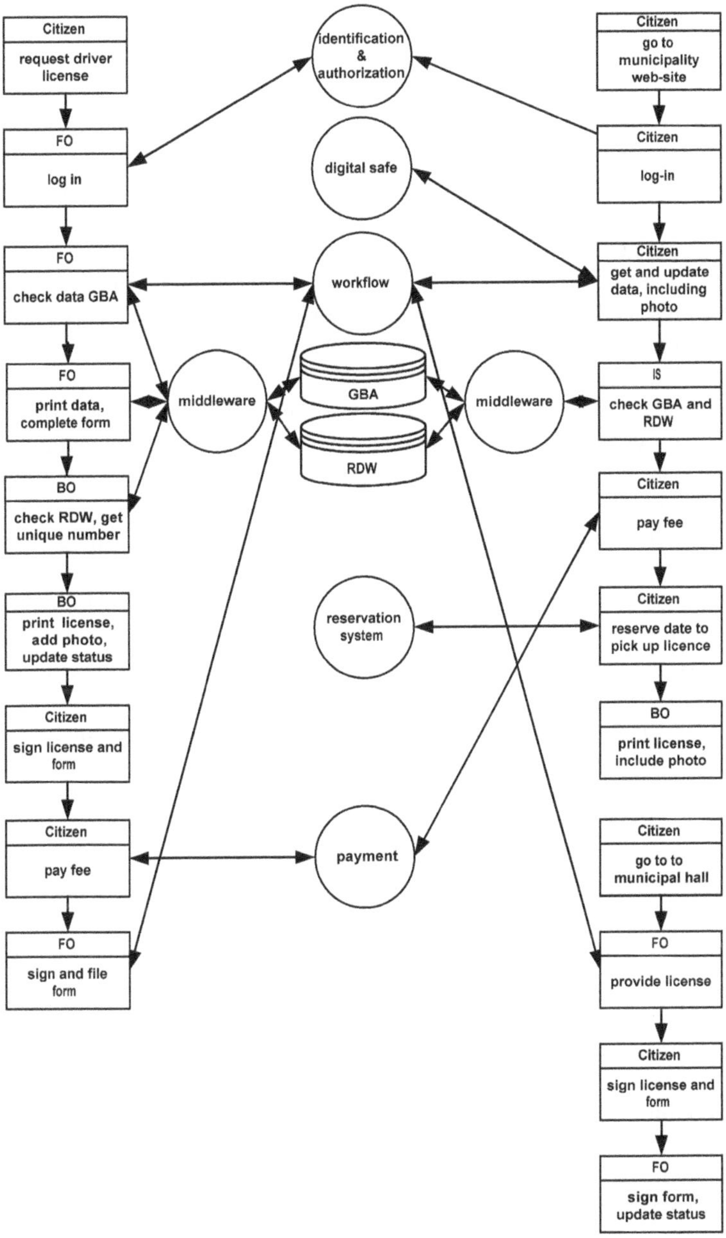

license. The front-office employee, abbreviated as FO, requests the old driver's license and other official papers and logs into the legacy information system. The FO requests data about the citizen from the GBA (in Dutch: Gemeentelijk Basis Administratie). The GBA is the Dutch authenticated registry of data about all residents living in a particular city or village. This registry contains citizens' data such as name, address, date of birth, sex, nationality, and so on. Many applications, such as passport or driver's license renewal requests, use data stored in the GBA and consequently need to communicate with the GBA. The FO compares the information in the old driver's license or other official papers with the information stored in the GBA. When the information is found to be valid, the FO prints the data on paper and fills in additional information from the existing driver's license. The FO gives this form to the back-office employee, abbreviated as BO. The BO enters the data on a terminal that is connected to the information system of the RDW (in Dutch: RijksDienst voor Wegverkeer). The RDW is the agency responsible for the central, nationwide registry of information about drivers living in the Netherlands. The RDW checks the data with the data in its own system. When the data are approved, the RDW sends a message to the BO containing a new unique driver's license number. The BO uses this unique number to print the information on a preprinted driver's license. After printing, the BO adds the passport photo on the license and brings the license to the FO. The FO employee checks the information again, asks the citizen to sign to acknowledge receipt, asks for payment, signs the delivery receipt, and finally files the information.

The component-based architecture under study should align the structure of the municipalities' processes to the demand for services for current ("as is") as well as potential future ("to be") situations. The future situation should allow citizens to request a driver's license online using the Internet. The tasks for the online request handling are shown on the right hand side of Figure 9.4. A citizen logs into the municipality Web site and enters data, including a digital photo, or gets the data from a digital safe. The information system (IS) automatically checks the entered data with the GBA and RDW. When the request is accepted, the citizen is asked to pay the fee and to reserve a date to pick up the license. The BO gets all the necessary data, prepares the license, and stores it so it is available for the FO. On the reserved date and time slot, the citizen arrives at the FO, signs the license, and takes it away.

The Arena simulation tool was used to develop a simulation and animation model of the existing situation was built by the developer. The correspondence with the existing situation was checked. A screenshot of this model is shown in Figure 9.5. The screenshot shows the employees and systems in the back office at the top right of the model. The front office employees and information systems are shown in the middle, below the front office. Citizens waiting in the municipality hall are shown at the bottom. The left of the model shows the existing external systems, RDW, VROM, and GBA, and the relationship to the FO and BO applications. When playing the simulation, the time-dependent interactions, such as messages sent between the systems, are shown. Communication time between information systems is too short to be visible in a simulation; therefore, a time delay is used to visualize the movement of messages and data packages between information systems.

Diagnosis and Solution Finding

The processes in the "as is" and "to be" situations were further analyzed to identify components using the approach described in the preceding section. Our business engineering methodology leverages the investments in legacy systems by analyzing the existing applications as components, linking them to business processes and expanding the functionality by adding new components. Components were identified by mapping components on tasks and taking into account the dependencies with other tasks and using our design guidelines. The resulting components and the mapping are shown in Figure 9.4, and the components will be discussed hereafter.

Figure 9.5 **Screenshot of the Simulation Model of the Current Situation**

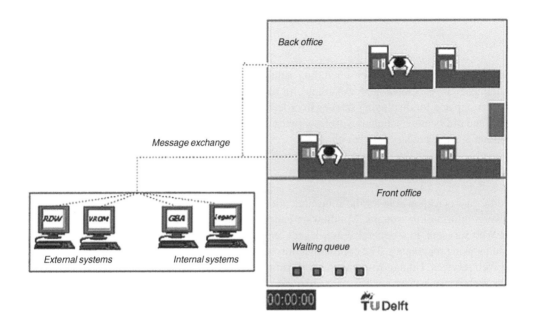

Identification and Authorization

With the identification component, citizens or employees in the BO and FO can identify themselves in order to get access to the other components. Identification can be implemented using a user name and password, but also using a chip card or biometrical method. Other components can ask the identification component for authorization data. The authorization, the provision of access to the functionality of a component, stays within each component itself. For example, when a user wants to get data from the digital safe, the digital safe component sends a request for information about the identification to the identification and authorization component. The digital safe component decides to permit access based on the information received from the identification and authorization component. The advantage of this construction is that the identification and authorization component does not need to store all data about authorization rules per component. In this way, cumbersome maintenance and control procedures can be avoided. This procedure follows our design guideline to store data at the source and reuse it in other processes.

Authorization is dependent not only on the role of a person, but also on the level of identification. For example, somebody identified using biometrics might get more access rights (e.g., update GBA) than somebody identified using only a username and password.

Digital Safe

The digital safe is a component that allows citizens to store and reuse personal and private data. The citizen has authorized access to all kinds of personal data, such as address, marriage status, employment, medical information, and insurance information, in this component and can provide permission to others to retrieve (some) data stored in the safe. In this way, data have to be entered only once and can be reused by authorizing access. The identification and animation of this component has led to discussions about the possible offering of a digital safe by government to all citizens in the Netherlands.

Workflow

The workflow is responsible for scheduling sequences of tasks and for controlling the use of other components. It is responsible, for example, for requesting identification first before proceeding to the next step and for displaying screens in order. Moreover, this component signals delays, sends alerts, and offers other standard workflow functionality. It also provides information about which documents are necessary for specific tasks.

Middleware

Middleware is responsible for the communication between humans and information systems and between information systems. Middleware can be implemented using messaging, Web servers, and Web services. In a general sense, legacy information systems can communicate with other systems using messaging. The communication with state-of-the-art components can be done using Web services. Human-to-computer (information system) interaction can be implemented using a Web server.

Messaging exchanges data between systems such as legacy systems and components without any human intervention. A messaging application translates data formats into other data formats and asynchronously exchanges data based on message queuing. When an information system is not available, the messaging component can queue messages and submit the message at another time when the receiving component is available. The data formats are stored in the messaging application, so that control and maintenance of these formats can be done at one (central) location.

Human-to-computer communication proceeds using Web servers. The human user interacts with the server using a client application, such as a Web browser, based on a request-response protocol.

Reservation System

A reservation system can be used to let citizens schedule an appointment with a government representative or department. Employees provide data about their availability for appointments and citizens use the reservation system to make appointments. A citizen can also get a confirmation of the appointment, once an employee has accepted it. Reserving time slots allows people to avoid long waiting queues at offices at the municipal hall. Instead, citizens can go directly to the office at the agreed time and be served immediately.

Payment

The payment component is responsible for financial settlement of the service provision. The goal was not to use a component, but to use a service provider offering this functionality. An external payment provider should take care of the execution of the financial settlement after receiving a minimum amount of data (amount, reference, municipality, and client data). Third parties like Bibit (www.bibit.nl/) and BNG (www.bng.nl/) in the Netherlands offer various forms of payment. They can take over the full responsibility for financial settlement after obtaining the necessary data and take care of sending reminders and even other means for obtaining payments.

Figure 9.6 **Screenshot of the Simulation Model Including Components**

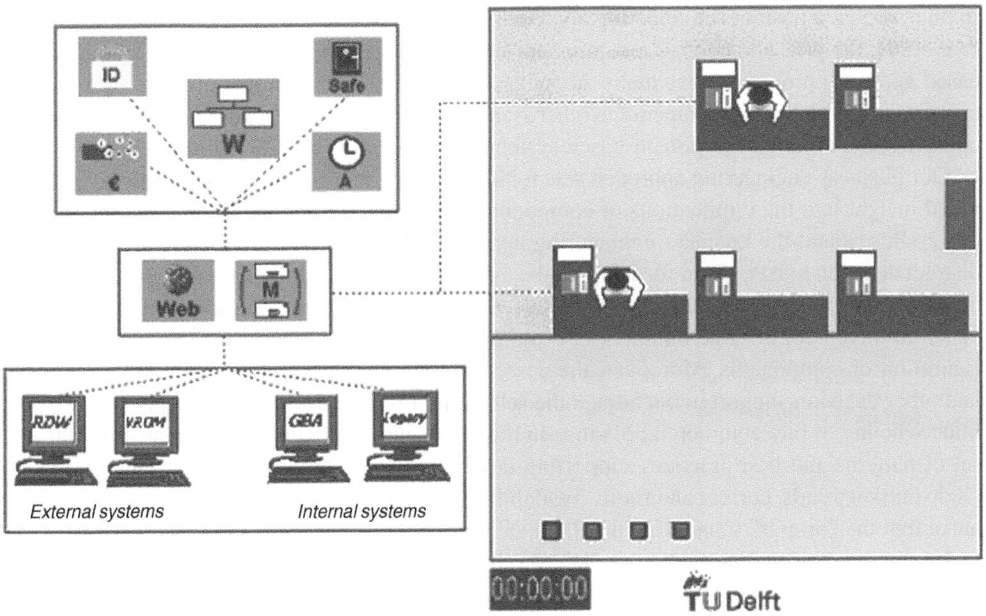

The following step was to build a "to be" model including a component-based architecture for service provisioning. A screenshot of this model is shown in Figure 9.6. The "as is" model is expanded toward an open, flexible, component-based architecture. The simulation is aimed at showing the business case for an open, flexible, component-based ICT architecture. The simulation model shows that components and legacy applications, developed at different times and by different software vendors, can work together. Therefore, investments in legacy systems can be protected. By just plugging in new components, organizations can make changes easily.

The functions of the components were simulated to ascertain that the model was independent of specific implementations. The model provided support to discuss the functionality of the software components. In this way the functional requirements were validated using the various expertise and disciplines of the actors involved.

Choice and Implementation

By means of the models, the quality attributes of the architecture were assessed in relation to the quality requirements. More flexibility is created as (1) new components can be added to and (2) existing components can be replaced in the simulated architecture; the simulation showed that (3) the current process and (4) a potential future process for requesting a driver's license could be supported with generic components. The information managers agreed that more flexibility would be created since new components can be added to and existing components can be replaced in such architectures. The managers also became aware that it is important that a component's interface to the outside world should be clearly defined and decoupled from its implementation. Coordination of the development of standards and architecture can facilitate such an approach.

IMPLICATIONS FOR RESEARCH AND PRACTICE

In this chapter, a business engineering approach was discussed and applied in a case study. In the case study, the pros and cons of a component-based approach were evaluated and a component-based approach proved to have many advantages. This does not mean that in all cases a component-based system would be superior to other systems. A future research goal should be to determine under what conditions component-based systems are superior to traditional development.

Our business engineering approach was focused on the identification of components and provided insight into the implications of component-based systems. Focusing on other characteristics could expand the business engineering approach presented here; however, this should not distract decision makers from focusing on the essential elements. Other characteristics that could be explicitly considered in a business engineering approach are relationships between components, involvement of large numbers of cross-organizational processes, and the reuse and configuration of components. Moreover, the case study showed the need for methods, guidelines, and other decision support to encourage the selection of best-of-breed components and to determine whether to buy commercial off-the-shelf components or develop components in-house. A set of patterns and best practices supporting developers could be very helpful. This should include market trends, current and future availability of components, and, moreover, a way to guarantee that the "proper" standard will still be valid in five, ten, or fifteen years.

In our business engineering approach, the focus was on coarse-grained, high-level components, legacy systems, their interrelations, and business processes and sequences of activities. An approach suitable for designing fine-grained components may benefit from the business engineering approach discussed in this chapter. The approach may require additional concepts that can be identified in future research. Our approach stopped with the identification of functional components. To complete the life cycle, further steps need to be added to capture, analyze, and design component interfaces, data structures, and algorithms. The translation from abstract components to concrete, implemented components has not been addressed yet. Future research can address the translation of an abstract to implementation model.

CONCLUSION

Organizations have been reluctant to adopt component-based systems. A business engineering approach can provide insight into the opportunities and implications of such systems. We have proposed a business engineering approach aimed at (1) defining and identifying components and (2) evaluating the pros and cons of component-based systems. The approach was tested in a case study.

We found that the identification of components needs to take into account the complex relationships between legacy systems, components, existing business processes, and hypothetical future business processes. Components can be identified by mapping components on tasks and by explicitly taking into account the interdependencies with other tasks. We also introduced a number of design guidelines to support this process which proved to be effective for deriving components in our case study. A structured approach to component identification is not enough; stakeholders' knowledge and experiences need to be capitalized and should also contribute to this process.

Simulation and visualization were used to involve stakeholders, to enable discussions, and to provide insight into the implications of component-based systems. We found that an animation model should capture various architectural layers, including the business process, application and technical infrastructures layers, and their dependencies. Animation was a suitable instrument to facilitate communication between stakeholders and to make plausible that a component-based system would be better than building a large new system and replacing old systems based on a number of quality attributes. More flexibility was created because (1) new components can be added to and (2) existing components can be replaced in such architectures; the simulation showed that (3) the current process and (4) a potential future process for requesting a driver's license using multiple channels could be supported with generic components.

During the case study, the approach proved to be effective. The approach does not offer a universal guarantee for success, however, since many other factors can influence the outcomes and success is dependent on the contribution of the knowledge and experience of stakeholders.

REFERENCES

Arsanjani, A. 2002. Developing and integrating enterprise components and services. *Communications of the ACM* 45, no. 10: 31–34.

Brown A.W. 2000. *Component-Based Development for the Enterprise.* Englewood Cliffs, NJ: Prentice Hall.

Budgen, D. 2003. *Software Design.* Harlow, UK: Addison-Wesley.

Crnkovic, I., and M. Larsson. 2001. Challenges of component-based development. *Journal of Systems and Software* 61, no. 3: 201–212.

Cross, N. 1994. *Engineering Design Methods.* Chichester, UK: Wiley.

Fan, M., J. Stallaert, and A.B. Whinston. 2000. The adoption and design methodologies of component-based enterprise systems. *European Journal of Information Systems* 9, no. 1: 25–35.

Fremantle, P., S. Weerawarana, and R. Khalaf. 2002. Enterprise services: Examining the emerging field of Web services and how it is integrated into existing enterprise infrastructures. *Communications of the ACM* 45, no. 20: 77–82.

Janssen, M. 2001. Designing Electronic Intermediaries: An Agent-based Approach for Designing Interorganizational Coordination Mechanisms. PHD diss. Delft University of Technology, Netherlands.

Janssen, M., J. Beerens, and R. Wagenaar. 2002. *Animatie van simulatiemodellen: informatie-architectuur gevisualiseerd.* Informatie, 52–56.

Kontonya, G., and I. Sommerville. 1998. *Requirements Engineering. Processes and Techniques.* Chichester, UK: Wiley.

Law, A.M., and D.W. Kelton. 1991. *Simulation Modeling and Analysis.* New York: McGraw-Hill.

Lee, J., K. Siau, and S. Hong. 2003 Enterprise integration with ERP and EAI. *Communications of the ACM* 46, no. 2: 54–60.

Levi, K., and A. Arsanjani. 2002. A goal-driven approach to enterprise component identification and specification. *Communications of the ACM* 45, no. 10: 45–52.

Meel, J.W. van. 1994. *The Dynamics of Business Engineering: Reflections on Two Case Studies Within the Amsterdam Municipal Police Force.* PhD diss., Delft University of Technology, Netherlands.

Mitroff, I.I., F. Betz, L.R. Pondy, and F. Sagasti. 1974. On managing science in the system age: Two schemes for the study of science as a whole systems phenomenon. *TIMS Interfaces* 4, no. 3: 46–58.

Morisio, M., M. Seaman, C.B. Basili, V.R. Parra, A.T. Kraft, and S.E. Condon. 2002. COTS-based software development: Processes and open issues. *Journal of Systems and Software* 61, no. 3: 189–199.

Parnas, D.L. 1972. On the criteria to be used in decomposing systems into modules. *Communications of the ACM* 15, no. 12: 1053–1058.

Pegden, C.D., R.E. Shannon, and R.P. Sadowski. 1994. *Introduction to Simulation Using SIMAN.* New York: McGraw-Hill.

Sametinger, J. 1997. *Software Engineering with Reusable Components.* Berlin: Springer Verlag.

Shannon, R.E. 1975. *Systems Simulation: The Art and Science.* Englewood Cliffs, NJ: Prentice Hall.

Sol, H.G. 1982. *Simulation in Information Systems Development.* PhD diss., University of Groningen, Netherlands, Netherlands.

Swain, J.W. 1999. Imagine new worlds: 1999 OR/MS today simulation software survey. *OR/MS Today,* 38–51.

Vreede, G.J. de, and A. Verbraeck. 1996. Animating organizational processes: Insight eases change. *Simulation Practice and Theory* 4, no. 4: 245–263.

PART III

COMPONENT-BASED DEVELOPMENT WITH COMMERCIAL OFF-THE-SHELF PRODUCTS

CHAPTER 10

SELECTING COMMERCIAL
OFF-THE-SHELF PRODUCTS

HARETON K.N. LEUNG

Abstract: Use of commercial off-the-shelf (COTS) products has become a popular software development trend. The success of a COTS-based development project is highly dependent on the ability of selecting the most appropriate COTS without using a relatively large effort. In this chapter, we will first identify the basic strategies in COTS product selection: best-fit and first-fit strategies. Then, we describe the key challenges in selecting COTS products and present the common evaluation techniques used for COTS products. We will review several direct assessment selection methods, such as the off-the-shelf option, COTS-based integrated system development, procurement-oriented requirements engineering, COTS-based requirements engineering, the infrastructure incremental development approach, and the comparative evaluation process. Strengths and weaknesses of these COTS selection methods will be compared. The indirect assessment method named domain-based COTS product selection method will be introduced and applied to a case study concerning the development of an online margin-trading system for a large, leading bank in Hong Kong using COTS products. The case study will demonstrate that the indirect assessment method reduces the complexity and improves the efficiency of COTS product selection.

Keywords: Commercial Off-the-Shelf Products, Selection Methods, Direct Assessment, Indirect Assessment

INTRODUCTION

Use of commercial off-the-shelf (COTS) products has become a popular software development trend. Shrinking budgets, rapid advancement of COTS development, and the increasing demands of large systems are the key drivers for the adoption of the COTS development approach. According to Jane's report, the United States, several western European countries, and Australia have made COTS mandatory in their defense industry (Jane's Information Group 2000). Some Asian countries are also following this lead. For example, a study analyzed fifteen COTS projects, performed at the Flight Dynamics Division at the Goddard Space Flight Center of NASA (Morisio et al. 2000).

A COTS product is defined as an independent unit that provides a set of related functions and is suitable for reuse. COTS products are "things that one can buy, ready-made, from some manufacturer's virtual store shelf (e.g., through a catalog or from a price list)" (Oberndorf 1997). COTS products should be available at a reasonable cost. Examples of COTS products include Graphical User Interface (GUI) builders, e-mail and messaging systems, and inventory control systems.

COTS products are different from software components in terms of their completeness. A software component is defined as a unit of composition with contractually specified interfaces and explicit context dependencies only. A software component can be deployed independently and is subject to composition by third parties (Szyperski 1997). In this chapter, we treat components as units that provide a single function.

A COTS product can be viewed as a coarse-grained component that provides a larger set of functions than a typical component. A COTS product may represent a subsystem, while a component generally represents a finer-grain entity.

A system that adopts COTS products to provide some of the required functionalities is called a COTS-based system (CBS). Compared with traditional software development, CBS development promises faster delivery with lower resource costs. The shift from custom development to CBS is occurring in both new application development projects and maintenance projects. Rather than building the whole system from scratch, a new system can be assembled and constructed by using existing COTS products. For example, COTS products for transaction processing and inventory control can be bought and integrated into an e-commerce system.

Developing a CBS involves selecting the appropriate COTS products, building extensions to satisfy specific requirements, and then gluing the COTS products and the in-house developed units together. It is critical to a project's success that the most appropriate or "right" COTS product is selected. A poor COTS product selection strategy can result in a short list of COTS products that can hardly fulfill the required functionality, and it might also introduce overheads in system integration and maintenance phases. On the other hand, if the effort required to select the appropriate COTS product is too high, then it may offset the benefits in using the CBS development approach. An effective, efficient COTS product selection process is essential to the success of a CBS development.

Selecting the appropriate COTS product is difficult because of the lack of a well-defined selection process, incomplete evaluation, rapid changes in the marketplace, inappropriate result analysis, and a large set of COTS candidates. Many COTS selection methods have been proposed. These methods can be classified into three categories: the intuition approach, the direct assessment approach, and the indirect assessment approach. In the intuition approach, software developers select COTS products according to their experience and intuition. Typically, information on COTS products may come from hands-on experience, witnessing vendor demonstrations, observing a user, and reading third-party literature or vendor's product information. This approach is subjective, with the results that some suitable COTS products may be omitted inadvertently.

Most of the recently proposed COTS product selection methods belong to the direct assessment approach, which selects COTS products directly from their source. Software developers using these methods consider all of the descriptions of the COTS products and then try to make decisions on the products' suitability. These methods all start with a searching phase followed by an evaluation phase that examines both the functional and nonfunctional aspects of the COTS products. Common selection criteria include vendor behavior, functionality, performance, interoperability, architecture, evolution, and quality characteristics such as usability, maintainability, and portability. Although these approaches are more objective than the intuition-based approaches, they are expensive because their efficiency is inversely proportional to the product of the number of modules in the system to be developed and the total number of modules in the candidate COTS products (Leung and Leung 2002). As more and more COTS products are pushed into the market, the time spent on choosing the appropriate COTS products could easily offset the advantages of using them.

In the indirect assessment approach, instead of selecting COTS products based on the information about the COTS, developers use other derived information to short-list the candidates. The domain-based COTS product selection (DBCS) method is an example of the indirect assessment approach, which makes use of domain models (Leung and Leung 2002). A domain model is a generic model of the domain of an application system. It captures all the features and characteristics of the domain. The DBCS method takes advantage of the detailed view of the relations between the available COTS products and the CBS.

The selection processes for COTS products and components are different, since a component that does not satisfy the requirements will not be selected, while a COTS may be selected even if it does not perfectly fit the requirements. A COTS product provides a set of functions, which, compared to the system requirements, may coincide with some of the functions required by the system, along with some additional functions that are not required. In some cases, even if a COTS product does not provide all the required functions, it is selected because there are no better candidates available.

The chapter is structured as follows. The second section identifies the basic strategies in COTS product selection, the key challenges in selecting COTS products, and the common evaluation techniques used for COTS products. The third section reviews the proposed COTS product selection methods. We also comment on their efficiency. The fourth section presents conclusions and research problems.

COTS SELECTION

Strategies

There are two basic strategies for selecting a COTS product, depending on whether the evaluator needs the best available COTS product:

- *Best-fit strategy:* the objective is to identify the *best* COTS product among all the candidates.
- *First-fit strategy:* the objective is to identify the first COTS product that satisfies all the requirements. If no COTS product satisfies all the requirements, then the best product from the available COTS products is selected.

The best-fit strategy will require analyzing all the COTS candidates, whereas the first-fit strategy may require less effort as it will stop once the first COTS candidate that meets the requirements has been identified. However, the first-fit strategy may not identify the best COTS product.

There are three major strategies to COTS evaluation: progressive filtering, keystone identification, and puzzle assembly (Anderson 1989; Maiden and Ncube 2000; Walters 1995; Kunda 2002; Maiden and Cornelius 1998). In progressive filtering a COTS product is selected from a set of potential candidates. This strategy progressively eliminates the candidates that do not satisfy the evaluation criteria. In the keystone selection strategy, a keystone characteristic, such as vendor or operating platform, is chosen before selecting the COTS products. Often, interoperability with the keystone is used to eliminate a large number of other products from consideration. The puzzle assembly strategy is based on the premise that a valid COTS solution will require fitting the various components of the system together as a puzzle. It applies an evolutionary prototyping technique to build versions that are close to the final system.

Challenges of COTS Product Selection

The success of CBS depends on the successful selection of COTS products to fit customer requirements. This activity is difficult for the following reasons.

• *Lack of a well-defined process.* Most organizations are under pressure to complete development as soon as possible and do not follow a well-defined COTS product selection process. Processes for evaluating, comparing, and selecting COTS products are often nonexistent or inconsistent. These deficiencies can reduce confidence in the selection decision and may lead to the use of wrong COTS products that delay a project's development, increase life-cycle costs, and reduce quality.

• *Incomplete evaluation.* Due to the "black box" nature of COTS (lack of access to the COTS internals), it is difficult to understand COTS products and therefore complete evaluation is impossible. Often, the supporting documentation for these products is incomplete or wrong. Testing can be incomplete, as it can only assess the COTS through its interface.

• *Rapid changes in the marketplace.* The user has little or no control over COTS product evolution. Frequent releases of COTS products and rapid changes in the marketplace make evaluation difficult. For example, a new release of the COTS product may remove a required function previously available.

• *Evaluation results may be misinterpreted.* Because there are many criteria that can be used to evaluate COTS products (e.g., reliability, correctness, vendor reputation, and support services), the evaluator may not always use the most appropriate method to consolidate the results. For example, a common approach to consolidating evaluation results is to use some kind of weighted sum method, which relies on knowing the right weighting to match the customer's expectation.

• *Large number of potential COTS products.* As more and more COTS products become available in the market, without an efficient COTS product selection method, the evaluator may require significant effort to identify the right COTS product. This investment reduces the benefit of using COTS products.

Multiple Attribute Decision Making

COTS product selection involves a multiple attribute decision-making (MADM) process. MADM refers to making preference decisions among the available alternatives that are characterized by multiple and possibly conflicting attributes (Yoon and Hwang 1995).

The goals of MADM are (1) to help the decision maker choose the best action or alternative, (2) to identify *better* alternatives among a set of alternatives, and (3) to rank the alternatives in a particular order of preference. MADM techniques share the following characteristics (Yoon and Hwang 1995):

• *Alternatives:* A finite number of alternatives are screened, prioritized, selected, and/or ranked.
• *Multiple attributes:* Each problem has multiple attributes, goals, or criteria. For example, the relevant attributes for buying a test tool may include functionality, cost, and quality.
• *Incommensurable units:* Attributes have different units of measurement.
• *Attribute weights:* Almost all MADM methods require information regarding the relative importance of each attribute, which is usually supplied in an ordinal or cardinal scale.
• *Decision matrix:* A MADM problem can be concisely expressed in a matrix format, where columns indicate attributes and rows list competing alternatives.

A number of MADM techniques have been applied in COTS product selection. The most common are the weighted sum method (Williams 1992), the analytical hierarchy method (Hokey 1992; Kontio 1996; Maiden and Ncube 2000) and outranking method (Anderson 1989; Morisio and Tsoukiàs 1997).

The weighted sum method (WSM) is based on the multiple attribute utility theory that any decision maker attempts implicitly to maximize some function by aggregating all the different points of view (Vincke 1992). A score is obtained by adding contributions from each alternative. Since two items with different measurement units cannot be added, a common numerical scaling system is required to permit addition among attributes values. The total score for each alternative can be computed by first multiplying the comparable rating for each criterion and the importance weight of the criterion and then summing these products over all the criteria. The weights are subjective and dependent on the characteristics of the project. The decision maker provides a set of weights that are believed to be appropriate for the particular situation.

The main advantage of the WSM is its ease of use and its assistance in helping the decision maker structure and analyze the decision problem. However, this method tends to involve ad hoc procedures with little theoretical foundation. These can lead to confusion about the most essential customer requirements (Maiden and Ncube 2000), causing the selection of products that have the highest aggregated scores but do not satisfy important criteria (Morisio and Tsoukiàs 1997). Another weakness is that it is difficult to define a set of criteria and corresponding weights such that either they are independent of each other or, if they overlap, their weights are adjusted to compensate for overlapping areas (Kontio 1996). Since many COTS software attributes are not independent of each other, WSM may not be suitable for aggregating COTS software evaluation attribute data.

A closely related method is the weighted average method (Phillips and Polen 2002). When the criteria are arranged in a hierarchy, then the weights in a level of the hierarchy should add up to 100 percent for normalization purposes. For example, if the level one hierarchy consists of two criteria, basic and management, then weights assigned to basic and management should add up to 100 percent. The global weight is determined by multiplying weight, in percentages, by the weights of the criteria in the hierarchy.

The analytical hierarchy process (AHP) method is based on the idea of decomposing a complex, multicriteria decision-making problem into a hierarchy of the selection criteria (Saaty 1997). The AHP helps decision makers structure the important components of a problem into a hierarchical structure. The AHP reduces the complex, multicriteria trade-off decisions to a series of simple pair-wise comparisons and synthesizes the results. Besides helping a decision maker to arrive at the best decision, AHP also provides a clear rationale for making a particular choice. In addition, it provides a means for measuring the consistency of the decision maker's judgments.

Outranking methods are a class of multicriteria decision-making techniques that provide an ordinal ranking of the alternatives (Mollaghasemi and Pet-Edwards 1997). Instead of building complex utility functions, it determines which actions are being preferred to the others by systematically comparing them on each criterion. The advantages of this approach are that it can consider both objective and subjective criteria and that it requires the least amount of information from the decision maker. As this method only identifies the ranking of the alternatives, however, it provides no information on how much better one alternative is over another.

OVERVIEW OF COTS SELECTION METHODS

Direct Assessment Methods

In this section, we provide an overview of some direct assessment methods. The methods reviewed are the off-the-shelf option (OTSO) (Kontio 1996), COTS-based integrated system development (CISD) (Tran et al. 1997), procurement-oriented requirements engineering (PORE) (Maiden and Ncube 2000), COTS-based requirements engineering (CRE) (Alves and Castro 2001), the infrastructure incremental development approach (IIDA) (Fox et al. 1997), and the comparative evaluation process (CEP) (Phillips and Polen 2002).

Off-the-Shelf Option (OTSO)

Kontio proposed the off-the-shelf option-selection method (Kontio 1996). The OTSO method assumes that the requirements of the proposed system already exist. But, in practice, the requirements cannot be defined precisely because the use of certain COTS products may require some changes to the requirements. The main principle followed by the OTSO method is providing explicit definitions of the tasks in the selection process, including entry and exit criteria. It also uses the analytic hierarchy process to consolidate the evaluation data for decision-making purposes. The inputs for OTSO include the requirements specification, design specification, project plans, and organizational characteristics. The outputs are the selected COTS product, the results of the evaluation, and the expected cost.

The OTSO selection method comprises three phases: searching, screening, and evaluation. The selection criteria are developed based on knowledge of the requirements specification, design specification, project plan, and organizational characteristics. The searching phase attempts to identify all potential COTS candidates that cover most of the required functionality. This phase emphasizes breadth rather than depth. The search criteria are based on the functionality and the constraints of the system.

The objective of the screening phase is to decide which COTS candidates should be selected for detailed evaluation. The screening criteria are similar to those of the searching phase. The less-qualified COTS candidates are eliminated during this stage.

In the evaluation phase, COTS candidates undergo a detailed evaluation. The evaluation criteria are defined by decomposing the requirements for the COTS products into a hierarchical set of criteria. Each branch of this hierarchy ends in an evaluation attribute, which is a well-defined measurement that will be determined during the evaluation. Although the set of criteria is specific to each case of COTS products selection, most of the criteria can be categorized into four groups:

- Functional requirements of the COTS
- Required quality-related characteristics, such as reliability, maintainability, and portability
- Business concerns, such as cost, reliability of the vendor, and future development prospects
- Issues relevant to the software architecture, such as constraints presented by an operating system, the division of functionality in the system, or the specific communication mechanisms that are used between modules

OTSO, however, is limited by the fact that some of the selection criteria may not have been clearly defined.

COTS-Based Integrated System Development

Tran, Liu, and Hummel proposed the COTS-based integrated system development model for COTS development (Tran et al. 1997). The CISD model is not solely for COTS product selection. It can also be used to generalize the key engineering phases of selecting, evaluating, and integrating COTS products for a CBS. The inputs for the selection process are the system requirements and information about the COTS products, and the outputs include a prioritized list of the COTS products and the architecture of the system. The CISD model consists of three distinct phases: identification, evaluation, and integration/enhancement. The COTS product selection process lies within the identification and evaluation phases.

The identification phase includes all the technical activities that are required to generate a prioritized collection of products for subsequent evaluation. It includes two subphases: product classification and product prioritization. In the product classification subphase, information on potential COTS products is collected based on the requirements of each application service domain. This phase is similar to the searching phase of the OTSO selection process.

In the prioritization subphase, candidate COTS products are screened and prioritized. Two important criteria for prioritization are interoperability and the ability to fulfill multiple requirements of the service domains. The first criterion ensures that the selected COTS candidates can be integrated readily, leading to a reduction in the overall time and effort. The second criterion gives a higher rating to products that support multiple domains, given that these products can reduce the number of interconnected interfaces and architectural mismatches.

The evaluation phase encompasses the process of creating prototype software and temporary integration and testing of the candidate COTS products. A detailed evaluation of the COTS products is performed on the following important attributes:

- Functionality
- Architecture and interoperability
- Performance

The integration/enhancement phase encompasses all of the development efforts that are required to interconnect the different selected COTS products into a single integrated system.

Procurement-Oriented Requirements Engineering

The procurement-oriented requirements engineering method guides a software development team in acquiring customer requirements and selecting COTS products that satisfy those requirements (Maiden and Ncube 2000). It uses a progressive filtering strategy.

The PORE method supports an iterative process of acquiring requirements and selecting COTS products. During each of the iterations, the software development team acquires information about the customer requirements that helps discriminate between the COTS product candidates. The team also undertakes multicriteria decision making to identify candidates that are not compliant with the requirements. Therefore, the team rejects some of the COTS candidates and then explores the remaining candidates by discovering possibly new customer requirements that might discriminate more thoroughly between the remaining candidates.

The inputs or selection criteria of the PORE method are the attributes of the COTS products, supplier requirements, and information about product branding, open standards, product certification, the development process, the supplier's Capability Maturity Model (CMM) level (Carnegie Mellon University 1995), and the product and the supplier's past record, reliability, security, and dependability. The output is the short list of COTS products.

PORE offers techniques such as scenarios to discover, acquire, and structure the customer requirements and formulate test cases that are used to check the compliance of the COTS products with the customer requirements.

COTS-Based Requirements Engineering

The COTS-based requirements engineering method was developed to facilitate a systematic, repeatable, and requirements-driven COTS product selection process. A key feature of this method is the definition and analysis of the nonfunctional requirements during the COTS product evaluation and selection (Alves and Castro 2001). The CRE method is goal-oriented in that each phase is aimed at achieving a predefined set of goals. Each phase has a template that includes some guidelines and techniques for acquiring and modeling requirements and evaluating products. The inputs of the CRE method include defined goals, evaluation criteria, information about the COTS candidates, and test guides. The output is the selected COTS products.

This method has four iterative phases: identification, description, evaluation, and acceptance. The identification phase is based on a careful analysis of five groups of influencing factors of COTS product selection (Kontio et al. 1995). They are user requirements, application architecture, project objectives and restrictions, product availability, and organizational infrastructure.

During the description phase, the evaluation criteria are elaborated in detail with an emphasis on the nonfunctional requirements. This is followed by a refinement of the description of the requirements.

In the evaluation phase, the decision to select a particular COTS product is based on the estimated cost versus expected benefits. The COCOTS (constructive COTS) cost model is used (Boehm et al. 1998). In particular, the *best* COTS product is identified by continuously rejecting noncompliant candidates. COTS products that do not meet the requirements are rejected and removed from the list of candidates.

The acceptance phase is concerned with the negotiation of a legal contract with vendors of the COTS products. During this phase, the evaluation team has to resolve legal issues pertaining to the purchase of the products and their licensing.

The selection criteria of the CRE method include:

- Functional and nonfunctional requirements
- Time restriction: the time available for searching and screening all the potential COTS candidates
- Cost rating: the cost of acquiring the COTS products. This includes expenses such as acquiring a license, the cost of support, expenses associated with adapting the product, and ongoing maintenance costs.
- Vendor guarantees: this addresses the issue of the technical support that is provided by a vendor. Consideration is given to the vendor's reputation and the maturity of its organization, and the number and kinds of applications that already use the COTS product.

A disadvantage of the CRE method is that the decision-making process can be very complex, given that there are a large number of potential COTS products and many evaluative criteria.

Infrastructure Incremental Development Approach

The infrastructure incremental development approach has been proposed for the development of technical infrastructure using COTS products (Fox et al. 1997). This approach is a combination of the classical waterfall and spiral development models in order to accommodate the needs of CBS development. The process of selecting COTS products in the IIDA relies on two phases: analysis prototype and design prototype.

In the analysis prototype phase, COTS candidates are selected from each COTS product family. A COTS product family is defined as a group of COTS products that perform similar functions and/or provide related services. Based on the general capabilities and basic functionalities of the COTS candidates, the qualified COTS products that fulfill the infrastructure requirement are identified in each of the COTS product families. However, the IIDA does not specify how the COTS product family is constructed nor does it provide possible sources for that information. The purpose of the design prototype phase is to select and evaluate the best COTS products from the earlier phase. Basic evaluation criteria include functionality and performance.

Comparative Evaluation Process

The Software Productivity Consortium has developed the comparative evaluation process (CEP) for evaluating and selecting COTS products (Phillips and Polen 2002). There are five top-level activities. With the first activity (*Scope Evaluation*), the expected number of COTS products to search, screen, and evaluate is determined. This activity supports resource planning. With the second activity (*Search and Screen Candidate*), the initial search criteria and thresholds are defined first. The search criteria are based on functionality and key constraints. A preliminary list of possible candidates that satisfy the search criteria is determined and then screened by applying minimum thresholds.

Afterward (*Define Evaluation Criteria*), detailed criteria necessary to support a repeatable and systematic evaluation are produced. The criteria focus on functional, architectural, management, strategic, performance, and financial characteristics of the candidates. Weights are also established for all the evaluation criteria with respect to each project's importance.

Evaluate Component Alternatives follows in which the short-listed candidates are assessed based on the defined criteria from the previous activity. Various evaluation scenarios are developed to assess the alternatives rather than just exercising the component's functionality.

Finally (*Analyze Evaluation Results*), rankings of alternatives are compared, based on the priorities. The decision model used is simple weighted average. The weights are subjective and dependent on the particular project emphases. The result of a COTS product is based on its criteria value and credibility rating.

There is a high level of similarity between CEP and OTSO. A unique feature of CEP is the use of credibility value scoring, which rates the confidence in what the evaluator knows about an alternative.

Summary of Direct Assessment Methods

Table 10.1 summarizes the inputs, selection procedures, selection criteria, and outputs of the COTS product selection methods. Although the six direct assessment methods have some differences in their finer details, the typical steps of these methods are as follows:

1. Inspect all the modules of each of the available COTS products to check whether they satisfy some or all of the functional requirements of the CBS being developed.
2. Check whether a COTS product also satisfies the nonfunctional requirements of the CBS. Nonfunctional requirements may include properties such as the interoperability of the modules of the COTS product with other systems.
3. Select the most appropriate COTS product that satisfies both the functional and nonfunctional requirements of the CBS.

Table 10.1

Comparison of COTS Product Selection Methods

	OTSO	CISD	PORE	CRE	IIDA	CEP	DBCS
Input	Requirement specifications; design specifications; project plans; organizational characteristics	System requirements; COTS products	COTS product attributes; supplier requirements; product development process	Defined goals; evaluation criteria; COTS products; test guides	COTS from each COTS product family	COTS products	COTS with domain mapping; system requirement
Selection procedure	Searching; screening; evaluation	Identification; product classification; product prioritization; evaluation	Acquires customer requirements; undertakes multicriteria decision making; rejects noncompliant COTS candidates; explores remaining COTS candidates to discover new customer requirements	Identification; description; evaluation; acceptance	Analysis prototype; design prototype	Scope evaluation; search and screen; define evaluation criteria; evaluate alternatives; analyze results	Identify modules in domain model; identify COTS modules applicable to the identified domain model; evaluation of nonfunctional properties

Selection criteria	Functional requirements; required quality characteristics; business concerns; relevant software architecture	Functionality; architecture/inter-operability; performance; fulfill multiple requirements of the service domain	Development process; supplier's CMM level; product and supplier's past record; reliability; security; dependability	Functional and nonfunctional requirements; time restriction; cost rating; vendor guaranties	Functional requirements; performance	Functional requirements; constraints	Functional requirements; nonfunctional requirements
Output	Selected COTS; evaluation results; cost models	Prioritized COTS products; system architecture	Selected COTS	Selected COTS	Selected COTS	Prioritized COTS products	Selected COTS

The efficiency of these exhaustive direct assessment methods is inversely proportional to the product of:

- the number of modules to be developed using COTS products, and
- the total number of modules in all the available COTS products.

As more and more COTS products become available in the market, the total number of modules in all of the available COTS products will become large. Therefore, the efficiency of the direct assessment methods can be expected to decrease sharply.

Indirect Assessment Methods

DBCS

The DBCS method is an indirect assessment method, which uses the domain model as an agent between the COTS products and a CBS (Leung and Leung 2002). It consists of two phases: setup and selection.

1. Setup phase
   When vendors roll out their COTS products, they need to provide a mapping of their COTS modules to those modules of the applicable domains. These mappings are available to the application system developers and can be accessed electronically.

2. Selection phase
   a. When selecting the COTS modules for a CBS, instead of selecting the COTS components directly, the corresponding modules in the domain model of a CBS are consulted.
   b. Through the mappings between a domain model and the COTS products, the corresponding COTS modules that are claimed to be appropriate for the CBS module are identified. Note that these modules are functionally applicable to the domain models. The mappings between the COTS products and the domain models can be managed via computing systems, and retrieving information about the COTS modules from the domain models can be done automatically.
   c. The nonfunctional properties of the identified COTS modules are assessed. This vetting procedure cannot be fully automated because some of the nonfunctional criteria will require human judgment.
   d. With reference to all of the assessment results, the most appropriate COTS modules are selected.

Several observations on the efficiency of the DBCS method can be made. In the setup phase, the modules of the COTS products are first mapped to domain models by the vendors. Since the vendors have full information about the functionalities and features of the COTS products, it should be easy for them to decide how the modules are to be used in different domain modules. The mappings from the COTS modules to a domain model are reused each time a CBS from that domain is to be developed. Moreover, the mappings between the COTS modules and the domain modules help the vendors to market their products because they can demonstrate easily how their COTS products can be applied in an application domain.

Conceptually, the relation between a domain model and all of the COTS products is one-to-many. Since the mappings are developed from the COTS-product side to the domain-model side, it is still a one-to-one relation. Consequently, the complexity in developing the mapping is reduced.

In the selection phase, the first step is to identify the corresponding modules in the domain model for a CBS. This step is simple because a domain module has captured all of the features of the domain. The relation between a module of a CBS and its domain module is one-to-one. It should be easy for the developer of a CBS to identify the corresponding modules in the domain model.

Although the process of selecting the COTS products for these modules depends on the number of mappings, it is still a simple step since information on the COTS products can be collected through the defined mappings. Furthermore, if the mappings are well managed, after the modules of the domain models are identified, the mappings between the COTS products and the domain modules can be retrieved by automatic systems. This would be an accurate, efficient method to identify those COTS products that satisfy the functional requirements of a CBS.

The DBCS method is an efficient method, as the one-to-many relationship between a CBS and all of the COTS products is reduced to two relations, namely, a many-to-one relationship between the COTS products and a domain model and a one-to-one relationship between a domain model and a CBS. The latter relation is a simple relationship and is handled easily. Although the former relationship is complex to deal with, the vendors who possess all of the necessary information are able to easily solve this problem. We have reported the quantitative proof that the DBCS method is a more efficient method than a direct assessment method (Leung and Leung 2002).

A Case Study

We have applied the DBCS method to the development of an online margin-trading system for a large, leading bank in Hong Kong using COTS products (Leung et al. 1999). The system deals mainly with the margin trades between trading parties, one of the core activities in the banking and financial industry.

In applying the DBCS method, the first requirement is the availability of a domain model for the specific application. Since an industrial-scale, margin-trading domain model was not available for our case study, we first created such a domain model. This domain model was built by an experienced developer who had been working on a margin-trading system in a leading bank for several years. He was familiar with the business, the main activities, the detailed operations, and the general architecture of a margin-trading system.

The construction of the domain model of margin-trading follows three steps:

- Gather domain knowledge
- Perform domain analysis
- Consolidate various domain models

The domain model was built using object-oriented technology and expressed in Object Modeling Technique (OMT).

In our study, we focused on the main function of the margin-trading system, namely, providing a trading environment for a dealer to perform a margin trade with various trading parties. It was decided to use COTS for the data security and currency handling modules of the margin-trading system.

Before applying the DBCS to identify the best COTS available, we needed to have a list of suitable COTS provided by the vendors, with the proper mapping to the domain model. As there was no such mapping available, we developed the mapping by ourselves. The nonfunctional criteria for the system included interoperability, performance, and ease of use.

The modules of two COTS products were then mapped to the modules of the margin-trading domain model. Afterwards, the software developers identified the COTS modules by following the steps of the DBCS method, using both best-fit and first-fit strategies on the two modules.

From our study, we conclude that:

1. The DBCS method can reduce the complexity and improve efficiency in COTS selection. It breaks down the complicated many-to-many relationship between COTS products and system requirements into a one-to-one relation and a one-to-many relation.
2. CBS development can save time. Two person-weeks of development effort was saved by using the two COTS products, compared to developing everything from scratch.

CONCLUSION

In this chapter, we have classified the methods for selecting COTS products into three classes: intuition, direct assessment, and indirect methods. Most of the existing methods are based on selecting COTS products either by intuition or direct assessment. The former approach has the weakness of being subjective and it may omit suitable COTS candidates. The efficiency of the latter approach is inversely proportional to the product of the number of modules of the CBS in question and the total number of modules in the available COTS products. This can lead to a large selection effort that may offset the advantages of using the COTS products in the CBS development. The indirect assessment method reduces the complexity and improves the efficiency of COTS product selection.

While many selection methods have been proposed, there has been little empirical study on comparing the effectiveness of these methods. We observe that many direct assessment methods adopt similar steps. It is not clear which method is best for a given situation. It would be of benefit to practitioners if more comparison studies were published. In addition, to ease the evaluation of selection methods, a benchmarking case should be developed so that all researchers can use the same case for comparison.

Another key problem that requires attention is the trade-off between searching for the right COTS product against accepting a less suitable COTS product. It is not clear how much effort should be devoted to the selection of COTS products in order to obtain the maximum benefit from CBS. A practical cost model for CBS needs to be developed to address this problem.

In selecting COTS products, quality and reliability are two key factors to consider. Practical methods for evaluating the quality and reliability of COTS products and their impact on the overall CBS should be developed. Some kind of rating method should be agreed on by both COTS producers and consumers. The use of rating methods implies the availability of metrics, which also need to be developed and agreed on by both parties.

REFERENCES

Alves, C., and J. Castro. 2001. CRE: A systematic method for COTS selection. Paper presented at *XV Brazilian Symposium on Software Engineering,* Rio de Janeiro, Brazil, October.

Anderson, E. 1989. A heuristic for software evaluation and selection. *Software Practice and Experience* 19, no. 8: 707–717.

Boehm, B., C. Abts, and E. Bailey. 1998. COCOTS software integration cost model: An overview. Paper presented at the *California Software Symposium.* Irvine, October.

Carnegie Mellon University, Software Engineering Institute. 1995. *The Capability Maturity Model: Guidelines for Improving the Software Process.* Reading, MA: Addison-Wesley.

Fox, G., K. Lantner, and S. Marcom. 1997. A software development process for COTS-based information system infrastructure. Paper presented at *The Twenty-Second Software Engineering Workshop,* NASA/Goddard Space Flight Center Software Engineering Laboratory (SEL), Greenbelt, MD, December.

Hokey, M. 1992. Selection of software: The analytic hierarchy process. *International Journal of Physical Distribution and Logistics Management* 22, no. 1: 42–52.

Jane's Information Group. 2000. *The Evolution of COTS in the Defence Industry.* October 9, www.janes.com/business/news/jdi/jdi001009_1_n.shtml.

Kontio, J. 1996. A case study in applying a systematic method for COTS selection. In *Proceedings of International Conference on Software Engineering,* 201–209. Los Alamitos, CA: IEEE Computer Society Press.

Kontio, J., S.F. Chen, and K. Limperos. 1995. A COTS selection method and experiences of its use. Paper presented at the *Twentieth Annual Software Engineering Workshop,* NASA Goddard Space Flight Center, Greenbelt, Maryland, December.

Kunda, D. 2002. *A social-technical approach to selecting software supporting COTS-based systems.* PhD Thesis., University of York.

Leung, K., and H.K.N. Leung. 2002. On the efficiency of domain-based COTS selection method. *Information and Software Technology* 44, no. 12: 703–715.

Leung, K., H.K.N. Leung, and F. Suk. 1999. *A COTS Selection Method Using Domain Model.* TR-20, Department of Computing, Hong Kong Polytechnic University.

Maiden, N., and N. Cornelius. 1998. Acquiring COTS: Software selection requirements. *IEEE Software* 15, 2: 46–56.

Maiden, N., and C. Ncube. 2000. COTS software selection: The need to make tradeoffs between system requirements, architecture and COTS components. In *COTS Workshop: Continuing Collaborations for Successful COTS Development,* International Conference on Software Engineering, Limerick, Ireland.

Mollaghasemi, M., and J. Pet-Edwards. 1997. *Technical Briefing: Making Multiple-Objective Decisions.* Los Alamitos, CA: IEEE Computer Society Press.

Morisio, M., C.B. Seaman, A.T. Parra, and V.R. Basili. 2000. Issues in COTS-based software development. In *COTS Workshop: Continuing Collaborations for Successful COTS Development,* International Conference on Software Engineering, Limerick, Ireland.

Morisio, M., and A. Tsoukiàs. 1997. IusWare: A methodology for the evaluation and selection of software products. *IEEE Proceedings of Software Engineering* 144, no. 3: 162–174.

Oberndorf, P. 1997. Facilitating component-based software engineering: COTS and open systems. Paper presented at the *Fifth International Symposium on Assessment of Software Tools and Technology,* Pittsburgh, Pennsylvania, June.

Oberndorf, P.A., L. Brownsword, and E. Morris. 1997. *Workshop on COTS-Based Systems.* Special Report CMU/SEI-97-SR-019. Carnegie Mellon University, Software Engineering Institute, November.

Phillips, B.C., and S.M. Polen. 2002. Add Decision Analysis to Your COTS Selection Process. *Crosstalk* (April): 21–25.

Saaty, T.L. 1997. Analytic hierarchy. In *Encyclopedia of Science and Technology,* 444–468. New York: McGraw-Hill.

Szyperski, C. 1997. *Component Software: Beyond Object Oriented Programming,* Harlow, UK: Addison-Wesley.

Tran, V., V.B. Liu, and B. Hummel. 1997. Component-based systems development: Challenges and lessons learned. In *Proceedings of the 8th International Workshop on Software Technology and Engineering Practice,* 452–462. Los Alamitos, CA: IEEE Computer Society Press.

Vincke, P. 1992. *Multicriteria Decision-Aid.* Chichester: Wiley.

Walters, N. 1995. Systems Architecture and COTS Integration. In *Proceedings of SEI/MCC Symposium on the use of COTS in systems Integration.* Software Engineering Institute Special Report CMU/SEI-95-SR-007, June.

Williams, F. 1992. Appraisal and evaluation of software products. *Journal of Information Science, Principles and Practice* 18: 121–125.

Yoon, K., and C. Hwang. 1995. *Multiple Attribute Decision-Making: An Introduction.* London: Sage.

CHAPTER 11

TRADING FOR COTS COMPONENTS TO FULFILL ARCHITECTURAL REQUIREMENTS

LUIS IRIBARNE, JOSÉ MARÍA TROYA, AND ANTONIO VALLECILLO

Abstract: Component-based development (CBD) moves organizations from application develop-ment to application assembly, involving the use of third-party, prefabricated pieces (commercial off-the-shelf components, COTS) and spiral development methodologies. Although a software component market is still quite slow to develop, effective use of software components is slowly becoming a valid technology for the building of software systems. Moreover, the complexity of the applications is continuously growing, and the amount of the information about components is becoming too large to be handled by human intermediaries. Therefore, automated trading of components will play a critical role in CBD. This chapter underlines the need of linking three areas of the COTS CBD: the documentation and specification of COTS components, the descrip-tion of COTS-based software architectures, and the trading processes for COTS components. A trading-based development method (TBDM), a three-tier method to build software applications as an assembly of COTS software components, is presented. A sample implementation is illustrated.

Keywords: Component Trading, Automated Trading, Trading-Based Development Method, Com-mercial Off-the-Shelf Components, Architecture

INTRODUCTION

In the last decade, component-based development (CBD) has produced a great interest due to the development of plug-and-play reusable software, which has led to the concept of commercial off-the-shelf (COTS) software components. Being currently more a purpose to achieve than a reality, this approach moves organizations from application development to application assembly. Con-structing an application now involves the use of prefabricated pieces, perhaps developed at different times, by different people, and possibly with different uses in mind. The final goal is to be able to reduce development times, costs, and effort, while improving the flexibility, reliability, and reusabil-ity of the final application due to the reuse of software components already tested and validated.

This approach is challenging some of the current software engineering methods and tools. For instance, the traditional top-down development method is not transferable to component-based development. This method is based on successive refinements of the system requirements until a suitable concrete component implementation of the final application is reached. In CBD, the system designer has also to take into account the specification of predeveloped COTS compo-nents available in software repositories, which must be considered even when building the initial requirements of the system, incorporating them into all phases of the development process (Mili et al. 1995; Robertson and Robertson 1999). Here, system architects, designers, and builders

Figure 11.1   **Fulfilling Components' Abstract Specifications From Concrete Specifications**

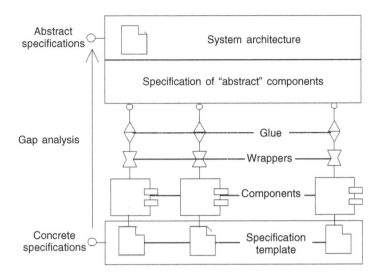

must accept the trade-offs among three main concerns: user's requirements, system architecture, and COTS products (Garlan et al. 2002; Ncube and Maiden 2000).

Current solutions are usually based on spiral methodologies—see, for example, Nuseibeh 2001— which progressively develop detailed requirements, architectural specifications, and system designs, by repeated iterations. These solutions are also related to the so-called gap analysis (Cheesman and Daniels 2001), shown in Figure 11.1. Here, the abstract software architecture of the system is first defined from the user's requirements, which describe the specification of "abstract components" and their relationships. These abstract components are then matched against those "concrete components" available in software repositories. The matching process produces a list of the candidate components that could take part in the application: both because they provide some of the required services, and because they may fulfill some of the user's (extrafunctional) requirements such as price and security limitations. With this list, the system architecture is reexamined in order to accommodate as many candidates from the list as possible. Then the system requirements are matched against those provided by the architecture, and revised if needed. Finally, wrappers may be used to adapt the selected COTS components (hiding extra services not required, or adapting their interfaces for compatibility or interoperability reasons), and some glue language can be used to compose and coordinate the component interactions (see Figure 11.1).

In this new setting, the real search and selection processes of COTS components have become the cornerstone of any effective COTS development. These processes currently face serious limitations, generally for two main reasons. First, the information available about the components is not detailed enough for their effective selection. In this case, the black-box nature of COTS components hinders the understanding of their internal behavior. Moreover, only functional properties of components are usually taken into account, while some other information crucial to component selection is missing, such as protocol or semantic information (Vallecillo et al. 1999), or nonfunctional requirements (Chung et al. 1999; Rosa et al. 2001).

Second, the search, selection, and evaluation criteria are usually too simplistic to provide practical utility. These component searching and matching processes are delegated to traders (usually based on human factors) that do not provide all the functionality required for an effective COTS component trading in open and independently extensible systems (e.g., the Internet), as discussed in Vasudevan and Bannon (1999).

There are at least two important issues in this perspective. The first one deals with a common and standard documentation and specification of both abstract components described in software architectures and those third-party components available in software repositories.

The second issue deals with the trading processes for COTS components. These processes may implement partially (or fully) the functionality required in the software architecture, by constructing the list of candidate COTS components and calculating all their possible and different combinations that fulfill partially (or fully) the architectural requirements from the assembly of candidate components. As a result of a trading perspective, the alternative component combinations of the software architecture could be shown to the system's designer, who could decide which of the alternatives better matches the original user's requirements.

This chapter looks into these COTS-CBD areas. First, it looks into the documenting of COTS components. COTS documents are useful for the search and selection tasks associated with the trading service. Second, the chapter looks into software architectures with COTS components. In this case, we think that the Unified Modeling Language-Real Time (UML-RT) is a suitable notation for COTS software architecture descriptions. Finally, to solve the gap analysis problem, we propose two associated processes: COTStrader (Iribarne et al. 2001) and COTSconfig (Iribarne et al. 2002). The COTStrader process is a tool that extends the Open Distributed Processing (ODP) trading service (ISO/IEC 1997) to look for COTS components. The COTSconfig process is a composition function that calculates all the possible component combinations from those stored in the list of candidates generated by the trader. In this chapter, we explain the connection of the above areas, mainly focusing on the trading service for COTS components. Accordingly, the chapter presents a trader-based development method to fulfill architectural requirements. This method is mainly focused on an experimental framework to test and justify the validity and the usefulness of trading processes in CBD.

The rest of the chapter is organized in six sections. The first one describes a COTS document and a simple example of a COTS-based application to illustrate the proposal. The second section describes some features of a trading process for commercial components. The third section describes a three-tier method to build systems with commercial components. Tier one looks at defining the system's requirements using a software architecture. Tier two looks at searching and selecting components that meet the architectural requirements using the trader service COTStrader. And tier three looks at producing configurations of the software architecture (COTSconfig) from those components found by the trading service. The fourth section describes the technology used to develop the processes associated with the proposed method. Then, the fifth section describes the related works. Finally, the sixth section contains some concluding remarks.

DOCUMENTING COTS COMPONENTS

COTS components are coarse-grained components that integrate several services and offer many interfaces. Component capabilities and usages are specified by interfaces. An interface is "a service abstraction defining the operations that the service supports, independently of any particular implementation" (Szyperski 1998).

Interfaces can be described using many different notations, depending on the information that we want to include, and the level of detail of the specification. In the Common Object Request Broker

Architecture (CORBA), an interface consists of the supported object public attributes, types, and methods. The Component Object Model (COM) follows a similar approach, but components may have several interfaces, each one describing the signature of the supported operations. The CORBA Component Model (CCM) also considers that component interfaces may describe not only the services they support, but also the ones they require from other components during their execution.

The current approaches at the signature level use the Interface Definition Language (IDL) to describe interfaces, which guarantee interoperability at this level among heterogeneous components. Interfaces can be written in different languages using different object models, living in different machines, and using different execution environments. Some IDL examples are those defined by CORBA, COM, and CCM.

On top of the signature level, the semantic level deals with the "meaning"—that is, the behavior (Leavens and Sitaaman 2000)—of the operations, though much more powerfully than mere signature descriptions. Behavioral semantics of components present serious difficulties when they are applied to large software systems: the computational complexity of proving behavioral properties of the components and applications hinders the interface's practical utility.

The semantic level can usually be described by using formal notations that range from the Larch family of languages (Dhara and Leavens 1996) using pre- and post-conditions and invariants to algebraic equations (Goguen et al. 1996), or refinement calculus (Mikhajlova 1999).

Finally, the protocol level just deals with the components' service access protocols, that is, the partial order in which components expect their methods to be called, and the order in which they invoke other methods (Vallecillo et al. 2000). This level, identified by Yellin and Strom (1997), provides more powerful interoperability checks than those offered by the basic signature level. Of course, it does not cover all the semantic aspects of components, but it is not weighed down with the heavy burden of semantic checks. At the protocol level, the problems can be more easily identified and managed, and practical (tool-based) solutions can be proposed to solve them.

At the protocol level, most of the current approaches enrich the IDL description of the components' interfaces with information about protocol interactions, using many different notations: finite-state machines (Yellin and Strom 1997), Petri nets (Bastide et al. 1999), temporal logic (Han 1999), or pi-calculus (Milner 1993).

An Example Using COTS Components

In order to illustrate our proposal, we will introduce a simple example that comes from the distributed Geographic Information Systems (GIS) arena. It consists of a common translation service between spatial images, usually known as Geographic Translator Service (GTS). Briefly, a sender component needs to send a formatted image to a receiver component, but instead of sending it directly, the sender uses a translator service to deal with all issues related to the image format conversion and compression. This simplifies both the sender and the receiver, taking away all those format-compatibility issues from them.

The way the service works is shown in Figure 11.2. First, the Sender forwards a translation request to the GTS, with the required service and its related information:

```
<image url="http:// . . . /download/">
        <name input="RiverImage" output="RiverImage"/>
        <format input="DWG" output="DXF"/>
        <compression input=".zip" output=".tar"/>
</image>
```

Figure 11.2   **A Geographic Translator System (GTS) Example**

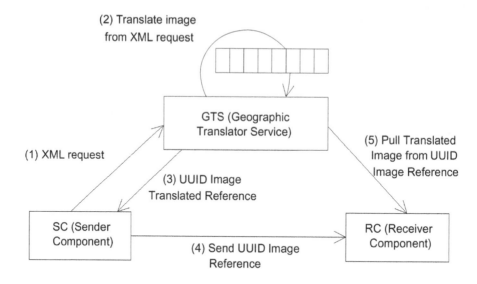

Following this request, the GTS component downloads a zip-compressed DWG image from the http site. Then it generates a DXF image file with the same name and stores it in a buffer. After that, GTS associates a unique identifier UUID to the translated DXF image. Finally, it returns the identifier to the sender component, which gets the required image by pulling the converted file from the GTS buffer.

For our discussion, we will just concentrate on the GTS subsystem. It uses a main component called Translator that provides the target translation service (see Figure 11.6).

COTS Documents

Similarly to software components, a mechanism to document commercial components is very useful in tasks of search, selection, evaluation, and assembly of components. For these processes, it is very important to use complete, concise, and unambiguous specifications of components in order to guarantee successful COTS software development.

A commercial component document (like an identity credential and a contract) could be used by developers to describe particular issues of the target component to build. System architects could also use this kind of information, recovered in a commercial component document, to describe the components' architectural requirements in the software architecture.

A COTS document is a Document Type Definition (DTD) template based on the World Wide Web Consortium's (W3C) XML Schema language, used to describe COTS components. Figure 11.3 shows an instance of an XML-based COTS document for a simple software component called Translator, which translates between spatial image formats.

A COTS document deals with four kinds of information: functional, nonfunctional, packaging, and marketing. This kind of information can help to determine the component requirements when describing the software architecture and can be used as the information type that a trader manages.

The first part describes the functional (i.e., computational) aspects of the services provided by

Figure 11.3 **A COTS Document Example**

```
<COTScomponent name="Translator" xmlns="http://www.cotstrader.com/COTS-
XMLSchema.xsd" . . . >
    <functional>
        <providedInterfaces>
            <interface name="Translator">
                <description notation="CORBA-IDL">
                interface Translator {
                    boolean translate(in string request, out string UDDI);
                    boolean get(in long UDDI, out string URL); };
                </description>
                <exactMatching href=" . . . /servlet/CORBA.exact"/>
                <behavior notation="Larch-JML">
                    <description> . . . </description>
                    <exactMatching href=" . . . /servlet/LarchJML.exact"/>
                    <softMatching href=" . . . /servlet/LarchJML.soft"/>
                </behavior>
            </interface>
        </providedInterfaces>
        <requiredInterfaces>
            <interface name="FileCompressor"> . . . </interface>
            <interface name="ImageTranslator"> . . . </interface>
            <interface name="XDR"> . . . </interface>
            <interface name="XMLBuffer"> . . . </interface>
        </requiredInterfaces>
        <choreography>
            <description notation="pi-protocols" href=" . . . /translatorProtocol.pi" >
            <exactMatching href=" . . . /servlet/PI.exact"/> <softMatching href=" . . . /servlet/
PI.soft"/>
        </choreography>
    </functional>
    <properties notation="W3C">
        <property name="capacity"> <type>xsd:int</type> <value>20</value> </property>
        <property name="isRunningNow"> <!—dynamic property—>
            <type>xsd:bool</type> <value href="http:// . . . /servlet/GTS.running"/> </property>
        <property name="keywords"> <type>xsd:string</type>
            <value> spatial image, format, conversion, compression, GIS </value> </property>
    </properties>
    <packaging>
        <description notation="CCM-softpkg" href=" . . . /AnImplementation.csd"/>
    </packaging>
    <marketing>
        <expirydate>2004–2-11</expirydate> <certificate href=" . . . /card.pgp" />
        <vendor>
            <companyname> . . . </companyname> <address> . . . </address> . . .
        </vendor>
    </marketing>
</COTScomponent>
```

the component, including both syntactic (i.e., signature) and semantic information. Unlike most object services (which contain only an interface), functional definition will host the set of interfaces offered by the component, and the set of interfaces that any instance of the component may require from other components when implementing its supported interfaces. The documentation may also list the set of events that the component can produce and consume, as defined in component models such as CCM, Enterprise JavaBeans (EJB), or Enterprise Distributed Object Computing (EDOC) (OMG 2001).

Since we did not want to commit to any particular notation of expressing the functional information contained in the XML templates, the "notation" attribute can be present in many fields of a COTS document, with several predefined values. This attribute can be used by clients and servers to agree with the values they want to use.

Behavioral information can be described directly in the document, or in a separate file by the "href" attribute, or even omitted (behavioral information is optional; only signature information is mandatory).

A third (optional) element called "choreography"—commonly known as protocol information (Canal et al. 2000; Vallecillo et al. 2000)—deals with the semantic aspects of the component that globally describe its behavior and that cannot be captured by the semantics of the individual interfaces. A protocol refers to the relative order in which the component expects its methods to be called and the way it calls other components' methods.

Syntactical (i.e., the interfaces), behavioral, and protocol descriptions can be referred to a couple of (optional) procedures that will allow the trader to do the matchmaking programs. In this example, LarchJML.exact is the name of a program that is able to decide whether two behavioral descriptions A and B, written in Larch-JML (Leavens et al. 1999), satisfy that A can replace B. Analogously, a second program, LarchJML.soft, is the one in charge of implementing the soft matchmaking process.

The second part of the COTS component template describes nonfunctional aspects (e.g., Quality of Service (QoS), nonfunctional requirements, etc.) in a similar way to ODP, that is, by means of service properties (ISO/IEC 1997). In order to deal effectively with nonfunctional requirements, we use some principles taken from a qualitative approach called nonfunctional requirements (NFR) Framework (Chung et al. 1999). This approach is based on the explicit representation and analysis of nonfunctional requirements. Considering the complex nature of nonfunctional requirements, we cannot always say that nonfunctional requirements are completely accomplished or satisfied. We have studied the importance of nonfunctional information and how to include it into COTS documents (Iribarne, Vallecillo et al. 2001).

The ODP way has been adapted to describe nonfunctional properties, that is, using "properties." They are the usual way (name, type, and value) in which the nonfunctional aspects of objects, services, and components are expressed in the literature. Dynamic properties can also be implemented in this approach, indicating the reference to the external program that will evaluate their current values. Keyword-based searches are allowed too, and they use the special "keywords" property. Complex properties and traceability can also be considered in a COTS document (see Iribarne, Vallecillo et al. 2001).

The third part contains the packaging information to download, deploy, and install the COTS component that provides the required service. It includes implementation details, context and architectural constraints, and so on. In this example, the CCM "softpackage" (OMG 1999) description style is used (see Figure 11.3). This information allows us to describe resources, configuration files, the location of different implementations of the component for different operating systems, the way those implementations are packaged, the resources and external programs they need, and so on.

Finally, some other nontechnical details of the service, and the component implementing it, are described in the marketing section, which includes licenses, certificates, vendor information, and so on.

TRADING FOR COTS COMPONENTS

Trading is a well-known concept for searching and locating services. In a trader-based architecture, a client component that requires a particular service can query a matchmaking agent—called the trader—for references to available components that provide the required kind of service. Moreover, enhanced traders with quality-of-service (QoS) facilities can provide the means of self-configuring multimedia applications. In this chapter, we will just concentrate on COTS component trading. However, most of our discourse is also applicable to all disciplines in which trading is required.

After analyzing specific characteristics of CBD in open systems, we present in Table 11.1 the features and characteristics that traders should have in order to provide an effective COTS component trading service in these open environments.

Existing traders mostly follow the ODP model (ISO/ITU-T 1996), and therefore they present some limitations when their features are compared against the previous list of requirements in Table 11.1. Based on the experience obtained from the existing industrial implementations of the trading service (e.g., Distributed Object Group and IONA [2001]), and based on some closely related works (e.g., Merz et al. [1994] and Vasudevan and Bannon [1999]), we can see that current traders:

- use homogeneous object models only
- use direct federation
- do not allow service composition or adaptation
- work with "exact" matches at the signature level only
- do not allow multiple interfaces
- are based on a push model only

COTStrader, a trader that can overcome these limitations, is specifically designed to deal with COTS components in open environments. COTStrader uses two kinds of templates to register and look for components: a COTScomponent template similar to the "COTS Document" and a COTSquery template, respectively.

In order to import (or get) a service from the repository, the client uses a COTSquery document, which contains the selection criteria that must be used by the trader to look for services (COTS components). Using this kind of document, the trader covers the repository, looking for similar COTS documents. The trading process returns a list of candidate documents, accomplishing the search criteria fixed in the client query document. Figure 11.4 shows a COTSquery example of searching one (or more) Translator component(s).

As we can see here, a COTSquery template consists of five main parts. The main features of the required service can be directly described into the document or even with an additional COTScomponent document referred inside the "COTSdescription" part, in the COTSquery document. This COTScomponent document is the one used by the trader to match it with the candidate document being analyzed.

Table 11.1

Features of a Trading Process for Commercial Components

Features	Description
Heterogeneous	A trader should not restrict itself to a particular component or object model, but it should be able to deal with different component models and platforms, such as CORBA, EJB, COM, .NET, etc.
Federation	Cooperating traders can federate using different strategies. The direct federation approach requires the traders to directly communicate (and know about) the ones they federate with. In the repository-based federation, multiples traders read and write to the same service offer repository.
Search engines	Traders may superficially resemble search engines, but perform more structured searches. In a trader, the matchmaking heuristics need to model the vocabulary, distance functions, and equivalence of classes in a domain-specific property space.
Softmatches	Traditional exact matches between imports and exports are very restrictive in real situations, in which more relaxed matching criteria should be used. Therefore, partial matches should be allowed when building the list of candidate components.
Extensible and scalable	Component behavior, NFRs, QoS, marketing information, and semantic data should also be considered. The information managed by the trader should be able to be extended by users in an independent way, and still the trader should be able to use all its functionality and capabilities.
Compose and adaptation	Current traders focus on one-to-one matches between client requests and available service instances. A compositional trader should also consider one-to-many matches, in which composing several available services, which together provide the services, can also fulfill a client request.
Multiples interfaces	Components simultaneously offer several interfaces and, besides the services, should be defined in terms of sets of interfaces. This fact has to be specially considered when integrating components, since conflicts may appear between components offering common interfaces.
Subtyping	Current traders organize services in a service type hierarchy in order to carry out the service matching process. Central to type matching is the notion of type subtyping (or type conformance). Subtyping needs to be defined in order to cope with syntactic and semantic information, protocols, QoS, etc.
Store and forward	If a trader cannot fully satisfy a request, either it automatically replies back to the client with a denial (automatic behavior) or it stores the request and postpones the reply until a suitable service provider is found (store and forward).
Push and pull	In a push model, exporters directly contact the trader to register their services with it. Bots and search engines, used to enhance current COTStrader, use a push model, crawling the Web looking for services and "pushing" them into the traders.
Heuristics and metrics	Users should be able to specify heuristic functions and metrics when looking for components, especially in the case of soft matchmaking.
Delegation	If traders cannot resolve requests they should be able to delegate them to other (smarter) traders. Delegation of the complete request or just parts of it is desirable.

Figure 11.4 **A Query Template Example**

```
<COTSquery name="TranslatorQuery">
    <COTSdescription href="http:// . . . /Translator.xml"/>
    <functionalMatching>
        <interfaceMatching> <exactMatching href=" . . . /servlet/exactmat"/> </
interfaceMatching>
        <choreographyMatching> <softMatching/> </choreographyMatching>
    </functionalMatching>
    <propertyMatching>
        <constraints notation="XQuery"> (capacity <= 17) </constraints>
        <preferences notation="ODP">random</preferences>
    </propertyMatching>
    <packagingMatching notation="XQuery">
        description/notation ="CCM-softpkg" and description/implementation/os/
name="WinNT"
    </packagingMatching>
    <marketingMatching notation="XQuery">vendor/companyname="IBM"</
marketingMatching>
</COTSquery>
```

The other four parts of the COTSquery document describe the selection criteria to be used. In the functional part, the client may specify whether the matchmaking process should be *exact* or *soft,* and optionally the matchmaking program to be used (the program originally stated in the target COTS component description is ignored) (Zaremski and Wing 1995). For example, in the query template shown in Figure 11.4, we can see how a soft matching action is only desired at a protocol (choreography) level, whereas at the syntactical level an exact matching action and a program are desired by the client.

If a client does not offer a soft or exact matching program in the query document, the trader looks for it inside the document of the candidate component (candidate document) that is being analyzed from the trader's repository. Otherwise, the trader looks for default matching programs related to it. The candidate document is refused by the trader if an exact matching was required and no program was found. The candidate document is included in the candidate list (to be returned) if a soft matching was required, but no program was found.

Property-based matching is done in the usual way by ODP traders, using constraints and preferences. Constraints are boolean expressions consisting of service property values, constants, relational operators ($<$, $>=$, $=$, $!=$), logical operators (not, and, or), and parentheses, which specify the matching criteria to include a component in the trader's list of candidates for the current search. We have used the notation defined in the W3C's XML QueryAlgebra proposal to write the expression. On the other hand, the preferences can sort out the list of candidates according to a given criterion using terms like "first," "random," "min(*expr*)" and "max(*expr*)," where *expr* is a simple mathematical expression involving property names (ISO/ITU-T 1996).

Finally, the packaging and marketing information is matched using expressions that relate the values of the COTSdescription query in the appropriate tags ("<packaging>" or "<marketing>"). In this example, the W3C's QueryAlgebra notation is used again to build the "select" expressions.

Figure 11.5 **The TBDM Architecture**

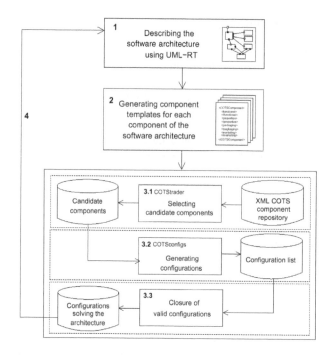

PROCESSES FOR A TRADING-BASED DEVELOPMENT METHOD

To assess the usefulness of the trading process for CBD, it has been integrated into a method to build COTS-based systems by automating most of the search and selection activities. In order to produce systems with commercial components, architects, designers, and builders must accept the trade-offs among three main concerns: user requirements, system architecture, and COTS products.

In this section, we will introduce all the processes dealing with a trading-based development method (TBDM), that is, a software development proposal to build COTS-based systems that require the use of quick prototypes of the system's software architecture. This method tries to solve an important problem at design level, known as gap analysis in the CBD literature (Cheesman and Daniels 2001). The main purpose is to approach the architectural design requirements of the components and those related with particular implementations available in the market of software components (i.e., commercial components). Some important tasks, tools, and methods, very common in requirements engineering (requirement elicitation, analysis, specification, and validation), are beyond the scope of this chapter, which is rather focused on the design level.

Figure 11.5 shows the schema of all connected tasks that conform to the automated method. The process initially describes the software architecture (SA) of the system, which defines its high-level structure, exposing its organization as a collection of interacting components (step 1). The SA decomposes the application requirements into a hierarchical criteria set, which usually includes component functionality, extrafunctional requirements, architectural constraints, and other nontechnical factors such as vendor guarantees and legal issues.

Subsequently, the process continues by extracting the component requirement information from the SA (step 2). This step produces a list of abstract services, which can easily be expressed by means of COTScomponent documents (i.e., abstract documents).

Using this information (i.e., the list of COTScomponent documents), the next step begins with the activities of component selection. In this case, the COTStrader can be queried to look for those COTS components that provide the desired requirements (step 3.1). The trader returns a list of candidate components to each abstract document. A candidate list contains the collection of those particular documents (i.e., COTS documents of existing implemented components) that match with the information of the abstract document being considered.

The process keeps on trying to build the system from these lists of candidate components. The COTSconfig process (step 3.2) carries out this purpose by calculating a list of all possible combinations between the candidate components. A valid component combination represents a closed configuration of the system that partially (or fully) solves the abstract component requirements of SA. A closed configuration does not require any external component to work, that is, all services required by its constituent components are provided by a component in the configuration. Therefore, a new process deals with the closing of configurations (step 3.3).

Finally, a list of all closed configurations is shown to the system designer (step 4), so that a decision can be made as to (1) the best configuration that matches the user requirements, (2) which components are still missing and hence need to be developed, and (3) the extent to which the initial software architecture should be changed (and whether it is worth changing) in order to accommodate to the COTS components found. The selection, validation, evaluation, and adaptation of configuration activities are beyond the scope of this chapter. Instead, we focus on the assessment of the usefulness of integrating a COTS trader with CBD methodologies (e.g., Capability Maturity Model (CMM) or Rational Unified Process (RUP) approaches using software components).

The following sections describe these steps in more detail, and the Geographic Translation Service example is used to illustrate the trader-based development method. The discussion that follows will refer to Figure 11.5.

Describing the Software Architecture

Complex software systems require expressive notations to represent their architecture. In general, the software architecture defines its high-level structure, exposing its organization as a set of interacting components.

Traditionally, specialized architecture description languages (ADL) have been used to provide a formal description of the structure and the behavior of an application's architecture (Medvidovic and Taylor 2000). The formality and the lack of visual support of most ADLs, however, have encouraged the quest for more user-friendly notations. In this respect, the Unified Modeling Language (UML) notation is clearly the most promising candidate, since it is familiar to developers and, to a certain extent, nontechnical people, it offers a close mapping to implementations, and it has commercial tool support.

The problem is that the current definition of UML does not offer a clear way of encoding and modeling the architectural elements typically found in the architectural description languages as discussed by Garlan et al. (2002) and Medvidovic et al. (2002), for instance. Until the new UML 2.0 is released (which is expected to support component-based development and run-time architectures of applications), the only widely accepted proposal for documenting software architectures available now is probably UML-RealTime (UML-RT) (Selic and Rumbaugh 1998).

Figure 11.6   **The GTS Software Architecture in the UML-RT Notation**

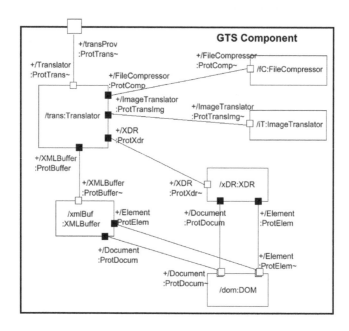

UML-RT is a visual modeling language with formal semantics for specifying, visualizing, documenting, and automating the construction of complex, event-driven, and distributed real-time systems. UML-RT uses some graphical notations to describe the software architecture, such as capsules (i.e., components), ports (i.e., provided and required interfaces), protocols (i.e., choreography), and connectors (to bind components through the ports).

Figure 11.6 shows the GTS software architecture using the UML-RT notation. This figure represents the first stage (step 1) of the TBDM method (shown in Figure 11.5).

As we can see, a general capsule is used to describe the whole software architecture. A UML-RT capsule can be composed of one or more capsules (i.e., components in our case). Please notice that the GTS software architecture capsule represents the GTS component capsule in Figure 11.2.

The +/transProv:ProtTrans~ port represents the boundary that communicates both the sender and receiver components with the inner part of the GTS capsule. This port connects directly with the +/translator:ProtTrans~ dual port, which is a part of the /trans:Translator component.

The GTS software architecture is composed of six components (i.e., capsules). The main component is /trans:Translator, which requires four additional components:

1. a file compressor called /fC:FileCompressor
2. a translator of spatial images called /iT:ImageTranslator
3. a component for intermediate representation of data called /xDR:XDR
4. a buffer called /xmlBuf:XMLBuffer

The GTS subsystem also requires two document object model (DOM) interfaces called Document and Element. They are used by the XDR and XMLBuffer components to support XML formats. These interfaces are available in software packages such as IBM XML4J or Sun JAXP.

Figure 11.7 **A Capsule Describing the Component Requirements**

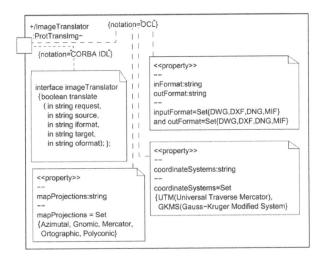

In the GTS software architecture, only an instance of the base component DOM is used, but Document and Element ports are duplicated to handle both /xDR:XDR and /xmlBuf:XMLBuffer components.

Moreover, there is some important information that must be recovered inside a capsule. This information, which is recovered by UML notes and tagged values inside a capsule (i.e., component), is related with that included in a COTS document. For example, Figure 11.7 shows the internal requirements imposed on the ImageTranslator component. To simplify, we just represent the signature level of interfaces and nonfunctional information, but the remaining information of a COTS document can be represented in a similar way.

The signature level of interfaces can be described by some particular IDL notations. Specifically, the CORBA IDL notation is used to describe interfaces. This description is directly included inside a UML note and connected with the corresponding port (a UML-RT port refers to interfaces). Also, an external tagged value—which is connected with the IDL note—determines the notation type to describe the interface's signature level (e.g., notation n = "CORBA IDL").

Properties are also described in a separate note. A property description begins with the "<<property>>" stereotype name. Next, the property description is indicated with a particular notation. As the interface shows, the description notation is represented by using an external tagged value. For example, the ImageTranslator capsule describes three properties in separate notes. It uses an external tagged value (notation = "OCL") connected with each property note. A "—" symbol is used to separate several parts in a property description note: (1) the "<<property>>" stereotype header; (2) the declaration of those types by the object constraint language (OCL) property description; and (3) the body of the property description.

Once the software architecture is drawn—using the Rational Rose RealTime package in our case—the information about the components, the services they offer and require, and their properties is extracted from the UML-RT diagram (i.e., capsule information, as we have discussed).

This process represents the second stage (step 2) of the TBDM method (Figure 11.5).

For that purpose, we have a process that parses the files produced by Rational Rose RealTime and generates a list of COTS documents (i.e., COTSdocument templates) with the description of

Figure 11.8 **A Template List of COTS Components**

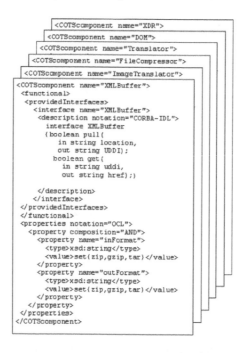

```
<COTScomponent name="XDR">
<COTScomponent name="DOM">
<COTScomponent name="Translator">
<COTScomponent name="FileCompressor">
<COTScomponent name="ImageTranslator">
<COTScomponent name="XMLBuffer">
 <functional>
  <providedInterfaces>
   <interface name="XMLBuffer">
    <description notation="CORBA-IDL">
     interface XMLBuffer
     {boolean pull(
        in string location,
        out string UDDI);
      boolean get(
        in string uddi,
        out string href);}

    </description>
   </interface>
  </providedInterfaces>
 </functional>
 <properties notation="OCL">
  <property composition="AND">
   <property name="inFormat">
    <type>xsd:string</type>
    <value>set(zip,gzip,tar)</value>
   </property>
   <property name="outFormat">
    <type>xsd:string</type>
    <value>set(zip,gzip,tar)</value>
   </property>
  </property>
 </properties>
</COTScomponent>
```

the components found in the software architecture. Figure 11.8 shows the list of six COTScomponent templates generated for the GTS software architecture (shown in Figure 11.6).

In addition to this, we have a generic tool that processes XML Metadata Interchange (XMI) files and produces the COTScomponent templates, since we did not want to commit to any particular tool or graphical notation.

Looking for COTS Components (Trading)

Besides obtaining the architectural needs, the next stage of the TBDM method looks over the component search and selection activities (step 3.1). This stage deals with the trader process (COTStrader). The trader generates a list of candidate components from the repository when it is queried with a client component template to be searched. In our case, the trader service is queried just six times using those document templates with the architectural requirements. These were extracted from the software architecture in the previous step. This search process will generate a list of candidate components for each query requested.

The trading service was described in the "Trading for COTS Components" section. As we could see there, the matching operations, which look for COTS components and generate a list of candidate components, start with soft matches (basically, just by looking for keywords). As the software architecture gets progressively refined, these initial soft matches get more and more exact in each iteration (see again Figure 11.5). Typical (and increasingly stronger) levels of matching are keywords, marketing and packaging information (operating systems, component models, etc.), quality properties, interface names, interface operations, and behavioral and semantic information. Although the latter level of matching is very useful in theory, our experience shows that it is difficult to go beyond the level of looking for quality properties. Software vendors do not even include the names of the interfaces that provide their services, or mention their semantics.

Building Alternative Implementations

As previously discussed, the trading service produces a list of candidate components (i.e., candidate list) that fulfills the architectural requirements. A separate process (COTSconfig) generates the collection of all possible combinations of components from those in the list of candidate components (step 3.2).

Although a configuration should resolve partially (or fully) the architectural requirements, not all of them are really valid to build the system. A COTS software component is identified by two sets of incoming and outgoing information flows, basically at the syntactic, semantic, and protocol level (i.e., services), which are referred to as two collections of provided and required services. Nevertheless, a component combination (configuration) with multiple services may generate some problems, such as service gaps and overlaps. Gaps happen when none of the components in a configuration provides any of the services required by the software architecture. On the contrary, overlaps happen when two or more components in the same configuration provide the same service. The aim is to find those configurations without service gaps or service overlaps.

Here below, we will discuss an algorithm that generates valid configurations. In order to explain this algorithm, we will use a particular component notation, focused only on the provided and required services of the component (i.e., on the functional information), but not on the properties, packaging, or marketing information of a COTS component (as there is no influence in a configuration). In relation to the functional information, the algorithm considers the services independently of its information level (i.e., the syntactic, semantic, or protocol level).

To simplify the discussion of the configuration algorithm, let us now consider a component C by two sets of services $C = (P,R)$, where P is the set of supported (or provided) services ($P = \{P_1, \ldots, P_n\}$), and R is the set of required services, $R = \{R_1, \ldots, R_m\}$. For simplicity, we are writing $C.P$ and $C.R$ to refer to both sets of services. At the signature level, P_is and R_js represent standard interfaces (e.g., CORBA or COM interfaces) composed just of a set of public attributes and methods. At the protocol level, P_i and R_j describe a "role." At the semantic level, they correspond to a description of an interface decorated with semantic information (e.g., with pre- and postconditions).

The GTS example will be used to explain the configuration algorithm. We are supposing that the COTStrader process has generated the list of eight candidate components shown in the right column of Figure 11.9. For the algorithm, $C_B(A)$ refers to the candidate list, B refers to the trader repository, and A refers to the software architecture. On the left column, we are show the six components of the GTS subsystem (see Figure 11.6).

For simplicity, we are using just two characters to name components and services. For example, the FileCompressor component will be written as FC, and a service as P_{FC}. Both C_2 and C_6 candidate components require two external services, R_{TL} and R_{FL} respectively. The first one represents a Tool interface, containing a collection of methods to transform spatial images (e.g., sizing, rotation, rolling, and so on). The second one represents a Filter interface, containing a collection of methods with some special effects on spatial images (e.g., noise effect, thresholding, edge detect, shading, segmentation, and so on). If these components are then considered for a configuration, this must be closed first in order to produce a working application. The last step of the process deals with this task (step 3.3 in Figure 11.5), closing the configurations with regard to the repository B.

Figure 11.9 **The Components of the GTS Architecture Against the Candidate List**

Component name	GTS architecture	C_B(GTS): Candidate components
FileCompressor	FC={P_{FC}}	C_1={P_{EL},P_{DO}}
ImageTranslator	IT={P_{IT}}	C_2={P_{EL},P_{DO},R_{TL}}
XDR	XD={P_{XD},R_{EL},R_{DO}}	C_3={P_{FC}}
XMLBuffer	BF={P_{BF},R_{EL},R_{DO}}	C_4={P_{FC},R_{EL},R_{DO}}
DOM	DM={P_{EL},P_{DO}}	C_5={P_{IT}}
Translator	TR={P_{TR},R_{FC},R_{IT},R_{XD},R_{BF}}	C_6={P_{IT},P_{FC},R_{FL}}
		C_7={P_{BF},P_{TR},R_{EL},R_{DO}}
		C_8={P_{XD},R_{EL},R_{DO}}

The configuration algorithm (i.e., COTSconfig process) tries to build a set (S) with all the possible configurations obtained from the candidate list $C_B(A)$, which was previously generated by the trading process (i.e., COTStrader process). Figure 11.10 shows a backtracking algorithm that implements this process. It produces—from the set of candidates, $C_B(A)$, and from the application A—the set S of valid configurations (line 11). The initial invocation of the algorithm is $S =$ Æ, Sol = Æ, and configs(1,Sol,S). Each configuration (line 9) is generated by trying all candidates, incorporating those interfaces $C_i.P_j$ not yet included in A, and discarding those already considered (lines 8 and 10). When the algorithm finishes, S contains all configurations. Because of the way in which the algorithm works, no service gaps or overlaps may occur, and therefore, it produces some valid configurations.

The complexity of this algorithm is $O(L2^n)$, where n is the number of interfaces offered by all candidate components in $C_B(A)$, and L is the complexity of the substitutability operator used (i.e., at the signature level, protocol level, or semantic level operator). To reduce the exponential complexity, we could change the algorithm into a "branch and bound" one, which uses some upper bounds to prune many of the options in the exploration tree, thereby improving notably the execution time of the algorithm.

Once all configurations have been generated, we need to close them in order to get a "complete" application (step 3.3). The closure process of a given configuration can be carried out by applying any of the existing algorithms that calculate the transitive closure of a set (i.e., a configuration) with regard to another bigger set (in this case, the repository). Therefore, we may need to invoke the COTStrader again to look for those external services until we get a closed configuration.

Figure 11.11 shows some results of the GTS example, generated by the configuration algorithm from the candidate list, shown in Figure 11.9. Here, only twenty-four configurations are valid, although other discarded configurations are shown for completeness. Columns 2 to 9 (labeled C_1–C_8 indicate the services provided by the components in each combination. Column 10 (labeled configurations) describes the configuration, hiding the appropriate service too (e.g., we represent the hiding services as "C_3–{P_{DO}}"). Columns 11 and 12 (labeled Res. and Cd) indicate whether the configuration respects the application's structure and whether it is a closed configuration, respectively. As for that, an application is closed if all services required by its constituent components can be served internally, that is, without requiring external services from the components outside the application. Note that valid configurations may not be closed. Although they do not contain gaps with reference to the original services specified in the architecture, configurations may still contain a COTS component that requires some external services not contemplated

Figure 11.10   **Obtaining All Valid Configurations**

```
1      function configs(i,Sol,S)
2              // 1? i ? size(CB(A)) traverse the repository
3              // Sol is the configuration being built
4              // S contains the set of all valid configurations A
5              if i ? size(CB(A)) then
6                      for j := 1 to size(Ci.P) do // all service in Ci
7                              // we try to include Ci.Pj service in Sol
8                              if {Ci.Pj} ? Sol.P = Ø then // Ci.Pj { EMBED Equation.3 }
9                                      Sol := Sol { EMBED Equation.3 }{Ci.Pj};
10                                     if A.P{ EMBED Equation.3 }Sol.P then // Is Sol a
11                                             S := S { EMBED Equation.3 }Sol; // if so, it
12                                     else // but if there are still service gaps . . .
13                                             configs(i,Sol,S); // search in Ci . . .
14                                     Endif
15                                     Sol := Sol – {Ci.Pj};
16                              endif
17                      endfor
18                      configs(i+1,Sol,S); // Next in CB(A).
19              endif
20      endfunction
```

in the original design. This situation is not common in real applications. For instance, if we install a software component in our computer, we will soon realize that it needs another additional (and apparently unrelated) component, which should be installed for the application to work.

The "respect" and "closure" concepts, together with the collection of operators used by the configuration algorithm, are defined in Iribarne et al. (2002).

For instance, configuration 1 contains all candidate components, except C_2, C_4, and C_6, and each component provides just one interface, except C_1, which offers two. This configuration is closed and it respects the application structure. Given the twenty-four configurations, five of them are closed, and twenty respect the structure.

Now it is a decision of the system's designers to select the configuration that best suits their requirements from this list of valid configurations or to revisit the original architecture.

It is important to observe that the process described here has been defined for complete applications. However, it could also be used for some parts of an application. In this way, we could allow the designer to decide which parts of the whole application to implement with COTS components from the repository, applying the process just to the selected parts.

On the other hand, the application of gap analysis is an important feature to assess the difference between stated requirements and existing components, making a compromise to the requirements in order to deliver the solution in a faster and cheaper way (Cheesman and Daniels 2001).

TECHNOLOGY USED

All the processes described in the trader-based development method have been implemented in Java. Rational Rose RealTime has been used to describe the software architecture, which adopts Bran Selic's original UML-RT version. The W3C's XML 1.0 and XML Schema notations have

Figure 11.11 **Some Results of the Configs Algorithm for the GTS Example**

	C1	C2	C3	C4	C5	C6	C7	C8	Configurations	Res.	Cd.
1	P_{EL}, P_{DO}	–	P_{FC}	–	P_{IT}	–	P_{TR}, P_{BF}	P_{XD}	$C_1, C_3-\{P_{DO}\}, C_5, C_7, C_8$	true	true
2	P_{EL}, P_{DO}	–	P_{FC}	–	–	P_{IT}	P_{TR}, P_{BF}	P_{XD}	$C_1, C_3-\{P_{DO}\}, C_6-\{P_{FC}\}, C_7, C_8$	true	false
3	P_{EL}, P_{DO}	–	–	P_{FC}	P_{IT}	–	P_{TR}, P_{BF}	P_{XD}	C_1, C_4, C_5, C_7, C_8	true	true
4	P_{EL}, P_{DO}	–	–	P_{FC}	–	P_{IT}	P_{TR}, P_{BF}	P_{XD}	$C_1, C_4, C_6-\{P_{FC}\}, C_7, C_8$	true	true
5	P_{EL}, P_{DO}	–	–	–	P_{IT}	P_{FC}	P_{TR}, P_{BF}	P_{XD}	$C_1, C_5, C_6-\{P_{IT}\}, C_7, C_8$	true	true
6	P_{EL}, P_{DO}	–	–	–	–	P_{IT}, P_{FC}	P_{TR}, P_{BF}	P_{XD}	C_1, C_6, C_7, C_8	false	true
–								–	NONE: P_{IT}, P_{BF}, P_{XD} missing (gaps)	false	false
7	P_{EL}	P_{DO}	P_{FC}	–	P_{IT}	–	P_{TR}, P_{BF}	P_{XD}	$C_1-\{P_{DO}\}, C_2-\{P_{EL}\}, C_3, C_5, C_7, C_8$	true	false
8	P_{EL}	P_{DO}	P_{FC}	–	–	P_{IT}	P_{TR}, P_{BF}	P_{XD}	$C_1-\{P_{DO}\}, C_2-\{P_{EL}\}, C_3, C_6-\{P_{FC}\}, C_7, C_8$	true	false
9	P_{EL}	P_{DO}	P_{FC}	–	–	–	P_{TR}, P_{BF}	P_{XD}	$C_1-\{P_{DO}\}, C_2-\{P_{EL}\}, C_3, C_4, C_5, C_7, C_8$	true	false
10	P_{EL}	P_{DO}	–	P_{FC}	P_{IT}	–	P_{TR}, P_{BF}	P_{XD}	$C_1-\{P_{DO}\}, C_2-\{P_{EL}\}, C_4, C_6-\{P_{FC}\}, C_7, C_8$	true	false
11	P_{EL}	P_{DO}	–	P_{FC}	–	P_{IT}	P_{TR}, P_{BF}	P_{XD}	$C_1-\{P_{DO}\}, C_2-\{P_{EL}\}, C_5, C_6-\{P_{IT}\}, C_7, C_8$	true	false
12	P_{EL}	P_{DO}	–	–	P_{IT}	P_{FC}	P_{TR}, P_{BF}	P_{XD}	$C_1-\{P_{DO}\}, C_2-\{P_{EL}\}, C_6, C_7, C_8$	false	false
13	P_{DO}	P_{EL}	P_{FC}	–	P_{IT}	–	P_{TR}, P_{BF}	P_{XD}	$C_1-\{P_{EL}\}, C_2-\{P_{DO}\}, C_3, C_5, C_7, C_8$	true	false
14	P_{DO}	P_{EL}	P_{FC}	–	–	P_{IT}	P_{TR}, P_{BF}	P_{XD}	$C_1-\{P_{EL}\}, C_2-\{P_{DO}\}, C_3, C_6-\{P_{FC}\}, C_7, C_8$	true	false
15	P_{DO}	P_{EL}	–	P_{FC}	P_{IT}	–	P_{TR}, P_{BF}	P_{XD}	$C_1-\{P_{EL}\}, C_2-\{P_{DO}\}, C_4, C_5, C_7, C_8$	true	false
16	P_{DO}	P_{EL}	–	P_{FC}	–	P_{IT}	P_{TR}, P_{BF}	P_{XD}	$C_1-\{P_{EL}\}, C_2-\{P_{DO}\}, C_3, C_6-\{P_{FC}\}, C_7, C_8$	true	false
17	P_{DO}	P_{EL}	–	–	P_{IT}	P_{FC}	P_{TR}, P_{BF}	P_{XD}	$C_1-\{P_{EL}\}, C_2-\{P_{DO}\}, C_5, C_6-\{P_{IT}\}, C_7, C_8$	true	false
18	P_{DO}	P_{EL}	P_{FC}	–	–	P_{IT}, P_{FC}	P_{TR}, P_{BF}	P_{XD}	$C_1-\{P_{EL}\}, C_2-\{P_{DO}\}, C_6, C_7, C_8$	false	false
–								P_{XD}	NONE: P_{FC}, P_{IT} missing (gaps)	false	false
19	–	P_{EL}, P_{DO}	–	–	P_{IT}	–	P_{TR}, P_{BF}	P_{XD}	C_2, C_3, C_5, C_7, C_8	true	true
20	–	P_{EL}, P_{DO}	–	–	–	P_{IT}	P_{TR}, P_{BF}	P_{XD}	$C_2, C_3, C_6-\{P_{FC}\}, C_7, C_8$	true	false
21	–	P_{EL}, P_{DO}	–	P_{FC}	P_{IT}	–	P_{TR}, P_{BF}	P_{XD}	C_2, C_4, C_5, C_7, C_8	true	false
22	–	P_{EL}, P_{DO}	–	P_{FC}	–	P_{IT}	P_{TR}, P_{BF}	P_{XD}	$C_2, C_4, C_6-\{P_{FC}\}, C_7, C_8$	true	false
23	–	P_{EL}, P_{DO}	–	–	P_{IT}	P_{FC}	P_{TR}, P_{BF}	P_{XD}	$C_2, C_5, C_6-\{P_{IT}\}, C_7, C_8$	true	false
24	–	P_{EL}, P_{DO}	–	–	–	P_{IT}, P_{FC}	P_{TR}, P_{BF}	P_{XD}	C_2, C_6, C_7, C_8	false	false
–						–	P_{TR}, P_{BF}	P_{XD}	NONE: $P_{EL}, P_{DO}, P_{FC}, P_{IT}$ missing (gaps)	false	false

been used to write the COTScomponent documents and develop the template schemas (the grammar of a COTS document), respectively. The COTStrader service has been implemented by using the IONA's ORB ORBacus and IBM XML4J, and the latter implements the trader repository.

A Web client and some servlets (working on the Apache Tomcat WebServer and under a Linux/Redhat platform) have also been implemented to support trading service from the Web site of our trading-based development method (www.cotstrader.com).

Finally, well-known formalizations have been used to implement certain parts of the proposal: for example, the object constraint language notation to describe the properties of a COTS template, and Leavens' JML notation (Leavens et al. 1999) to describe the semantic specification of COTS component interfaces (the "behavior" tag in Figure 11.3). Finally, a subset of the pi-calculus notation (Milner 1993) has been used to describe protocols (the "choreography" tag in Figure 11.3).

RELATED WORK

The contributions presented in this chapter are related to two main research lines: research based on component acquisition and research based on the building of systems from commercial components.

Component Acquisition

Component acquisition is related to the component search and selection processes from software repositories. These studies take into account architecture requirements (also known as applications engineering) and the component specifications available in well-known software repositories (also known as domain engineering).

Several studies focus on component acquisition. Here, we are underlining three of them. First, Rolland (1999) proposes a technique that captures requirements through transition diagrams (called maps) based on four basic models: the "as-is model, "to-be" model, COTS model, and integrated match model. This approach, however, does not propose any particular way of specifying COTS components, nor does it give any indication of how to carry out the syntactic and semantic matchmaking process between components.

Second, Goguen et al. (1996) present and discuss a set of criteria for searching and selecting components from a repository. However, this technique deals only with components that offer simple interfaces, and therefore the problems of service gaps and overlaps do not appear.

Finally, Seacord et al. (2001) propose a process to identify component ensembles that satisfy the specification of system requirements focused on a knowledge basis of the integration rules of the system. This technique does not make use of a trading model, as discussed in the section titled "Trading for COTS Components."

Building COTS-Based Systems

Another related research line deals with processes aimed at developing software applications with commercial components. First, Seacord et al. (2001) propose some processes for the identification of components, focusing on the knowledge of the integration rules of the system. This proposal lacks a concrete way of documenting commercial components; however, it is one of the few works that deal with real examples of commercial components. This work is developed in the COTS-Based Systems (CBS) Initiative at the Software Engineering Institute (SEI) at Carnegie Mellon University (Pittsburgh, Pennsylvania).

Second, the Concepts to Appliccation in System-Family Engineering (CAFÉ) and Engineering Software Architecture and Platforms System Families (ESAPSb) projects (available at www.esi.es/ Cafe and www.esi.es/esaps) can be cited. Although there are several lines of interest, we emphasize the work of Cherki et al. (2001). The authors describe a platform called Thales for the building of software systems based on COTS parts. This proposal also makes use of Rational tools to define the software architecture, and a diagram of classes prevails instead of UML-RT, as carried out in the trader-based development method. This work also lacks trading processes for COTS components.

CONCLUSION

CBD deals with the building of software systems by searching, selecting, adapting, and integrating COTS software components. Although a software component market has been quite slow to develop, we are perceiving how the effective use of software components is slowly becoming a valid technology for the building of software systems (e.g., Componentsource is successfully selling and licensing many components every month). Moreover, the complexity of the applications is continuously growing, and the amount of information available is becoming too large to be handled by human intermediaries. Therefore, automated trading processes seem to play a critical role in CBD.

In the present chapter, a trading-based development method (TBDM) has been proposed to build software applications as an assembly of COTS software components. This work is due in part to the need of linking three areas of COTS component-based development: (1) the documentation and specification of COTS components, (2) the description of software architectures with COTS components, and (3) the trading processes for COTS components.

To document COTS components, we have first proposed the use of XML document templates (called COTScomponent) for the specification of commercial components. In the case of software architectures, we think that the UML-RT notation is suitable to describe software architectures with COTS components. Finally, we have discussed that the current trading processes are not sufficient to support COTS components, given that there is no connection with existing software architectures. TBDM, an automated method to build COTS systems, solves this problem. It mainly uses two functions (or stages): (1) the COTStrader function, a tool that extends the ODP trading service to look for COTS components, and (2) the COTSconfig function, a tool that generates combinations of components (called configurations) from those in the candidate list—found previously by the COTStrader function. The configurations are taken as solutions that fulfill the architectural requirements of those abstract components defined in the software architecture of the system. The software architecture's description represents an early stage of the TBDM method, which uses the UML-RT notation.

As a future line, metrics and heuristics should be considered so that the trader can generate ordered sequences of candidate components based on certain criteria established by the user or the administrator of the trader community. A connection with other traders should also be implemented to search or register components in a federated trading. Finally, a COTS trader should also be in accordance with some Web services technologies, integrating it with WebServices Definition Language (WSDL) documents, the Universal Description, Discovery, and Integration (UDDI) repositories, and the Semantic Web.

ACKNOWLEDGMENTS

The authors would like to thank the anonymous referees for their insightful comments and suggestions. This work has been partially supported by Spanish CICYT Projects TIC2002–04309-C02–02 and TIC2002–03968.

REFERENCES

Bastide, R., O. Sy, and P. Palanque. 1999. Formal specification and prototyping of CORBA Systems. *Lectures Notes in Computer Science* 1628: 474–494.

Canal, C., L. Fuentes, J.M. Troya, and A. Vallecillo. 2000. Extending CORBA interfaces with protocols. *Computer Journal* 44, no. 5: 448–462.

Cheesman, J., and J. Daniels. 2001. *UML Components. A Simple Process for Specifying Component-Based Software.* Boston, MA: Addison-Wesley.

Cherki, S., E. Kaim, N. Farcet, S. Salicki, and D. Exertier. 2001. Development support prototype for system families based on COTS. *TR ESAPS Project,* www.esi.es/esaps.

Chung, L., B. Nixon, E. Yu, and J. Mylopoulos. 1999. *Non-Functional Requirements in Software Engineering.* Boston, MA: Kluwer Academic Publishers.

Dhara, K.K., and G.T. Leavens. 1996. Forcing behavioral subtyping through specification inheritance. In *18th International Conference on Software Engineering,* 258–267. Berlin, Germany. Los Alamitos, CA: IEEE Computer Society Press.

Garlan, D., S. Chen, and A. Kompanek. 2002. *Reconciling the* needs of architectural descriptions with object-modeling notations. *Science of Computer Programming,* 44, no. 1: 23–49.

Goguen, J., D. Nguyen, J. Meseguer, D. Zhang, and V. Berzins. 1996. Software component search. *Journal of Systems Integration* 6, no. 9: 93–134.

Han, J. 1999. Semantic and usage packaging for software components. Paper presented at ECOOP'99 Workshop on Object Interoperability, Lisbon, Portugal

IONA. 2001. ORBacus trader: ORBacus for C++ and Java. *Technical Report,* IONA.

Iribarne, L., J.M. Troya, and A. Vallecillo. 2001. Trading for COTS components in open environments. In *27th Euromicro Conference,* 30–37. Los Alamitos, CA: IEEE Computer Society Press.

———. 2002. Selecting software components with multiple interfaces. In *28th Euromicro Conference,* 26–32. Los Alamitos, CA: IEEE Computer Society Press.

Iribarne, L., A. Vallecillo, C. Alves, and J. Castro. 2001. A non-functional approach for COTS components trading. Paper presented at the *Workshop on Requirements Engineering,* Buenos Aires, Argentina.

ISO/IEC. 1997. Reference model for open distributed processing. ISO/IEC DIS 13235, ITU-T X.9tr, ISO/IEC/ITU-T.

ISO/ITU-T. 1996. Information technology–Open Distributed Processing–ODP trading function. Rec., ISO/IEC DIS 13235, ITU-T X.9tr, ISO.

Leavens, G.T., L. Baker, and C. Ruby. 1999. JML: A notation for detail design. In *Behavioral Specifications of Businesses and Systems,* ed. H. Kilov, B. Rumpe, and I. Simmonds, 175–188. Boston, MA: Kluwer Academic.

Leavens, G.T., and M. Sitaraman. 2000. *Foundations of Component-Based Systems.* Cambridge: Cambridge University Press.

Medvidovic, N., D.S. Rosenblum, J.E. Robbins, and D.F. Redmiles. 2002. Modeling software architectures in the Unified Modeling Language. *ACM Transactions on Software Engineering and Methodology* 11, no. 1: 2–57.

Medvidovic, N., and R.N. Taylor. 2000. A classification and comparison framework for software architecture description languages. *IEEE Transactions on Software Engineering* 26, no. 1: 70–93.

Merz, M., K. Muller, and W. Lamersdorf. 1994. Service trading and mediation in distributed computing systems. In *14th International Conference on Distributed Computing Systems,* 450–457. Los Alamitos, CA: IEEE Computer Society Press.

Mikhajlova, A. 1999. Ensuring Correctness of Object and Component Systems. PhD diss. Åbo, Finland: Åbo Akademi University.

Mili, H., F. Mili, and A. Mili. 1995. Reusing software: Issues and research directions. *IEEE Transactions on Software Engineering* 21, no. 6: 528–562.

Milner, R. 1993. The polyadic pi-calculus: A tutorial. In *Logic and Algebra of Specification,* ed. F.L. Bauer, W. Brauer and H. Schwichtenberg, 203–246. Berlin, Germany: Springer-Verlag.

Ncube, C., and N. Maiden. 2000. COTS software selection: The need to make tradeoffs between system requirements, architectures and COTS components. Paper presented at the *COTS Continuing Collaborations for Successful COTS Development.* Limerick, Ireland.

Nuseibeh, B. 2001. Weaving together requirements and architectures. *IEEE Computer* 34, 3: 115–117.

OMG. 1999. *The CORBA Component Model,* www.omg.org, Object Management Group.

————. 2001. *A UML Profile for Enterprise Distributed Object Computing V1.0.*, www.omg.org/technology/documents/formal/edoc.htm, Object Management Group.

Robertson, S., and J. Robertson. 1999. *Mastering the Requirements Process.* Harlow, UK: Addison-Wesley.

Rolland, C. 1999. Requirements engineering for COTS based systems. *Information and Software Technology* 41, no. 14: 985–990.

Rosa, N.S., C.F. Alves, P.R.F. Cunha, and J.F.B. Castro. 2001. Using non-functional requirements to select components: A formal approach. Paper presented at *Fourth Iberoamerican on Requirements Engineering and Software Environments.*

Seacord, R.C., D. Mundie, and S. Boonsiri. 2001. K-BACEE: Knowledge-based automated component ensemble evaluation. In *27th Euromicro Conference,* 56–62. Los Alamitos, CA: IEEE Computer Society Press.

Selic, B., and J. Rumbaugh. 1998. Using UML for modeling complex real-time systems, www-106.ibm.com/developerworks/rational/library/139.html.

Szyperski, C. 1998. *Component Software: Beyond Object-Oriented Programming.* Harlow, UK: Addison-Wesley.

Vallecillo, A., J. Hernandez, and J.M. Troya. 1999. Object interoperability. *Lectures Notes in Computer Science* 1743: 1–21.

Vallecillo, A., J. Hernandez, and J.M. Troya. 2000. New issues in object interoperability. *Lectures Notes in Computer Science* 1964: 256–269.

Vasudevan, V., and T. Bannon. 1999. WebTrader: Discovery and programmed access to Web-based services. Paper presented at the *Eighth International WWW Conference,* Toronto, Canada.

Yellin, D.M., and R.E. Strom. 1997. Protocol specifications and component adaptors. *ACM Transactions on Programming Languages and Systems* 19, no. 2: 292–333.

Zaremski, A.M., and J.M. Wing. 1995. Signature matching: A tool for using software libraries. *ACM Transactions on Software Engineering and Methodology* 4, no. 2: 146–170.

EDITORS AND CONTRIBUTORS

William F. Acosta received his BS degree in computer engineering from the Pennsylvania State University and is currently a PhD and MS candidate in computer science at the University of Notre Dame, where he is an Arthur J. Schmitt Fellow. He worked in industry as a software developer and consultant, specializing in building distributed and Web-based applications using component and object-oriented technologies. During his time in industry, he developed several distributed component applications, including the e-commerce engine of a large retailer. Currently, his research interests include peer-to-peer architectures and network overlays for distributed applications, efficient resource discovery for distributed systems, and distributed Web-caching. He is a member of ACM (Association for Computing Machinery), IEEE Computer Society (Institute of Electrical and Electronics Engineers), and USENIX (Advanced Computing Systems Association).

Colin Atkinson received a PhD and MSc in computer science from Imperial College, London, and received his BSc in mathematical physics from the University of Nottingham in 1983. From 1991 to 1997 he was an assistant professor of software engineering at the University of Houston–Clear Lake (UHCL). He then became a professor at the University of Kaiserslautern, Germany, and a project leader and consultant at the affiliated Fraunhofer Institute for Experimental Software Engineering (IESE). Since April 2003 he has held the Chair of Software Engineering at the University of Mannheim, Germany.

Jan Bosch is a vice president and head of the Software and Application Technologies Laboratory at Nokia Research Center, Finland. Earlier, he headed the software engineering research group at the University of Groningen, The Netherlands, where he holds a professorship in software engineering. He received an MSc from the University of Twente, The Netherlands, and a PhD from Lund University, Sweden. His research activities include software architecture design, software product families, software variability management, and component-oriented programming. He is the author of *Design and Use of Software Architectures: Adopting and Evolving a Product Line Approach,* (co-)editor of several books and volumes in, among others, the Springer Lecture Notes in Computer Science series and (co-)author of a significant number of research articles. He has organized numerous workshops and served on many program committee (PC) and was the PC co-chair of the Third IFIP/IEEE Working Conference on Software Architecture (WICSA-3), the general chair for WICSA-4, and PC co-chair for the 8th International Conference on Software Reuse.

Christian Bunse received the PhD degree in computer science from the University of Kaiserslautern, Germany, and his BS (Vordiplom) and MS degree (Diplom) in computer science with a minor in medicine from the University of Dortmund, Germany. From 1993 to 1995 he was a faculty research assistant of the Software Technology Transfer Initiative at the University of Kaiserslautern. He is currently the head of the department for object-technology and component-based software development in the embedded domain at the Fraunhofer Institute for Experimental Software Engineering (IESE) in Kaiserslautern.

Sergio de Cesare holds a PhD in business information systems from Liberia Universitá Internazionale degli Studi Sociali (LUISS) Guido Carli in Rome. He is currently a lecturer at Brunel University (West London, UK). His research focuses on business modeling and information systems development. More specifically, he has published in the areas of object-oriented and component-based approaches. He has served on numerous program committees and organized various international events, including a series of workshops on Semantics of Enterprise Integration at the Object-Oriented Programming, Systems, Languages, and Applications (OOPSLA) 2001, 2002, and 2003.

Ajantha Dahanayake is an associate professor in the Department of Information and Communication Technology at the Faculty of Technology, Policy and Management, Delft University of Technology, the Netherlands. She previously served as an associate professor in the Department of Information Systems and Algorithms at the Faculty of Information Technology and Systems. She received her BSc and MSc in computer science from the University of Leiden and her PhD, in information systems from Delft University of Technology. She had served in a number of Dutch research and academic institutions. Her research interests are distributed Web-enabled systems, Computer Aided Software Engineering (CASE), methodology engineering, component-based development, and m-business. She is the research director of the research program Building Blocks for Telematic Applications Development and Evaluation (BETADE).

Ali Doğru has worked on design- and methodology-related research and development projects since 1990. He directed Design for Environment tool development efforts at New Jersey Institute of Technology in 1997 and 1998. Currently he is a member of the Computer Engineering Department, Middle East Technical University, Turkey, where he has directed the Software Engineering Laboratory. He conducted consulting for large-scale software development projects and technological training for engineering organizations in different countries. Dr. Doğru obtained his BS in electrical engineering from Technical University of Istanbul, his MS in electrical engineering from the University of Texas at Arlington, and his PhD in computer science from Southern Methodist University.

Luis Iribarne received his BSc degree in computer science from the University of Granada, and the MSc and PhD degrees in computer science from the University of Almería, Spain. From 1991 to 1993 he was a lecturer at the University of Granada. In 1993 he collaborated as an Information Technology Service Analyst at the University School of Almería, and he served for nine years as a lecturer in the Polytechnic School at the University of Almería. From 1993 to 1999 he worked in several national and international research projects on distributed simulation and geographic information systems (GIS). In 2001 he joined the Data, Knowledge and Software Engineering Group and then became associate professor at the University of Almería in 2002. His research interests include component-based software development, commercial off-the-shelf (COTS) components, trading, Web services, and Unified Modeling Language (UML) design.

Marijn Janssen is an assistant professor in the field of information systems and government at the section of Information and Communication Technology at Delft University of Technology. He has been a consultant for the Ministry of Justice of the Netherlands and received a PhD in information systems. His main research interests are the design and modeling of living architectures in networks of organizations.

Erik Kamsties has been senior research assistant at the Institute for Computer Science and Business Information Systems (ICB) at the University of Duisburg-Essen since 2002. He is leading a group of researchers in the field of product line engineering. Earlier, he was leader of the requirements engineering competence team at the Fraunhofer Institute for Experimental Software Engineering (IESE) in Kaiserslautern, Germany. He received a PhD in computer science from the University of Kaiserslautern and an MS degree (Diploma) in computer science from the Technical University of Berlin, Germany. His research interests include requirements engineering, in particular natural language requirements, object-oriented analysis, software product line engineering, requirements-based testing, and empirical software engineering. He is program cochair of the Requirements Engineering: Foundation of Software Quality (REFSQ) workshop series.

Ronny Kolb works as an applied researcher in the department Software Product Lines at the Fraunhofer Institute for Experimental Software Engineering (IESE) in Kaiserslautern, Germany. He works in several research and industrial projects in the context of product line engineering and has experience in transferring product line engineering into practice. His main research interests are quality assurance for software product lines and the design and analysis of product line architectures. He received a MS in computer science from the Friedrich-Schiller University Jena.

Hareton K.N. Leung is an associate professor in the Department of Computing, The Hong Kong Polytechnic University. He currently serves as the director of the Laboratory for Software Development and Management, which focuses on software process, quality improvement, and other applied software technology research. The lab has worked with local software professionals on the improvement of software practices and technology transfer. Dr. Leung has conducted research in software testing, software maintenance, quality and process improvement, and software metrics. A member of IEEE, IEEE Computer Society, and Hong Kong Computer Society, he currently serves on the editorial board of *Software Quality Journal* and the program committee of many international and local conferences on software quality, software metrics, and maintenance. He is also a reviewer of *IEEE Transactions on Software Engineering, IEEE Software, IEEE Computer, Communications of ACM, ACM Transactions on Software Engineering and Methodology,* and *Journal of Software Testing Verification and Reliability.*

Mark Lycett holds a BSc in computing and business management (Oxford Brookes, UK), MSc in information systems (Brunel University, UK), and a PhD in information systems (Brunel University, UK). Before returning to education, he spent a number of years in industry and has both worked on and managed a number of national and international feasibility and development projects. His research concentrates on all aspects of business and software engineering, and he is currently engaged in ongoing research and consulting with a number of blue-chip companies, small businesses, and defense agencies. He has more than thirty publications in leading journals and international conferences. In addition, he regularly contributes to industry publications such as *Computing, Computer Weekly, Director,* and *Financial Times IT.*

Robert D. Macredie (BSc, PhD) has worked with a range of organizations, from large, blue-chip companies to small businesses and government agencies. His key interest lies in the way in which people and organizations use technology, and his research aims to determine how work can be more effectively undertaken by improving the way that we understand how people and technology interact in organizational settings. He is professor of interactive systems and head of the School of Information Systems, Computing and Mathematics, Brunel University, UK. He has worked on a range of issues associated with people, technology, and organizations and has more than 150 published research contributions in these areas.

Gregory Madey received his PhD and MS degrees in operations research from Case Western Reserve University and the MS and BS degrees in mathematics from Cleveland State University. He worked in industry for several firms, including Goodyear Aerospace, Gould Oceans Systems, and Loral (now part of Lockheed Martin). He is currently an associate professor and director of graduate studies in the Department of Computer Science and Engineering at the University of Notre Dame. His research includes topics in distributed systems, Web-services and service-oriented architectures, Web portals for scientific collaboration, Grid computing, Web intelligence, Web mining, agent-based modeling and simulation, and swarm intelligence. He has published in various journals, including *Communications of the ACM, IEEE Transactions on Engineering Management, Journal of Management Information Systems, Decision Sciences, The European Journal of Operational Research, Omega, Expert Systems with Applications*, and *Expert Systems*. He is a member of the Association for Computing Machinery, Association for Information Systems, IEEE Computer Society, Informs, and the Society for Computer Simulation.

Dirk Muthig heads the Department Software Product Lines at the Fraunhofer IESE in Germany. He is responsible for the research strategy in the area of PuLSE (ProdUct Line Software Engineering) and has experience in transferring product line engineering into practice across all life-cycle stages since 1997. Numerous publications were derived from this work, among them publications at ICSE, ICSR, SPLC, and in IEEE Software. He gives a lecture on software product lines at Kaiserslautern University of Technology and has also presented tutorials at several international conferences, as well as for industry. He received an MS and a PhD in computer science from the Kaiserslautern University of Technology.

Alan O'Callaghan is a researcher in the Software Technology Research Laboratory at De Montfort University, UK, where he has lectured for the past fifteen years. He is also a practicing consultant in software architecture, component-based development, and object-oriented design, in which capacity he has worked on some of the largest software systems in Europe. Besides being a member of the BCS (British Computer Society), the ACM, and the IEEE he is a member of both the World Wide Institute of Software Architects and the Hillside (Europe) Advisory Board—Hillside being the sponsoring organization of the Patterns Movement. He has written two books (a third is a work in progress) and more than forty journal articles as well as two pattern languages, and he is a frequent speaker on both the academic and professional conference circuits.

Henk Sol is the dean of the Faculty of Management and Organization, University of Groningen, the Netherlands, and a professor of business engineering and ICT. Previously, he was the dean of the Faculty of Technology, Policy and Management, Delft University of Technology, the Netherlands, and at the same time the chair of systems engineering. He also served as chair of the Department of Information Systems of the Faculty of Information Technology and Systems. He is the founder of the Faculty of Technology, Policy and Management, as well as the founder of the Delft Institute for Service Engineering (DITSE). He is a pioneer in simulation and decision support research.

Zoran Stojanovic is a researcher with the faculty of Technology, Policy and Management, at Delft University of Technology, the Netherlands. His research interests are in the areas of component-based development, Web services, enterprise and system modeling, geographic information systems (GIS), and location-based services. He received his graduate engineering degree and master of philosophy degree in computer science and GIS from the Faculty of Electronic Engineering, University of Nis (Yugoslavia). He has been working since 1993 as a researcher and teaching assistant in the fields of computer science, software and system engineering, first at the University of Nis and since February 2000 at the Delft University of Technology. He is an author of a number of research publications.

José María Troya received his MSc and PhD in physics from the Madrid Complutense University. From 1980 to 1988 he was associate professor at that university and in 1988 became full professor at the University of Málaga, where he leads the Software Engineering Group. His research interests include parallel programming, distributed systems, and software architectures. He has worked on several national and international research projects, written articles for the most relevant computer conferences and journals, supervised numerous PhD theses, and organized several workshops and international conferences. He is a member of ACM and IEEE.

Antonio Vallecillo holds BSc and MSc degrees in mathematics and a PhD degree in computer science. Most of his professional experience comes from the computer industry, where he has worked for more than ten years for several international companies, both in Spain and in the UK. Since 1996, he has worked at Málaga University, where he is currently an associate professor and has also been the head of the University IT Services. His research interests include component-based software development, open distributed processing, and the industrial use of formal methods. He is the representative of Málaga University at ISO (International Standards Organization), the OMG (Object Management Group), and AENOR (Associatíon EspaD´ola de Normalización y Certificación, the Spanish National Body for Standardization) and a member of several professional organizations, including the ACM and the IEEE.

René W. Wagenaar is a full professor of information and communication technology at Delft University of Technology in the Netherlands. He has more than fifteen years of experience in ICT, both from various positions in the academic community and from working in the ICT industry. He has published many scientific papers, conference contributions, and chapters in books. His main interests are e-service architectures within the public sector and private business networks.

Jörg Zettel received his MS and PhD degrees in computer science from the University of Kaiserslautern, Germany. From 1996 to 2003, he was research assistant at the Fraunhofer IESE in Kaiserslautern. Today, he is working as an analyst for the Hessische Zentrale für Datenverarbeitung (HZD) in Wiesbaden, Germany. His research interests include computer-aided software engineering, software process modeling, component-based software engineering, and agile software development.

SERIES EDITOR

Vladimir Zwass is the Distinguished Professor of Computer Science and Management Information Systems at Fairleigh Dickinson University. He holds a PhD in Computer Science from Columbia University. Dr. Zwass is the Founding Editor-in-Chief of the *Journal of Management Information Systems;* one of three top-ranked journals in the field of information systems, the journal has recently celebrated twenty years in publication. Dr. Zwass is also the Founding Editor-in-Chief of the *International Journal of Electronic Commerce,* ranked as the top journal in its field. Dr. Zwass is the author of six books and several book chapters, including entries in the *Encyclopaedia Britannica,* as well as of a number of papers in various journals and conference proceedings. He has received several grants, consulted for a number of major corporations, and is a frequent speaker to national and international audiences. He is a former member of the Professional Staff of the International Atomic Energy Agency in Vienna, Austria.

INDEX